Go Back to Sea

An insight into a marine engineer's life and a vocation to the priesthood

The Reverend Canon Keith R Corless

CARTHOUSE
PUBLISHING

Published by
Carthouse Publishing
The Rocket Carthouse
1 Tanners Close
Brockworth
Gloucestershire GL3 4QN

ISBN 978-0-9554750-0-9

Typesetting and jacket design by
Thurbans Publishing Services, Haslemere, Surrey
Printed by TJ International, Padstow, Cornwall PL28 8RW

DEDICATION

To shipmates of years past;
My wife Jean, and our family;
and
The many wonderful parishioners,
service to whom as a parish priest
has been so rich a privilege.

CONTENTS

LIST OF PLATES

NB. All original sketches were hand drawn by the author
whilst working aboard ship in the engine room.

ACKNOWLEDGEMENTS

I would like to thank the many people who have encouraged me in the writing of "Go back to sea…" among whom were:

Members of my family for their support and computer assistance
Jon Barsdell – a friend and advisor
Michael Evans C Eng – a friend and advisor
Richard Joseph – my publishing mentor

And I acknowledge with gratitude the valuable contribution
to this work of:

Fotoflite of Kent (formally Skyfotos) for the use of ship photographs, also the useful historical reality of journals of the past such as 'The Motor Ship' as well as the Newnes Technical Marine Engineering series, from both of which sources illustrative material has been used.

In my years in ministry as a full time Parish Priest, one of the questions I've been most frequently asked by those who have known something of my marine engineering background was: 'How did you come to leave the Merchant Navy and go into the Church?' quickly followed by the supplementary one from those knowing a little more about me: 'And why did you go back?' The answers are to be found in the pages of this book.

The book's beginning has its root in a personal lament expressed many years ago that while much nautical material was constantly coming forward for publication, a great deal of it was written from the angle of those serving in every department of a ship except the engine room! I'd said then that one day I would make an attempt to redress the balance and, the opportunity having arrived, I've penned some sea-faring stories as experienced from an engineer's point of view.

That in it all, the extraordinary issue of the discovery of a vocation to the priesthood of the Church, and the dilemmas faced in fulfilling it, also appears, gives a unique human slant to the narrative.

If you choose to read on then, you will find that what in many senses is a nautical book is also one revealing a very human story where some great emotional depths are plumbed, and the attendant agonies of serious decision-making are exposed. For some people, the knowledge that the fulfilling of a priestly vocation is, as in my case, sometimes a struggle, has come as a surprise, as it may to you, a reader of this story. In what people have sometimes said, they clearly thought a clergyman came ready-made at birth, with the uniform of the 'dog collar' already in place! And equally clearly they have thought clergy to be different to others, in a sort of 'protected species' sort of way! It's almost as if they've seen the dog collar acting like a force-field, warding off the evils that beset ordinary people in ordinary life.

Reading this narrative will quickly disabuse anyone of the idea that acquiring a dog collar is either, an easy business or, that it is in any sense a way to stress-free security!

A lady I once knew in parish life is on record as saying, in the context of a sad domestic situation, "Well, it's different for you Rector," implying that she did believe I enjoyed a secure remoteness from harsh reality. That from this book's story I could assure her that I was actually as 'normal' as anyone else, was a revelation to her, and when I could endorse it with the evidence of personal tragedy in what was then the recent death, in my arms, of my father aged but sixty, she really felt she could have confidence in me after all!

Of course, not all stories of the development of a vocation to the priesthood are as topsy-turvy as this one, and indeed some perhaps have been as smoothly developed as the 'dog collar' at birth idea suggests. Years ago many sons did follow in the steps of their clergymen fathers in an almost seamless progression, but equally, many followed other paths, some of which being very rocky ones indeed, and all will have involved the facing of the tensions, if not agonies, of very serious decision-making.

So plunge on into the following pages. Those with a marine engineering interest will find plenty to enjoy, and those who are simply fascinated by a very human story will find much to savour in that respect. For the non-technical, some of the engineering descriptions can be easily by-passed in the course of reading, but where they can be read in full even if some of the detail seems a little puzzling, their inclusion will help give the narrative its fullest substance, and open more clearly an appreciation of the human story it is.

Read on then, and enjoy, a revolutionary brush in South America and a fruitless call for passengers at Tristan da Cunha. Fret with us in the Suez crisis, and endure our corned beef voyage round Africa. Experience the dilemmas over faith, and church-going, and feel the tensions of making difficult decisions about the future. Savour then, some church work-experience and the laughs that went with it in Dublin. Live through personal rebellion at theological college, and feel the realities of ordination while living with guilt! Then marvel at a meeting and the bishop's urging to 'Go back to sea!' Join a ship again and then live with the discovery by others of one's church past! Explore too, other human situations, such as meeting a young man in Poland who had tried to escape from the communist bloc; hospitalisation in Brazil; relations with Indian seafarers; having one's wife aboard in bad weather and an astonishing contrast in journeys; not to mention the drama of 'fire down below!'

GLOSSARY

In the narrative, some terms of a nautical, or technical character are used, and the reader may find these explanatory notes helpful:-

Fo'c'sle –
The fore deck of a ship at the bows. It dates from the days when ships were built with an actual castle type structure at the front and back for military purposes. Although long discontinued as a feature in naval architecture the word forecastle continued in use, being frequently abbreviated to fo'c'sle.

Indicator Cock –
This is a screwed 'tap' on the cylinder of an engine to which an instrument called an indicator is fitted enabling a graph of the pressures occurring in the cylinder during a working cycle to be recorded. Those fitted in diesel engines are usually left open when the engine is first turned using compressed air, this being a safety factor in case oil has collected internally from a leaking fuel valve. Once the engine has turned over, the cocks are closed and full manoeuvring can begin.

'Lecky' –
The informal name for the ship's electrician.

Middles' Platform
The popular expression for the main intermediate platform on the larger marine engines, situated approximately half way between the bottom floor plates and the platform at the cylinder tops.

Poop –
This refers to the raised deck at the after end, or stern, of a ship. It is where the 'aftercastle' would once have been.

Salvage –
This is the term used for the recovery, or saving of a broken-down or stranded ship and/or its cargo, by another vessel. Considerable sums of money can be claimed by the rescuers in either, reward or, compensation terms.

Scotch boiler –
This is a large cylindrical vessel fitted internally with one or more large corrugated tubes known as furnaces in which either coal or oil is burnt. The furnaces fit into vertical steel boxes known as combustion chambers, and from them small return tubes bring the hot gases back to the front of the

boiler where they are led, via a chimney or funnel, to the atmosphere. The boiler is filled with water, the level of which must be maintained above the tops of the combustion chambers in order to obviate the risk of overheating and explosion. The remaining internal volume above the water level is the steam space. A Scotch boiler with its large volume of water and the fire and heat kept within its tubes, is quite adequate for the provision of low pressure steam, but where higher pressures are required as in steam turbine plants, the system is reversed.

A relatively small volume of water is supplied in the boiler's tube banks, and the furnace design allows the fire to burn around them. Thus boilers are easily defined as being of either the fire tube or, the water tube type.

Turning gear –
This is a device to both lock the propeller shaft on the one hand, and allow it to be turned in a controlled way on the other. A large wheel fitted to the end of the crankshaft has gear teeth cut in its circumference. Adjacent to it is fitted a unit with a small gear, driven by an electric motor (or steam engine in older versions). This unit is fitted on tracks allowing it to be moved in to engage the gears, or out to disengage them. Once engaged the propeller shaft is effectively locked, thus preventing it from being turned by any wave action of the sea on the propeller blades. It also means that when the small gear is rotated, driven by its electric motor, it will turn the large wheel it is meshed with and therefore the crankshaft itself, and other working parts of the engine. Different parts of the machinery are thus rendered accessible for maintenance work and this can be carried out safely secure in the knowledge that the shaft cannot be rotated inadvertently. In a large marine engine, for the turning gear to rotate the crankshaft through one complete revolution, it can take between four and five minutes. When the turning gear is engaged, a warning sign is always displayed at the control station to ensure that no attempt is made to start the engine until the gears have been disengaged!

'Tween deck –
This is a supplementary deck fitted in between two other, usually more principal ones.

In the engine rooms of ships the 'tween decks run the length of the machinery space on either side of the main engine, the areas they provide often then being utilised for the siting of lubricating oil storage tanks, workshop and store facilities and, in motor ships, the positioning of the large reservoir bottles for the holding of the compressed air required when manoeuvring.

Part One

AN EVENTFUL VOYAGE

As a teenager I spent many hours absorbing the bustling atmosphere of Southampton Docks and unsurprisingly, the call for me to 'go to sea' emerged.

Shortly afterwards I enrolled with the British Tanker Co and I embraced my two years as an engineer apprentice at technical college in Swansea.

This training led to my first voyage, a nine month trip on the MV British Baron, giving me an initial grasp of life at sea.

However, it was only when engine troubles set in during my second trip, on the larger MV British Reliance, that the enriching and exciting realities of my 'calling' really became clear…

The expensive crash of breaking crockery in the midship pantry announced that the ship had put to sea! To clear what had been our berth in Cape Town's bunker dock, now urgently required for an incoming ship, a hasty 'all hands' breakfast had been called. It had meant an early Sunday morning start for everyone. Soon after breakfast, and once smartly underway it meant that the catering staff performing the clearing up were rather taken by surprise when our ship, the tanker MV British Reliance, first plunged, then reared in crockery-smashing style, as she met the surging South Atlantic seas running that day outside Cape Town's long harbour moles. Doubtless the stewards reasoned that the event had at least saved them the chore of washing up, but what the Chief Steward thought was another matter; one no doubt a good deal less sanguine. His crockery indent to the company in London would need some careful phrasing!

Underway, and heading due west the ship, deep laden with sixteen thousand tons of Mena crude (crude oil from Mena al Ahmadi in the Persian Gulf) for delivery to a refinery at La Plata near Buenos Aires, quickly settled back into her voyage routine after her bunkering stop at the Cape. And happily, as the

The MV British Reliance, the ship featured in the story of the eventful voyage. The vessel is seen here passing the White Cliffs of Dover.   www.fotoflite.com

day past, the weather eased. It was too late to save the stewards' crockery but it was going to be a blessing for the engineers.

The year was 1956, and our ship was typical of tankers of that period being of the traditional 'three island design' – forecastle, midship bridge and poop structure with the funnel, and her attractive profile was further graced by the provision of two tall masts. She was powered, as were many vessels of that time with a Doxford opposed piston diesel engine, and she had the usual broad mix of steam and electrically driven auxiliaries. Steam was provided by a pair of Scotch type boilers each with three furnaces, and electrical power by direct current generators driven by in this case, Mirrlees diesel engines. I was aboard as one of two engineer apprentices, my colleague being Keith Gander, a lad from London and with whom I shared a cabin on the boat deck of the ship's midship accommodation. By then we had both been with the company (British Petroleum formally The British Tanker Company – BTC for short and affectionately if irreverently known by seafarers as 'Better Times Coming') for some time.

The first two years of our apprenticeship had been taken up with an engineering course at technical college in my case it being in Swansea and my colleague's in London, this being followed by a first trip to sea which had brought us together. That trip had been a nine month voyage on a slightly smaller ship than we were now on, it being the twelve thousand ton capacity MV British Baron powered by a four cylinder Doxford. Thus we had begun to accumulate a little experience but, my word, that we were going to gain a great deal more in the next couple of weeks was an understatement. On the 'Reliance' the engine whose troubles would so enrich our experience was an

An early Doxford marine engine showing the fully open construction.

impressive construction. It stood quite as high as a domestic house and with, in our case, her six cylinders, it had a length of a good fifty feet. Its working principle was essentially simple but impressive to watch in operation. Each cylinder unit had two pistons which, as they came together, compressed air. The air thus heated by the compression then ignited fuel oil injected through valves in the middle of the cylinder. The resulting expansion of hot gases drove the two pistons apart, and the cycle was then endlessly repeated. A lower piston was connected to a crank shaft, the upper piston similarly so by means of long side rods, and it was the sight of these upper pistons working, with their big beams and rods dancing in an entrancing spectacle of reciprocating motion which was such a fascinating and beloved feature of the Doxford design of engine. Now alas, our engine had a problem.

Having left Cape Town early on a Sunday morning, by the morning of the following day we were well over three hundred miles out in the South Atlantic. Shortly after 10am the Fourth engineer on watch had been alarmed to hear a frightening knock develop in the main engine. He promptly rang 'Stop' on the engine room telegraph to alert the bridge, and then operated the controls to shut the fuel off in order to bring the engine to a stop. I was in our cabin when I became aware that the hint of vibration always present in the ship when the engines were at work, had ceased. From our porthole I could see that it was clear the ship was by then only carrying her way as the sea was no longer surging past and indeed, even as I looked, it was plain she was beginning to fall gradually broad sides to the swells and the unpleasant sense of deadness so characteristic of a ship without power, was creeping into her movements. Although no alarms had sounded or any formal orders for attendance had been made, we all knew that in the event of a 'stop' we should turn-to to see if help was needed.

Leaving our cabin I saw framed in the after door of the accommodation the familiar red, white, green and white, black topped funnel of our ship noting that it was already sweeping long arcs across the horizon as the stopping ship, now broad side on, rolled to the swells. And on the flying bridge a trickle of off-duty engineers were making their way aft to the engine room to investigate our problem. Sliding down the maze of ladders we all foregathered on the bottom plates and I was intrigued to see the Chief engineer was already there. I couldn't help thinking that he cut a slightly incongruous figure, wearing as was his wont when at sea a frayed woolly 'cardi' and a pair of carpet slippers. A portly man who looked older than his years, one wouldn't have thought him as one at that stage of his career to be much given to hurrying but clearly he had that Monday morning in response to the Fourth's urgent telephone call proclaiming the alarming news that, "she's got a bloody great knock in number five!"

An example of the later Doxford engines featuring the fully enclosed crankcase.

With the engine now stopped the lubricating oil system had been shut down and the Fourth had already removed the light alloy inspection doors for the number five unit. Inside, the round ends of the huge webs of the crankshaft and the great bottom end bearings of the motion gear could be seen and, in the dark, the slowly draining oil glistened cheekily in the light of the torch which the Chief shone abstractedly around as he stared glumly, and obviously worriedly, inside.

The original Doxford engine design had featured a fully open crankcase as was so familiar with reciprocating steam engines, and the visual impact of each cylinders units' three cranks and attendant connecting rods whirling round must have been utterly stunning especially when seen in conjunction with the upper pistons' dancing ballet. In those earlier engines with their somewhat slower speeds, oiling round was largely achieved by gravity feed from reservoir points supplemented by hand operated oil cans, but the development of greater speeds and the advent of higher pump-driven oil pressures necessitated the crankcase having to become fully enclosed. This was achieved by fitting steel plates fixed to the frames of the engine but as access to the crankcase was always required for maintenance purposes the plates were pierced with inspection apertures each being sealed when the engine was running by light round alloy doors. The loss of Doxford's mechanical visual drama many felt to be regrettable but for us, visual interests of any sort were irrelevant for we were about to indulge in some serious physical intimacies with our engine's working parts!

INITIAL CHECKS; THEN THE PROBLEM IS REVEALED...

Now the engine was stopped the Fourth engineer's fellow watch-keeper had been detailed to get the turning gear in (this was a gear device which both locked the propeller shaft against it being turned by any surging action of the sea on the propeller blades, while it also enabled the crankshaft to be turned so that moving parts of the engine could be rendered accessible for inspection and maintenance). A couple of us were despatched to assist the electrician in collecting lead lamps from the stores and getting them rigged up to illuminate the crankcase. When all was ready the Fourth took a hammer and disappeared into the crankcase to 'ring' the nuts on the three connecting rod bottom end bearings. The noise given when the nuts received a smart tap was a ready indication of their tightness. A comfortingly solid sound suggested that all was tight and healthy whereas a lighter, more echoey one was a clear indication of a nut having slackened back or that its bolt had stretched. Such things happening would allow the bearing to open slightly and therefore move on the crank pin as the shaft revolved, the movement revealing itself audibly as a knock.

We all waited and listened as the Fourth clambered round wielding his hammer. Soon he reappeared declaring that all seemed fine at that level and as he wiped a drip of oil from his nose with an even oilier hand he said the knock had indeed seemed actually higher up in the crankcase. Accordingly our attention turned to the connecting rod top ends where they linked with the lower piston and the two side rods and, with his hammer in his hand and a deep breath in his chest the Fourth disappeared through the upper inspection door back into the hot crankcase. All the bearings there seemed to be in order however, so when the Fourth, looking even oilier, was safely out again, the Second ordered the turning gear to be started up and he instructed everyone to watch different parts of the motion gear looking for anything untoward in their movement or action. Thus with our lights illuminating the oily gloom we watched as the great cranks and rods began to ease round and then, suddenly, an awed voice said, "Strewth! – there it is…"

Eyes followed a pointing finger and indeed there it was; as the great cylindrical skirt of the lower piston slid into view in the crankcase it was seen to be cracked round a good part of its circumference. "Bloody wars," breathed the Second, "that just doesn't happen!" Being merely an inexperienced apprentice I was mystified by such amazement until someone reminded me that in the Doxford design of engine the lower piston was given much stouter dimensions than its upper counterpart in order to give some weight equivalence to the upper piston's beam to which the long side rods were connected. The establishment of weight equivalence ensured smooth running when the engine was working but with the lower piston skirt cracked and its structure therefore prey to distortion it had meant the broken edge had been connecting violently with the bottom of the cylinder liner on each upstroke making for anything but 'smooth running'! And the question was, why had it happened? With the wall thickness something in excess of three inches of good cast iron a crack like the one before us had got to have a good explanation. Clearly then the work of lifting pistons lay before us. In some Doxford maintenance notes the matter of lifting pistons is addressed with an almost offhand nonchalance thus: 'the removal of both upper and lower pistons in any cylinder need not take more than twenty minutes'. In the ideal conditions of a snug dock or a safe anchorage such a confident assertion is doubtless perfectly true but, to carry out the work at sea with the vessel rolling, it really is a task which can pose some serious challenges and risks!

The Second engineer gathered everyone for a briefing session. He was a Glaswegian and he cut a most striking figure being both tall and broad of shoulder and sporting swarthy, film star features. He exhibited an air of calm deliberation about everything he did and this was to prove a leadership trait about to pay dividends to us. The initial tasks he wanted attending to were purely domestic. We had to get our two Scotch boilers back on to oil fuel firing, four of their total of six furnaces having been on main engine exhaust gas for economy purposes; and we had to settle the engine's water services to harbour circulating temperatures now that we'd stopped. Then, he said, we'd be split into two working parties, one to lift the top piston and get it safely positioned on the overhauling beams at that level at the engine, while the other group would work in the crankcase to prepare the lower piston for its lifting operation. Put like that it sounded all very straight forward but a glance at the Chief suggested another story. He had the look of one who'd just been sand-bagged and as he took his portly figure off up the ladders to take to his cabin couch and his cigarettes I caught his muttered words, "my retiring trip too…" We were to hear that lament a good deal in the course of the next fortnight. As he disappeared and we set about our duties the Second turned to the phone to have a word with those on the bridge about the weather. We all appreciated the fact that it had eased somewhat since our departure from Cape Town, but for all that we were rolling quite badly. However, no deterioration was forecast so that when the Second gave us the news confidence was high that we'd accomplish what we had to do successfully.

Thus work began. The work on the top piston in the airier part of the engine room was not too bad. The side rods were disconnected, the big

gantry crane running on tracks in the engine room casing above being used to lift the keeps from their bearings. At the same time the hoses carrying the piston's cooling water were removed as were all the nuts holding the big guides and soon, a call for all hands announced the unit was ready for lifting.

The 'all hands' call was a welcome one for the crankcase party. In there, the work of getting the lower piston disconnected from its cross head unit had been more arduous. Although with the lubricating system shut down there was no free flowing oil, all the surfaces were still filmed with it, and, in consequence, very slippery. In addition everything was still hot from the engine's recent running and our discomfort was compounded by the necessity to constantly brace ourselves against the rolling of the ship. Being one of those working there as I clambered on the mighty cranks amongst the connecting rods I remembered the

Work inside the crankcase preparing a lower piston for lifting. The visual clarity of this sketch has been achieved using artistic licence to remove the whole crankcase cover plate, but in reality it would be happening inside the circular inspection door, that being the only one removed.

sailor's adage from windjammer days to 'keep one hand for yourself and one for the ship', realising it was still as applicable as ever even if its context had changed. No longer was it a matter of fisting canvas high aloft on a gale-lashed topsil yard, rather it was struggling with slippery tools in the hot slippery innards of a big ship's engine, but the adage's truth remained. We were nearly done in the crankcase when the 'all hands' call came to assist with the lifting of the upper piston and the Third sent us off to help. Leaving the crankcase we were pleased to find it distinctly cooler up on the top platform now cluttered with tools, and looking curiously more spacious where hand rails had been removed to facilitate the work, and to allow the unit to be craned across to its overhauling position.

As soon as everyone was assembled and ready to steady the unit the Second gave the signal for the lift to begin. Above us, the crane whirred and slowly, the assembly of the piston, beam and guides began to rise and, as it did so, we all became suddenly very conscious of the rolling of the ship. Glancing up I noticed how a shaft of sunlight through the skylight was sending shadows chasing madly on the white paintwork of the casing, and we found ourselves looking knowingly at each other aware that we'd never hold the massive weight once it was free of the restraint of the cylinder.

Stopping the lift the Second deliberated for a moment with lips pursed and then made an announcement which brought a smile to our faces.

"I'll ring the bridge," he said. "We'll get the mates down, and the deck hands, and we'll rig strops and tackle lines in four directions then with that lot tailing on we'll hold her alright."

The wait while this suggestion was passed to the bridge and then acted on gave us a welcome break and some of us popped up to get a breath of fresh air out on deck.

Stepping out of the engineers' entrance on the starboard side we leant on the teak- topped rail of the poop deck drinking in the fresh sea air. The broad vista of the sea lay before us, its great swells rolling us in stately fashion as they lifted us in their passing. Looking forward at the midship accommodation I noticed the mates had hoisted the two black balls above the bridge this being the international signal to inform any vessel which chanced upon us that we were without power and therefore 'not under command'. The 'balls' were in fact big, round, wicker-work baskets, painted black; at night they were lowered and replaced by two red lights. We were going to see a lot of both in the next two weeks or so.

Back in the engine room we waited for our helpers to arrive. The Second was anxious to crack on with the job; it would be good to have the pistons lifted by lunchtime. Then, a movement above caught our eyes. It was the first of the deck crowd making a timid entry to the engine room. In they came, their paint splattered dungarees and sun burnt faces, and in the case of the mates, collars, ties and gold-braided reefer jackets, making them all look awkwardly out of place in our world of steel, heat and oil. Assembling gingerly along the top platforms they looked as uncomfortable as soccer fans dropped off by mistake at an Ascot enclosure. The Second, enjoying his moment of command over his deck counterparts, issued his orders. Professional rivalry between mates (the navigators) and engineers, was well known at sea (we would experience a significant confrontation later in the voyage) but for the moment we really did have our deck colleagues as putty in our hands and the Second was clearly enjoying making the most of it.

With strops fitted round the partially lifted piston, tackles were attached and four groups of men, deck and engine, cheerfully mixed, took the strain. The lifting was resumed. Kneeling on the plates to monitor progress the Second, his hand waving encouragingly in an upward direction, announced, "She's clearing now," and was promptly bowled over as the piston emerged and the whole unit swung with the roll of the ship despite the restraint of the holding teams. Fortunately he was unhurt and scrambling to his feet, fearful of damage to the side rods, he energised the teams with a shout probably heard in far-off Cape Town of "HOLD IT!" Pulling manfully we got the feel of the unit's weight and gradually it was cleared of the rods and inched over to the starboard side where the girders were situated to bear it safely for maintenance.

THE PROBLEM WORSENS...

Then, while a couple of us were left to strip the top piston's rings, with the attendant laborious cleaning of their grooves to perform, the rest turned their attention to removing the damaged lower piston.

A short ladder was propped in the gaping maw of the still warm cylinder and an engineer scrambled nimbly down with a long eye-bolt to screw in the threaded hole provided in the centre of the piston head. Wire strops were passed down and the crane hook lowered to accept them and, with the ladder removed the lift commenced. It hadn't gone very far when it stopped. Immediately there came a faint voice from inside the engine saying, "carry on," while the Second, peering down into the cylinder made upward gestures with his hands to the electrician handling the crane controls. He, in his turn looked bleakly at his finger which had the 'lift' button firmly pressed. Then, something made him glance up and with a startled yelp he cast the handset from him as if it had bitten him. His cry made us all look up and we were appalled to see that the great steel girders which formed the basic structure of the crane, were actually flexing downwards obviously under a terrible strain. 'Lecky', realising that simply letting the 'lift' button go, didn't ease the problem, grabbed the handset as it swung back, and pressed the 'lower' button. Immediately the wires slackened off and to our relief the crane resumed its normal appearance, but the awful significance of the cause of this drama instantly transcended our concerns for the crane. Clearly, the piston was jammed in the cylinder.

The deck crowd, who had been impatiently waiting to assist in its removal, sensing a long delay, could be seen picking their way gingerly through the tools and dismembered hand rails as they melted away like spring snow before an April sun. The Second went down to the control desk and I watched him take the phone to the Chief's cabin to give him the bad news. Shortly after, carpet slippers on the ladders saw an even glummer Chief come down and much anxious talk ensued as the problem was debated.

Meanwhile, lunch was served. As with all such big breakdown situations work would continue until it was completed so the stewards brought lunch into the engine room and we enjoyed it, picnic fashion, sat on the floor plates of the fan flat at the after end of the engine room where the steam driven fans hummed and throbbed as they supplied air to the boiler furnaces beneath. As we ate our meal the conversation focused, not unnaturally, on what we could do in the face of the set-back.

"It might be a towing job," someone said, but that was laughably dismissed as the company wouldn't countenance a salvage situation. Another said it was not unknown in such circumstances to disconnect the bottom end bearings of the offending unit, chain them up securely in the crankcase and then run the engine on five cylinders instead of six.

Another, even more radical possibility, was that we leave the piston jammed in the cylinder and then embark on a major dismantling task to free the cylinder complete with piston and then fit our spare one. As it was said my eye darted to where the spare cylinder liner was positioned right at the top of the engine room. There it sat in its fixtures, and although being seen everyday, so irrelevant an object was it that it was unseen in exactly the way familiar ornaments become 'unseen' on the home mantelshelf. Ships often went from the builders to the breakers with such items of spare gear never used and so the thought of actually using ours was I guessed, a pretty astonishing one.

The stewards had now served coffee and the Second, who I knew had been with the Chief amidships, rejoined us. As he sipped his drink he outlined a strategy we were going to try. It involved using the turning gear to bring the cross head up to the piston and then, combining its effort with that of the crane we might be successful. Over coffee, cigarettes had been lit and as the smoke haze rose, swirling lazily as it caught shafts of light from the skylights above as the ship rolled, it struck me as having a spiritual quality about it as one might imagine the incense of the sanctuary rising like an offering. I trusted any Godly attention would receive it as such for I sensed we were going to need Divine inspiration if not actual intervention.

Lunch eaten I popped up to the changing room and while there I saw through the ports the black signal balls swinging in lazy arcs against the fresh wind-blown blue of the sky. Their depressing colour endorsed the depressing feeling a stopped ship always conveys. It really was a feeling with a death-like quality about it which, after all, wasn't entirely inappropriate since our source of 'life' had indeed 'died' for a while and even at that moment lay crucially dismembered.

Back down below preparations were made to implement the Second's strategy. The crane was precisely positioned and the slack taken up on the strops. An engineer was stationed at the turning gear and a code of signals agreed to ensure the 'push' and 'pull' would be absolutely together. I was stationed in the crankcase with the Third, and once the crosshead was in position to bear, the signal was given. The turning gear motor hummed, the crane motor whirred and, to everyone's delight the piston began to move.

Delight however was short-lived.

The upward movement stopped. A cry of "stop" echoed around and motors were switched off. In the light of his lead lamp I caught sight of the Chief peering up at the crankcase door. He had the stricken expression of a mouse before a pouncing cat. "He's worried about the main bearings," confided the Third. "Pressures like this can damage the white metal and then we really might be a towing job."

A spare cylinder liner, stowed right at the top of the engine room just beneath the skylights. Hand chain blocks would have to be used to lower it to a position where the engine room gantry crane could be brought into use.

The Second appeared clambering up beside us and with the little encouragement we'd experienced he'd got the bit well and truly between his teeth. The piston was going to come out! He ordered us off to the workshop store to break out an enormous bottle jack, his plan now being to use wooden blocks to protect the crosshead and use the force of the jack to back up the pull of the crane. The poor Chief seemed on the verge of having a fit of the vapours, and in the end, carpet slippers on the ladders told us he was off to take to his cabin and his cigarettes. There he would await good news of our efforts on the one hand, or the fate of his pension on the other, for which he now clearly feared the worse.

When all was ready we tried again and, to everyone's inexpressible relief it worked. It took a long time of patient jacking and blocking but it worked and at last, the cracked piston was at the top of the cylinder just inside the lip as a restraint from it swinging free and taking charge. Dinner, eaten on the flan flat, had long come and gone and it was now late on the Monday night which meant that if we were going enlist the aid of the deck staff, the sailors would now be in a position to claim overtime pay. Such expenditure being unthinkable it was agreed that as the rolling had eased a little we'd undertake to try to complete the removal of the piston ourselves. And as a welcome encouragement the steward appeared, bearing not the usual night watch's supply of sandwiches, but a treat of a fry-up supper instead. During our break I nipped up again to the changing room and now through the ports I could see the daylight signal had been replaced with the night one of two red lights on the hoist above the bridge. There they swung jewelling the night with a hint of menace as the black had suggested depression in the day. Back down below, invigorated by our supper, we formed two teams, port and starboard. Strops were positioned and tackles rigged and two teeth-gritting teams took the strain as the piston was lifted clear. It was quickly craned over to its overhauling position on the top platform and we relaxed. However, as it was not just a case of re-ringing the existing head, but a complete dismantling of the unit in order to fit a new skirt, it was then necessary to use the crane to lift it so that with wooden spars as levers we could cant it over to lie on its side on the top platform. The piston's construction was essentially simple only the size and weight of its component parts making it unwieldy. The unit comprised the piston head itself to which was bolted the flanged end of a stout rod. Then a 'skirt' was fitted over the rod to rest on the piston head, it being bolted to a smaller flange at the other end of the rod. All that had to be done was to remove those nuts and then, with tackles rigged, pull the skirt clear.

The night wore on and everyone was feeling weary but the work could not stop and in a sense to brighten the moment, we were in for a surprise. As the skirt was drawn back a cascade of lead coloured balls of assorted sizes spilled out onto the platform. I gawped with the bemusement of inexperience, but the old hands quickly realised what it meant especially when we looked at the rod's big flange bolted to the piston head. There, several nuts were missing and their studs, including the few still with their nuts on had the appearance of smooth round rivet heads. It meant that when the ship had been in dry dock and her engine had been dismembered for overhaul, on reassembly these nuts could not have been tightened properly and secured with locking wire. Thus as the engine had been running, nuts had progressively worked loose then to fly up and down with each stroke of the piston, the effect on them being not unlike that achieved with molten lead in the shot tower I remembered visiting at the Festival of Britain in 1951. Nuts that had remained in place were pounded into the rivet head shapes before us and the consequence of it all was that the stresses involved through inadequate tightness had cracked the skirt. It was all quite intriguing and the great consolation was that we were in no way to blame. When the Second broke the news to him the Chief's relief knew no bounds and he had yet another cigarette, this time in celebration! Tuesday was getting well into its stride by then and once the damaged skirt was secured and we'd chiselled off the rounded nuts and studs of the piston head in order to free the rod, work became simply tedious as distinct from dramatic. The spare skirt, like the spare cylinder another apparent ornament of the engine room but thankfully much more accessible, had to be broken out of its painted up fastenings, and likewise a new piston head was brought into play. At noon a Nelsonian touch enlivened the moment in the form of a rum issue for those who wished it, it being reckoned as a good way to energise ever wearying limbs.

At the controls; about to start up.

The work of the cleaning and preparing of the spare gear we were utilising seemed to take ages, and of course the cylinder itself had to be cleaned of carbon rings around the central combustion area as well as having to be thoroughly examined for any damage resulting from the knocks its bottom lip had received from the cracked skirt. The hours slipped from Tuesday to Wednesday but, gradually however, things were coming together. The lower piston was reassembled ensuring the flange nuts were properly attended to and, with the heads of both upper and lower pistons sporting shiny new rings, the matter of putting the engine back together could begin.

Finally, shortly after another alfresco meal on the fan flat on Wednesday evening, preparations could begin for starting up. The restored pistons, now back in the engine, were warmed through with preheated distilled cooling water, and the lubricating oil system was started up. The engine was then turned several times using the turning gear and when all seemed satisfactory the air valve was opened up from the big reservoir tanks situated in the 'tween decks above. With air on at six hundred pounds per square inch and a final check round, a ripple of excitement passed through our weary frames as we foregathered by the control station. The Second nodded in the direction of the telegraph and someone swung it enthusiastically back and forth round the dial bringing the handle to rest at 'Dead Slow Ahead'. As soon as the bridge responded, the Second's muscular hand took a firm grip on the air start lever, pushing it firmly over. A whooshing of compressed air above proclaimed the turning of the engine, and the Second brought the lever back. An engineer on the middles' platform was then busy closing the six indicator cocks on the cylinders and, as soon as he reappeared, the Second repeated the movement of the air lever. As the engine turned, he now moved the fuel valve setting lever as well. The engine fired, the air lever was brought back and a steadying throb proclaimed our engine was alive again. After a short run she was stopped in order to make a final check on the repaired unit and then, we were off again.

Some of us were then allowed to seek the luxury of our bunks, but the Second and two juniors stayed up for the rest of the night to 'run her in' and it was not until 9am on Thursday that 'Full Ahead, Full Away' was rung on the telegraph. Our voyage to La Plata had resumed, but I was intrigued to hear later that in the time of our stoppage the Benguela ocean current pushing up from the Southern Ocean along the West African coast had carried the ship nearly three hundred miles off our course. It was I thought something to reflect on; we could say we'd accomplished a mighty work in effecting our repair but mightier forces were indeed all around us.

DRAMA IN THE RIVER PLATE...

With the drama of our three day breakdown behind us we'd pressed on to cover the five-thousand miles or so to South America and having arrived at the River Plate pilot station, we'd begun passage in the buoyed channel of the great estuary. It was night time when we arrived and picked up the pilot but for all that his presence suggested landfall, so immense is the estuary the coast was still a long way off, and there was not a twinkle of any homely or welcoming lights anywhere to be seen. Now we were on pilotage the 'stand-by' watch custom applied, an extra hand being detailed for duty down below, and it had fallen to me to join the Third engineer and his junior during their midnight to four watch. Little did I know of the dramas we were 'standing by' for! The estuary being so big and the pilotage so long, the 'stand by' atmosphere actually had a very relaxed feel to it. The main engine pulsed steadily with vibrant life, and when shortly before three am mugs of tea appeared, and supper box sandwiches began to be munched, there was almost a holiday picnic air to the proceedings.

The Third stood, arms akimbo, his mug grasped in a projecting hand, his thighs resting comfortably against the rounded edge of the control box, while his eyes ranged ceaselessly over the quivering needles of the gauges on the big lozenge shaped board above him. His watching only broke away when he took appreciative sips from his mug of tea or he chose where next to bite his beef sandwich. His junior was stood further for'ard tea in one hand, sandwich in the other while he studied the temperatures of the engine cooling water returns as they tumbled in their sight glasses, and I was leaning comfortably on the engineer's desk my elbow cushioned by the log book, and my tea to hand in the pen tray. It was all very homely and peaceful which made the moment a drama was to unfold all the more dramatic. Suddenly, the Third jerked erect as if someone had jabbed a bradawl in the seat of his boiler suit and, slamming his mug down, he took off past me to leap up a ladder giving access at the after end of the engine to the narrow grating mid-way up the crankcase from which the upper inspection doors were reached. These upper doors were fitted with an opening porthole and the grating's access to them was directly in the way of the number five crankcase, the site of our recent breakdown problems. Thus it was with great dismay that I watched the Third knock back the port's holding dog and fling it open only to have his head engulfed in a thick blast of creamy grey smoke. Our recently repaired number five lower piston was, it seemed, in trouble again after all. However, the Third clearly thought differently. With great presence of mind he slammed the port shut again and, shaking his head free of smoke he promptly slid down to the floor plates and in a flash disappeared round to the back of the engine. Seconds later, and going now even faster than before, he reappeared heading straight for the control station. As he arrived wild-eyed, he gave an informative yell, "the thrusts on fire!" Alas the full significance of this was, by my inexperience, denied me at that moment, but that it was something very serious was perfectly clear. As the Third manipulated the controls to stop the engine I came to life intending to operate the telegraph, but so quick were his actions he beat me even to that. Then, turning from the telegraph without waiting for the bridge to reply, he leapt for the telephones, grabbing the one to rouse the Chief to apprise him of our new crisis.

Up on the bridge, as we discovered later, our sudden ringing of 'Stop' had caused a degree of confusion. All had been truly peaceful in the warm darkness of the wheelhouse. A good helmsman had been at the wheel and the pilot had the flashing lights of the channel buoys in a confident visual and mental grasp, and had even then just been judging things for a slight course adjustment in view of a bend ahead. The officer of the watch had been pleasantly relaxed as he let the pilot bear the immediate burden of our navigational progress and then, suddenly, their haven of tranquillity had been rudely disturbed by the strident rasp of the telegraph announcing 'Stop'.

On the bridge their concerns had focused on three things namely, how much way the ship would carry to give her steerage in view of the channel bend approaching; how the set of the tide would influence her movement and finally, how quickly an anchor could be dropped. Orders to turn the hands to for anchoring had been dispatched immediately and then eyes had strained in the dark watching the bows, and the channel buoys, as the ship gently slowed. It had become readily clear that she was deciding her own destiny. With all the determination of a sleepy head meeting its pillow for the night, she had eased her forefoot snugly and firmly into the estuary mud on the bend of the channel. Enough of ocean wandering she had seemed to say, a nice rest on a comfortable mud bank for a while would do very nicely. Thus not only were we broken down but, aground as well!

Down below, in response to the Third's summons, the Chief had appeared. He was distraught. In his carpet slippers but now, with his woolly 'cardi' on over his pyjama top, he seemed to have aged even more. As he took in the enormity of our new and appalling situation he must have felt convinced that his pension really had vanished into the ether.

A VERY LUCKY ESCAPE...

Other engineers were streaming down and as I dashed about closing coolers down and adjusting temperatures I listened in amazement to snatches of conversation which suggested we were all very lucky to be there at all. It seemed that the Third, realising his initial suspicions of failure with our piston repair were wrong, had then checked the thrust bearing and, through its inspection port had seen actual flames being dragged around as the propeller shaft revolved. The amazing thing was that as the thrust unit was integral with the engine crankcase, a space fully charged with hot oil mist, the presence of naked flames should have guaranteed a crankcase explosion. Every engine carried a warning plate saying amongst other things, 'Early detection of overheating and prompt slowing down or stopping of the main or auxiliary engines as circumstance permits will prevent the occurrence of the conditions favourable to fire or explosion'. It really was staggering. There we were not merely having overheating but, an actual fire! We should have exploded; amazingly it hadn't happened!

However, there was no time to waste talking about what might have happened. A number of us were mobilised to get the thrust block opened and, once its big cover was lifted with chain blocks the damage was revealed. White metal on the faces of the bearing pads had melted as a result, quite clearly of frictional heat. Some of the metal had actually fired which had created the flames the Third had seen through the inspection glass while other of it had formed molten globules which, being dragged round by the revolving collar and jammed between it and the steel base of the pads had resulted in the normally glass-smooth face of the collar being badly scored. That this had happened at all could only have been because the oil supply to this important unit had failed, and the reason for that would have to be traced at some point but, more immediately, decisions had to made about whether repairs were feasible. While the seniors debated courses of action I looked at the opened up unit and realised that we were dealing with something relatively rare as an experience and one therefore, as a young cadet, the company would expect me to learn as much from as possible. The thrust bearing in a ship is not unlike one of those internal parts in the human body

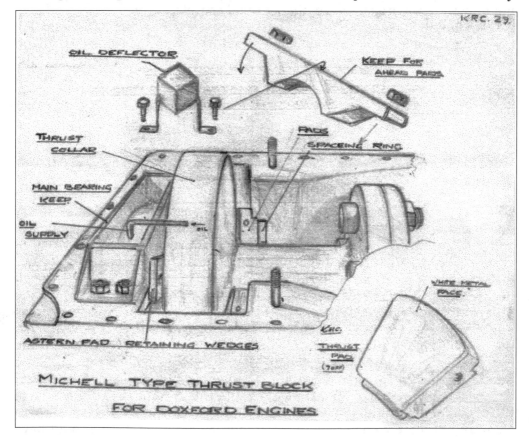

A sketch of the thrust block of the British Reliance. It was drawn for inclusion in notes the company expected apprentices to keep.

32

which function unseen and unthought-of but upon which the liveliness we all like to present as life, entirely depends. The thrust bearing's importance can be understood quite simply when one visualises an engine driving a shaft with a propeller on the end immersed in water. Once the engine starts and the propeller revolves, it 'pushes' against the surrounding water and, that 'push' will then transmit along the shaft and distort the working parts of the engine. As this would damage or even wreck the engine, something is required to allow the shaft to revolve whilst absorbing the 'push' safely. The way that this is most commonly done and was exactly so in our case is to have a disk, or collar as it is known, machined on a section of the shaft having a greater diameter that the shaft itself. This enables pads to be fitted on each side (both sides being required for ahead and astern running) and because the frame in which the pads are fitted is securely mounted to the ship, once the shaft and its collar revolve the 'push', or thrust, of the propeller is then transmitted through the pads to the frame and thence to the ship. The pads have special white metal bearing surfaces for the shaft collar to run against and the only essential thing is to ensure a copious supply of oil to ensure smooth running and to minimise and dissipate the build-up of frictional heat.

The disastrous evidence of what can happen in the event of the oil supply having a thrombotic stoppage while the shaft is turning, now lay starkly before us in the form of molten and burnt white metal, and the consequent scoring of the ahead face of the shaft's great collar. It was a grim sight. While debate amongst the seniors about what was to be done was going on the question of how it had happened persisted. As there hadn't been any trouble elsewhere in the engine's extensive lubrication system suspicion fell on the pipe that led from the rest of the system to the thrust unit itself, and the Second ordered a spare hand to get cracking to dismantle it. The pipe carried oil to a point where it discharged openly against a diamond shaped deflector ensuring a generous flood fell over the thrust collar to run endlessly down between it and the pads on either side. Being such a critical point of lubrication the pipe was fitted with a fine filter but when this was opened up it and the pipe, were found to be solidly choked. Expressions of surprise and anger mingled richly as, under prodding with a length of wire, wads and strands of cotton waste appeared.

THE FINGER OF BLAME POINTS TO FALMOUTH AGAIN – THE CHIEF'S RELIEF

As the ship didn't carry cotton waste and, more to the point, the only time any of the oil system's pipe work had been opened up was when she'd been in the dry dock at Falmouth two months or so before, the finger of blame for our troubles clearly pointed in that direction. All we could assume was that traces of waste used in cleaning operations by the dry dock fitters, had been left in the system and, as it was on the discharge side of the lubricating pump rather than the suction where the system's main filters would have collected it safely, it had simply been pushed together in the one free flowing pipe – the one to the thrust block, eventually choking it solid. Finding the source of the problem was gratifying, the more so as it clearly meant no accusatory finger at any future inquiry could point at the ship to lay any blame there. The Chief was visibly relieved, his pension seeming to float down to be within his grasp again but, it was a hollow satisfaction for us as it in no way changed the burden of the work which lay before us.

Attention turned again to that in earnest and the Second instructed that the big bridging keep fitted above the pads to hold them in place be removed. It was then clear that the only way to remove the pads which, as things having cooled down a little allowing the molten white metal to set, were now effectively welded to the face of the collar, was to engage the turning gear and ease the shaft round. With the keep removed the pads would then come round with the collar and could be knocked clear as they emerged. It was soon done and, with the damaged pads put aside the enormity of our task was clear. The ahead face of the great collar some six inches deep, and three feet in diameter was savagely scored all the way round. A repair would, ideally, see the thrust shaft section being removed and taken ashore to be set up in a big lathe to enable the face to be skimmed flat again but, as this was impossible in our situation the only method we had recourse to was to work on it in situ and by hand. This would mean filing and polishing the collar face to restore its surface, and using a big 'U' gauge to ensure the collar's width was accurately maintained all the way round. Due to the confined area of working the seniors agreed a strategy of splitting us into two groups to work six on and six off until the job was done. Every file in the ship was found and brought down to the site of operations and with two men, one on each side of the propeller shaft and perched uncomfortably, half in and half out of the casing, the work of filing began. It was going to be a long job.

Having been on duty all night I was put amongst those having the first six hours stand down and I made my way wearily up out of the engine room. Out on deck I looked round; it seemed depressing. There was absolutely nothing to be seen, no land, no other ships, not even a bird or two. We were alone in a mud-brown watery vastness, rippled by a gusty wind and dotted with a few dark objects that were buoys marking the channel.

Over breakfast, conversations revealed that a tug was coming down from BA to join us and there was much debate as to what she'd do. If she got us off the bank we would of course be a towing job anyway for broken down as we were we would be helpless and therefore we represented a salvage prize. One could imagine the thoughts racing in the minds of her crew; great riches could be about to fall into their eager hands...! On the other hand her role might be more important in a standby context for emergencies, as stuck on the channel bend as we were we must have represented something of a navigational hazard to other shipping.

However, such thoughts were not mine to worry about and I sought the haven of my bunk for some joyous rest before I would have to take up a file down below. As it always does in the face of change, life quickly assumed its own new if unfamiliar routine. The work of two men on the thrust was replaced for greater convenience by one working in concentrated bouts of energy and then being relieved. Thus passed the hours of the six of each phase. Meanwhile the other operations of the engine room, maintaining the boilers, electrical generations and the domestic services as a whole, were carried out by those standing down for a rest from the seemingly endless filing. The log books recording this activity were delivered regularly to the Chief's cabin for him to make up the fair copies for the company and, it was on one such delivery visit that I happened to make, that he stubbed a cigarette out and while reaching for another asked me worriedly how the work was going on down below. I felt sorry for him because although we now knew neither of our major problems were in any way our fault nevertheless, it was the Chief's engine that was broken down, the ship it powered was aground, a cargo charter was in tatters and he was ultimately responsible for the repair we were attempting. Looking at his woebegone face I spoke as encouragingly

The Royal Mail Line ship Alcantra easing past the British Reliance, aground in the River Plate. The tug, Captain Ray, can be seen at the tanker's bow.

as a mere cadet could do; he looked as if he could benefit from a comforting hug but I had to draw the line at that. Leaving him to his worries and his cigarettes I went from his sea cabin to go down below again.

Outside I found several of the crew gathered excitedly by the rail and following pointing fingers I was intrigued to see a Royal Mail liner working her way towards us. She proved to be the Alcantara fresh out from home with the mails and passengers bound for Buenos Aires and we waved cheerfully to her people on her starboard side as she moved gingerly round us. Those aboard her must have been fascinated to have such a close view of a stricken tanker making, as we must have done, an interesting diversion for any passer by. However, we must have been soon forgotten for they clearly got down to diversions of their own as became clear a few hours later.

I had not long come up from the engine room after another six hour spell when more excitement outside brought me from my cabin. Looking around I expected to see another ship working her way past us inward or outward bound. However, it was no ship that was claiming everyone's attention but something rather more amusing. Looking over the side there for all to see drifting past our hull on an ebbing tide were condoms. Dotted whitely in the mud coloured waters there seemed to be dozens of them! "Strewth; would you look at that!" someone breathed, incredulously, adding dryly, "those passengers on that mail ship 'aint 'arf been busy. 'At it' like ruddy rabbits by the look of it!" We laughed, and thought of them all having a last fling before they'd be docked in BA. Seeing the evidence of their fun floating past us, we realised of course that the Alcantara would by then have long been berthed in the docks and, for those who'd enjoyed it, the 'fun' would in fact already be history and, as likely as not, forgotten history at that.

For our part, far from forgotten, our history was in the making as we endeavoured to achieve a repair that would set us free from the River Plate's cloying mud so, leaving the condoms to their watery fate we turned from the rail to get on with it.

THOUGHTS TURN TO BREAKING FREE OF THE MUD...

Meanwhile we'd all begun entertaining the sneaky feeling that the longer we stayed stuck the ship was snuggling her forefoot ever more comfortably in the mud, determined to make the most of her untimely rest! With the drawing on of the hours into the third day of our stranding, our weary efforts began to produce a result that confirmed our belief that indeed we'd 'do it'. Admittedly, when it had been said at the outset of our work it had been rather hesitantly proclaimed, but now it rang loud and clear. The filed and polished area of the collar had grown steadily larger, and as a section would be declared finished the turning gear would be started to ease the shaft round to present a new one. The files were regularly carded (cleaned with a wire brush) in order to keep them as free from filing swarf as was possible, and our fingers became inured to the painful knocks they experienced from catching the edge of the great collar as the files swept back and forth. This was of course simply because of the awkwardness of the angle we were working at. Usually the work of filing is carried out in the flat plane with work held at a comfortable height in a bench vice, and fingers holding the file can be kept well clear on each side, but here we were working in the vertical plane on the face of the shaft's collar, and enduring at the same time, the added discomfort of doing it stood half in and half out of the thrust's casing; painful knocks were simply inevitable. However, now that progress was manifestly clear and success could be really anticipated, smiles were replacing frowns, and grumbles were ousted by the jolly banter of triumph.

With the work advancing so well, thoughts were being aired about getting ready to start up. The tug, The MV Capitan Ray, which had kept company with us since its arrival, had made frequent offers to try to pull us clear, but these had been politely declined on the basis that we'd make our own effort first and only if it failed would her help be accepted. However, the seniors felt that the ship had been fast enough in the mud not to want to budge very easily so talk had turned to the idea of lightening her by off-loading some of the cargo. This

had been discussed with the company in London who had in the end agreed to make the arrangements, with the result that we soon found ourselves joined by a small coastal tanker. She snuggled up alongside, and once we'd increased steam production in the boiler room, pumping operations could begin. Discharge hoses were slung from a 'midship derrick, coupled up to our visitor and soon after the rhythmic thudding of our cargo pumps resounded throughout the ship as oil began to be off-loaded.

Down below with the filing and polishing work nearly complete, attention had turned to the fitting of new thrust pads and, the very important aspect of cleaning out the casing. Any residual filing swarf, pieces of white metal from the ruined ahead pads, or any general dirt from our constant clambering about, could create a frictional hazard when we'd be running again. Thus cleaning was most thoroughly attended to, and this applied particularly to the pads of the other

Informing the bridge of progress, and intentions about engine management.

side of the collar, ones that took the thrust (that 'push') when the ship was going astern. Although undamaged the astern pads we realised were going to be called on with a vengeance. In order to break our bows free of the mud we'd obviously have to run the engine in reverse and, no doubt, long and hard at that! It meant that our repair to the ahead side would not be put to the test immediately but we wanted no repetition of our troubles through damage to the astern-running face of the collar! A big 'U' shaped gauge had been carefully used to check that the thickness of the collar was uniform and true all round, and new pads had been broken out of their storage hideaway in the 'tween decks. Seeing them emerge it was sobering to realise that these were also items of spare gear which could go from a ship's fitting out to the breakers without being seen let alone used, so relatively rare are thrust block problems. However, ours were now warmly welcomed to the light of day indeed.

Once they'd been thoroughly cleaned they were bedded to the collar's face this being done by coating it with engineer's marking blue and then having pressed the pads to it, scrapers were used on the soft white metal to remove high spots shown up where the marking blue had transferred. When all seven pads were finished they were fitted in their holding channel in the casing and adjusted to leave the correct clearance of twelve thousandths of an inch from the collar. Lubricating oil was then liberally applied, and the shaft revolved with the turning gear and then, at last, the Second gave the order, "box her up". The casing top was chainblocked down and secured but the inspection port was left open as someone was to be stationed there when we would start the main engine, so that at the first sign of any trouble there'd be no delay in stopping!

Attention turned to getting the engine ready for starting up, and a tangible air of triumph at our achievement, although tempered slightly with anxiety as to its outcome, permeated the engine room as compressors and pumps were started up. Meanwhile, up on deck we'd discovered that our visiting tanker had now departed with a goodly proportion of our cargo, although it had to be said, when looking over the side, it didn't appear to have made any difference to us. Presumably the cloying mud was possessed of a powerful suction like grip, which was keeping us down, but equally it was generally felt that if our own propeller was turning and with some help from the Capitan Ray, that and the added buoyancy factor might do the trick.

Thus at a moment when river flow and tidal height were firmly in our favour and with the Capitan Ray out in the stream attached and ready to tug as a good tug should, the moment of truth approached. With us ready below, readiness on the bridge was confirmed by telephone. Starting air was opened to the main engines. The Third took station on the thrust block with a lead lamp to shine in the inspection port's aperture and a generous flow of oil glinted in its light as it gushed from the cleaned out pipe. At the front of the engine the Second squared up to the control box, and with a final glance over the gauge board, and then around at our expectant faces, he nodded at the telegraph.

"Give 'em 'Dead Slow Astern'," he said.

Someone swung the handle back and forth round the dial bringing it to rest on the required setting and, as the bridge pointer responded the second swung the big reversing lever back towards him to its astern setting. Then, with his left hand he pushed the starting air lever firmly over. The familiar whooshing of compressed air took place above us, and all eyes watched the revolution counter needle quiver into the astern running sector as the engine turned. Pulling the lever back the Second straightened up to wipe his hands, while on the middles' platform an engineer ran along closing the cylinder indicator cocks.

A shout of 'OK' and a wave from the platform announced that the cocks were closed, and the Second thrust the air lever over again followed, as the engine turned, by the fuel lever. As the engine fired he brought the air control back and slowly eased the fuel valve lever notch by notch along its curved toothed rack. The engine settled to a slow rhythmic throb. "Check with the Third," shouted the Second, and I dashed to the after end to peer beneath the fuel pumps at the figure on the thrust casing, lamp in hand and eyes locked on the oil-splashed goings-on inside the inspection point. In response to my call, a thumbs up waved briefly, and I ran back to report. "We'll give her ten minutes like this," said the Second, "then we'll stop and check, and if she's OK we'll give her a run at 'Full Astern'." The Fourth rang the bridge to let them know and we all settled, watching the gauges and the needle of the revolution indicator quivering among the low figures in the astern sector.

The minutes passed like hours, until the Second, eyeing the clock said, "right – ring 'Stop'." The bridge responded immediately. The Second centred the fuel lever, and then dashed round to consult with the Third. Hands reached in through the port anxiously caressing the shaft collar, and to everyone's relief all seemed well. Back at the controls and wiping his hands over and over with the nervousness of the moment, the Second said, "OK – this is it. Ring 'Half Astern' first, and we'll take her up gradually."

Bells rang, air whooshed and away went the engine again and, bit by bit the speed was brought up. The floor plates began to vibrate as they always did when running astern and a sense of drama was eerily real. We could imagine the scene outside. The mud-coloured water would now be creamed like Bailey's liqueur streaming for'ard from our propeller, thrashing round trying to draw us back. Out in the stream, the Capitan Ray would be doing its bit, and surely but surely the mud must be going to yield. The Second eased the fuel lever further, and 'Full Astern' was rung and answered.

Floor plates jigged and hearts danced in mouths, and seconds seemed like whole minutes until suddenly, a strident ringing brought all eyes flashing to the telegraph. The bridge had rung 'Stop'! Was it we wondered because they were giving up on a failed effort, or ...? The phone rang, and the Second, leaving the controls grabbed it and we knew as a great grin creased his face, we were off. We'd done it! Smiles and backslapping went all round, but only for a moment as of course, with the ship now free we had to ensure she could be controlled, for we were, when all said and done, in an estuary channel, not the open sea! The Capitan Ray for all she'd no doubt helped, had done only that, and she couldn't claim us as a salvage prize, our own engines having done the prime work of achieving our release. However, if we weren't on the ball and we got in more difficulty the tug's crew might yet get their salvage bonanza they'd been yearning for! Accordingly therefore, we were going to have to start the engines for ahead running and now put our repair firmly to the test. The bridge were informed that a slow speed policy only would be attempted, and they now assumed control of the ship ringing down for us to give them 'Half Ahead'. The exuberance of the past few moments vanished with the realisation our repair was going to come into play. The Second started her up, and we watched anxiously for any sign of distress from the Third atop the thrust casing. Minutes past and all was well. Tensions eased and the Third, calling someone to replace him, went to chat with the Second. All indeed seemed to be well, thus we slowly, but steadily, made our way on up the estuary, to the land and, in towards our berth at La Plata. There a very disappointed Capitan Ray helped us into the dock before departing, her crew no doubt dreaming dreams of what might have been.

THE INFAMOUS MEAT PLANT...

Our entry to La Plata's wide, creek-like dock, off the main river, had had one brief moment of alarm. A clutch of us were gathered at the control station dealing with the manoeuvring required by the bridge when suddenly, everyone realised that our noses were all twitching – very defensively! An alien and unpleasant smell was enveloping us and, with our anxieties at fever pitch for the wellbeing of our thrust block, the same question was in everyone's mind – did the smell proclaim FIRE?! A junior sprinted to check at the thrust, but the engineer on duty on the casing, lead lamp in hand, waved him cheerily away; all was well. Giving us the thumbs up, as he turned to come back we saw him pause and move sideways and back again, and sideways and back, as if in a graceful ballet routine! Then sporting a big grin but holding his nose, he came back to report that the smell was in fact coming down an air vent. It was strongest when he stood under the vent than when out of its line, and as the vent in question was one of the few to have a powered fan in, the smell was indeed coming in upon us with a vengeance from something or somewhere up on deck or beyond.

Once alongside and with 'Finished With Engines' rung, we went to see where we were, and to satisfy our curiosity about the now all-pervading smell. Coming up from the engine room we found we were moored on the starboard side, and sprawled out before us were the familiar towers, tanks and pipes of a refinery complex. There was nothing of much interest there but, from the port side we found ourselves looking across the dock at an enormous factory complex. It was a meat processing plant we were told, and the appalling smell came from great belching chimneys, their foul smoke coming directly our way because, most unfortunately, we were on the downwind side. We stared across, marvelling more and more at the scale of it, as we absorbed the detail in the scene. In the distance at what we could see was the starting point of the plant's operations, there was an expansive yarded area in which big, high-sided lorries were delivering cattle. Russet coloured beasts were plain to see jostling in great metal pens from which ramps led, presumably to entrance doors out of our line of sight. We could assume that the animals were urged up, and into the plant and then, we could only guess at the various goings-on in the long chain of enormous buildings before us. In the middle the belching chimneys suggested their own unspeakable things, and it was probably we thought something to do with the rendering down of bones. "For glue" someone reckoned sagely. Whatever else went on could be judged by the activity from the final block. There, from great cavernous doors conveyor lines emerged with on some, swaying processions of carcasses, and on others crated boxes. "They'll be corned beef" the glue-guesser observed, as sagely as before. The conveyor lines led towards a big Federal Line cargo ship, which we fondly imagined was loading for the home market and we thought of homely mums and wives off to the butchers for a bit of meat for dinner, quite oblivious to the enormity of the sheer tonnage of it on the hoof, tripping innocently into the incredible plant before us!

A VISITING OPPORTUNITY – BUT NOT GRIPPINGLY POPULAR...

Sometime later we were informed that the meat plant was open to visitors, and our two deck apprentices promptly set off to sample its delights. It was interesting I thought that one of them soon returned, ashen faced, reporting that he'd felt unable to venture very far into the factory's bloodied innards! His companion did complete the tour but spoke in such sober terms of the whole experience, that any interest amongst the rest of us quickly evaporated like mist on a summer's morn. And everyone wished that the awful smell would vanish, as easily and as completely, as our interest.

Interest was much greater in seeing if any of us could actually get a visit made to Buenos Aires itself, some 75 kilometres from La Plata. It seemed a long way and time for shore leave was short, as we were not to be in port very long so, for some of us who were free to go we were delighted to be offered a lift by one of the ship's agents returning to the city after visiting the ship on official business. As we rode in his car we got the feeling that life in

Argentina must have been an unpredictable business, as he kept pointing out bare roadside plinths and roof top cills where statues of the country's ruling dictator, Peron and his wife, had recently been removed. "If you come again," he said, "you'll probably find them back up. Revolutions are a way of life here." I remembered his words for they did indeed turn out to be true.

Meanwhile, aboard the ship, Lloyd's surveyors had been visiting in order to check our thrust repair, and we were delighted to hear on our return that the work had been passed with flying colours. The Chief was a different man now, his anxious frowns which had been setting on his brow like concrete had miraculously gone, and smiles sprang easily to his lips again for his pension was safe in his hands once more!

A CURIOUS LEGACY OF WAR...

We sailed from La Plata with no regrets, only too thankful to be leaving the meat plant and its dreadful smell behind. *En route* to the sea the outward bound channel took us to the Uruguayan side of the estuary, and there we were intrigued to pass close to what from a distance looked like a lighthouse of an Emmet-cartoon design. It was however the once proud upper-works of the German battleship Graf Spe and they now looked very forlorn as they jutted from the muddy waters in which the hull lay immersed, sat on the sea bed exactly where she had been embarrassingly scuttled in the war. Chased by the Royal Navy anxious to remove the threat she posed to British Shipping, she'd sought sanctuary in neutral Uruguay's Montevideo Harbour. However, knowing that the rules of war engagement gave her only a limited time in such neutral safety, and knowing the Royal Navy was waiting for her out at sea, her commander solved his dilemma in the most astonishing way, by easing his ship out of the confines of Montevideo Harbour and then promptly taking its life by scuttling her, followed by his own in an act of distorted honour, as a suicide. Reflections on such war time dramas, interesting as they undoubtedly were, had to be brief however, for we were heading out to sea with a thrust block to really put to the test as we sailed for the Persian Gulf, via Durban for bunkers.

Once we were full away on passage, normal watch keeping routines were quickly established again, with merely the added responsibility for us of keeping a special eye on the thrust, but as the shaft revolved steadily, the oil flowed and there was no sign of it misbehaving, everyone relaxed.

However, a rumour that even if we were happy, the company was not, started going around the ship. The rumour like all such rumours was put out on the 'galley radio', this being every ship's fountain of, usually wildly incorrect information, and which had its origins in snippets of conversation the saloon stewards heard (or thought they heard) whilst serving the officers at meal times. The rumour had it that the company was so concerned about the ship and the seriousness of our recent breakdowns, that they were going to work her back to home waters so that, in the event of anything else going badly wrong, she could be quickly deposited back at the ship yard at Falmouth to be properly sorted out. Meanwhile, we pressed on across the South Atlantic and the voyage was uneventful, other than a relatively short stop at one point to deal with a piston problem. It was a case of some overheating, and by comparison with our other troubles, dealing with this one by stopping the ship and lifting the offending unit's pistons to clean and re-ring them, was relatively a routine matter of a few hours work. And on this occasion we had the bonus of something to actually laugh about.

For a long time as we'd ploughed our lonely furrow across the vastness of the sea we had rejoiced in the cheerful company of a squadron of those ocean wanderlusts the albatrosses. Now, with the vessel stopped, the great creatures had settled on the swells looking quite put out. Floating idleness is not for them. Their true element is the air, where being on the wing is, indeed, their very life. We'd all watched them, marvelling time and again at the way they glided hour after hour with scarcely a beat of their great wings, soaring and swooping over the ocean swells. Such birds frequently became welcome escorts to many a ship going about her business in the trackless seas of the Southern hemisphere, and the distances their wide wings carried them is truly staggering. For ours, now paddling uncomfortably on the water, there was however one advantage. Their enforced immobility meant that galley scraps could be more easily picked up instead of having to be snatched on the wing from the washing machine vortex of our wake! It was in this situation we were to find the bonus of a good laugh.

A morning's work had seen the pistons lifted and rather than waste time scrubbing up and

Piston Maintenance – as it should be! In calmer weather the engineers had no need of deck-side help, and the work was free of 'complications'. On this occasion the procedures were more in line with text book descriptions of 'straightforward' job.

donning uniforms for lunch in the saloon, we elected once again to picnic on the fan flat by the top of the boiler room. At the hands of our stewards courses came and went. The soup was fine and the roast quite passable; the sweet however, was another matter. It was duff – irreverently referred to as 'Board of Trade duff'. Years ago the Board of Trade was the body politic of maritime affairs, having a far ranging brief covering all aspects of life and work at sea. Its regulations covered health and safety, cargoes and officer competence, and a particular interest found expression in catering. Here, among the Board's prolific guidelines were recommendations as to the nature of duff for the nourishment of seafarers. Duff is a dish which when served ashore might be recognised as Spotted Dick steamed pudding, but which, when made at sea following the Board of Trade's culinary guidelines, seemed to fall into another recipe category altogether. Such duffs as we knew invariably had the consistency and character and, curiously, the shape to match, of cannon balls!

WE SINK AN ALBATROSS...

Thus when the stewards appeared bearing the spherical duffs they were waved away with the usual jests that we weren't one of England's Wooden Walls wanting cannon shot to deter the enemy, and we passed to the coffee instead. To enjoy this, with a breath of air as well, before resuming work on the engine we went to sit out on deck. Sheltering in the lee of the after accommodation, we sat on the poop deck bracing ourselves with our feet against the rails as the ship rolled, and through which we watched the albatrosses riding the swells and clearly impatient for us to get under way again. It was then it happened. As we sipped our coffee we saw the galley boy further aft go staggering to the rail bearing a couple of laden pails of 'gash' from lunch to be tipped 'over the wall'. Amongst it all were of course the cannon balls of duff, and we watched as they fell seawards given a long arc of fall as the stern rose and rolled on a stately swell. Also watching, and suddenly very alert, were the albatrosses. Getting a duff in his sights one of them, unfurled its great wings and, thrashing with its feet as well, it homed in with astonishing speed catching the duff as it splashed in the sea. Hooking it back out, and rearing its head in a great flurry of spray, we watched entranced as the albatross caught the duff in its beak, swallowed it whole, and, promptly sank! A look of sheer disbelief shadowed its face as it then beat its immersed wings and paddled frantically with its feet to keep its head poking above the surface. We cheered and clapped at such entertainment, and advised the birds that any complaints about the grub should be made direct to the Cook who, had appeared at that moment from his galley, to see what all the racket was about. "Should be ashamed of yourself, Cook," we said. "Look what your duff's done!" and we pointed to the dismayed albatross awash beneath our stern.

Happily it recovered well, for by the time later that afternoon when we were able to start up and get back 'on passage' the stricken bird seemed none the worse for its brush with Board of Trade victals, taking to the wing again as gracefully as ever. Thus life for albatrosses, as well as for us, assumed an orderly state once more.

However, things were less orderly it seemed elsewhere in the world. Radios aboard ship were picking up news (more reliable than that gleaned from the 'galley' rumour band) that there was a sense of unrest building up in the Middle East, its focal point being in Egypt and its concern being the running of the Suez Canal. We did wonder, in an idle way, whether if it developed, it would affect us very much, but our interest was at no deeper level than that of mere cabin chatter over a beer or two.

In truth no one thought we'd be going to Suez for quite some time anyway, as the normal voyage routine of a ship like ours was to operate on a year long basis from dry dock to dry dock. The pattern was that on leaving a shipyard after overhaul a vessel would work up during a few weeks of coastal voyaging in home waters, and then go off 'deep sea' which for tankers like ours, often meant east of Suez. Then, after several months, the company would begin a charter pattern to work the ship back towards home and another dry docking about a year on. Admittedly in our case there had been our serious breakdowns with the subsequent rumour of being taken homewards for safety's sake but, as the engine was by then giving every appearance of working well at last, and we were only a third of the way into the year's trip, the consensus of opinion was that the company would be deciding to keep her out. Suez troubles if there were any brewing, were ones we could comfortably ignore, and besides, it was best to dismiss them because thoughts of going north suggested thoughts of home. These were always as unsettling in their uncertainties as they were sweet and pleasant in their dreaming.

A CURIOUS STOP...

Meanwhile, the ship, her engine running well surged on taking us round the Cape of Good Hope into the Indian Ocean and on up to Durban for a short stop there to take on bunkers. From there we pressed on up the coast and across the Arabian Sea and towards the Persian Gulf and it was then that we experienced a very curious stop. In the Gulf, the weather was calm – almost eerily so, in fact. Later, looking back, we might have seen in it the significance of some sort of omen! Evening dinner was being served, but conversation was sparse as people responded in their own quiet way to the prevailing eerie atmosphere. The white-coated stewards went quietly about their work, and apart from their Jeeves-like shimmering, the only other visible movement was the surface trembling of water in glasses and carafes on the tables responding to the gentle vibrations of the engine. It was therefore to the dismay of the engineers that such trembling was suddenly seen to stop! The levels fell as still as the surface of a village pond when ducks and small boys had ceased their activities for the day and gone home to roost, or their tea! It was ominous for it could mean only one thing – there was trouble down below. I watched the Second, who held a laden fork between plate and lip, as a look of resignation passed over his face. Then the fork completed its ascent and, pushing his chair back, he rose to his feet and strode resolutely from the saloon. We all followed.

Down below we found that those on 'tea relief' had become aware of a curious knock, one more like a 'slapping thump' they expressively described it, and it appeared to be towards the front of the engine. There was nothing for it but to get the inspection doors off and, with the turning gear in, carry out a check on the bearings and the running gear. However, all seemed well. It was agreed then to start up again and everyone was stationed at strategic points to listen.

Once the engine was running, sure enough we could all hear the 'slapping thump!' so another stop and an inspection followed but, as all was well, diagnostic strategies had to become more daring! It was now proposed that we start up again only this time we'd leave the forward doors off so that with lead lamps in hand we could watch what was happening. The engine was started, and to minimise the splash from the lubricating oil which could now spray freely (and hotly!) from the open doors, the revolutions were kept well down. Thus the engine ran, eyes peered and ears listened. The sight of the massive cranks and rods whirling and glinting in the light of our lamps was unforgettable, but more seriously, we were trying to identify a problem, not just enjoy the view! It became readily clear that the 'thump' was in the number one crank pit, so the engine was stopped and a closer examination made there. Questions were then raised as to why there appeared to be an unusual accumulation of oil at the fore end. Lubricating oil emerging from the bearings, its work done, fell into the crank pits whose angled bottoms allowed it to run to a central collecting point where it drained to a sump below the engine. That oil had accumulated at the fore end was therefore unusual indeed.

In the end, someone raised the issue of the trim of the ship, and a consultation with the mates on the bridge quickly followed with the result that they confirmed that with the present state of their de-ballasting activity prior to our loading port arrival, the ship was indeed, slightly down by the head! Things now began to fall into place. Being down by the head, and with the sea so strangely calm, oil in the engine was not draining as it normally did, and it therefore appeared that the bottom end bearing of the main crank in the number one unit was, at its pass of bottom dead centre, catching the pooled oil with the same noisy impact as that of a failed diver's belly-flop entry to his pool! The mates got cracking and adjusted the ship's trim in the engine's favour, and order and serenity were restored. It would never have happened had it not been so incredibly calm, and thus it could be viewed as one of those happenings which fall outside the realm of text-books, and thus it was one well worth filing away in the mind's memory-bank of unusual experiences, these often being the most important ones to have!

THE ORDERS COME...

With that problem solved, we pressed on up the Gulf and, as we neared our loading port, the orders arrived giving the destination for the cargo. To our surprise it wasn't South America, or Australia, or the Far East, but, Hamburg! Indeed then the company was getting the ship back nearer home after all, thus proving the 'galley radio' to have been remarkably reliable for once, and thus too it meant a canal transit was looming up and our interest in the rumours of unrest there suddenly assumed an importance far greater than that which mere cabin chatter had suggested.

In the event, our Suez excursion of that moment proved to be something of an anti-climax! Once loaded, bunkered and stored in the Gulf, all achieved without any problem or hint of trouble, we set off on the trip round to Suez and the Canal. There, we found everything perfectly normal, which seemed to give the lie to all the rumours of hostility and trouble being stirred by Col Nasser, a new Egyptian leader and his people. Or was it, someone wondered darkly, just the 'lull before the storm?' Little did they know how right they were! – and that eerie calm we'd experienced in the Gulf, we would come to look back on as a portent indeed of troubles a-plenty brewing up nicely!

Col Gamel Abdel Nasser was then a very new and dynamic leader. He

More crankcase work – checking for a 'slapping thump'!

47

had led the Army Coup of 1952 deposing King Farouk of Egypt, and making himself president of the first Egyptian Republic. In consequence, he was a rising star of great magnitude in the Arab world as a whole! Under his leadership a programme of reforms began to lift the people of Egypt out of feudal backwardness, and while the nations of the west could applaud modernising initiatives, a very different view was taken when Col Nasser talked of reordering the running of the Suez Canal to better fund them. At that moment however, all was still quiet and we thought little of any political shenanigans, in whatever corridors of power they may be taking place, being only too pleased to enjoy just another Canal transit. Leaving Egypt, we passed through the Mediterranean and out into the Atlantic turning north to cross Biscay for the English Channel. There, as we romped along, we all tried to ignore the uncomfortable sensations created by the fact that 'home' was so tantalisingly close but, we were not stopping to savour it! And thus we arrived at Hamburg.

The engine had run faultlessly of course, dispelling any thoughts of a need to seek the ministrations of the shipyard at Falmouth, or anywhere else for that matter, and indeed, at Hamburg, while we discharged the cargo, another inspection survey was carried out on our thrust repair which it passed with flying colours. This was enormously gratifying, but it only served to endorse the growing realisation that the company would be sending us straight back whence we'd come, there to earn our keep and them some profit, with a bit more 'deep sea' voyaging. And sure enough, when the orders came, they were for the Persian Gulf, post haste and no messing!

CANAL-ZONE HOSTILITY...

It was when we arrived back at Port Said that we found things had changed dramatically. There was now a brittle tension in the air. It was as tangible as frost on a winter's morn. Military activity was clearly visible ashore, and it had to be said it did seem uncommonly menacing. We realised with a jolt, that the rumours of unrest we'd heard, and talked about for so long, were suddenly taking on the hard face of reality, and our cynic's assessment of the calm we'd known in the Canal, but four weeks or so earlier, had been correct – it had been a pre-storm lull, and the storm was clearly brewing before our astonished eyes. It was all very disconcerting. Requiring bunkers, we were manoeuvred into a harbour berth for that facility and, once in and tied up, we took stock of our position with tension-heightened interest. We were berthed in a small basin across the water-way from the handsome, colonnaded Canal Authority building, tied up by which we noted, was an Egyptian gun boat. With her guns pointing at all angles she resembled a rather dishevelled porcupine, and the fact that washing was actually slung between two of them, gave her a somewhat trigger-happy air. The sense of anxiety for us that this conveyed, was then roundly emphasised by the appearance in the bunker dock of gun-toting turbaned tribesmen. Several came aboard, prowling the decks in a most menacing manner. Bearing antique-looking rifles slung on their shoulders, and with bandoliers of fearsome bullets criss-crossing their chests, they looked as if they'd been bussed-in fresh from some desert tribal skirmishing, or camel rustling!

The respect we usually enjoyed for being British, and on a British ship at that, which we did rather take for granted when in foreign parts, was clearly gone. We felt uncomfortable. Such unpopularity seemed as odd for being unusual as it was unnerving in its newness. Odder still was the fact that the Egyptians didn't even seem to want our money anymore; the eager bum-boat traders, and the pally, 'You-buy-dirty-postcards-Johnny?' characters, had all made themselves strangely scarce.

It was all quite confusing and, perhaps to our shame, we thought less of why it was happening and, more simply, of how things might be hurried along to let us get out of the place intact! That the Egyptians might well have a grievance about the running of the Canal, where its profits went and whose authority in its affairs should be most valid, considering it cut right through their very country, were issues we were happy to leave to the remote and distant figures of the politicians. However, we might have been more concerned and attentive to the things unfolding even then before us, had we had any inkling of the military debacle that was going to happen. That those in Government in Britain and France were worried by Colonel Nasser's muscle flexing, and an Arab stranglehold on the West's precious oil supplies that might result was one thing, but to plan the clumsiest of invasions of Egypt, as they were even then beginning to wonder about doing, was quite another. A military attempt to protect the West's interests was to be a sorry failure, and it rightly saw the unseating of the then British Prime Minister, Anthony Eden. That however was all yet to happen. We knew simply, after a very jittery wait in Port Said, we were anxious only to get moving south and away to the safety of distant waters – the more distant the better, even though it meant a visit to the Gulf first.

With our bunkers safely aboard, we were advised to stay at the berth as its situation near the mouth of the Canal itself meant that we could be the south-bound convoy's lead ship, as soon as one was assembled and it was clear to proceed. All we had to do was wait patiently for the arrival of the north-bound convoy, then in transit.

Thus we waited. The gun-toting tribesmen grew more menacing, and the tension in the air tightened by the hour until, at last, the upper-works of ships could be seen over the raised, eastern sand bank of the Canal. The north-bound convoy was arriving and, to our surprise, not to say relief, it was actually being led by a British warship, announcing her arrival with cheerful little whoops from her siren. She looked as trim and as smart as if she was engaged on a

Sovereign's Spithead review. Her white ensign streamed out impressively from her stern, and her sailors were lined smartly at harbour stations along her rails in a stunning show of unflustered efficiency. We watched her admiringly. "That'll show 'em," someone breathed, nodding casually by way of comparison at the 'porcupine' across the harbour. With the Navy around the tension distinctly eased, and it was with lighter hearts and a merry air on our lips that, as soon as the last north-bound ship had passed, we cleared the scowling bandit figures off the decks, and got under way.

SAILING FROM THE GULF, AND BAD WEATHER SETS IN...

Once in the Gulf, at our loading port, we found that the hostility we'd experienced in Egypt was, to our relief, largely absent. Outwardly, all appeared perfectly normal and quite routine. The Arab shore workers dealt with the pipes and the loading of the cargo with their usual deftness, and all the stores ordered by our Chief Steward were delivered in full but, for all that, there was just a hint of something amiss in the air. Some of the usual exchanges of banter with the shore lads didn't seem to quite come off anymore. The jocular words were rarely understood, the language barrier seeing to that, but humour was always recognised and appreciated for its own sake, becoming so usefully the oil of good relations. Now, that was gone, and although outwardly everything was as before, one couldn't help but feel that things might change for the worse at any minute. The orders we'd received were for another run to La Plata, and we found ourselves balancing the uncomfortable realities of Middle East hostility on the one hand, with the evil odours of the meat plant on the other! The balance tipped of course, pretty convincingly, on the side of the meat plant; and anyway, with a bit of luck, the wind might be blowing the other way this time!

Thus we sailed, cleared the Gulf and headed south down the African coast. Nearing Madagascar, a flurry of interest was aroused by the sight of a particularly striking cloud formation. It took the form of an enormous arc across the sky resembling a giant rainbow – but one which had gone through the wash and lost its colour! While a group of us were marvelling at the sight, the Second mate passed, pronouncing authoritatively as he went, "It's a 'line storm'," and adding over his shoulder as he disappeared up the bridge ladder, "We'll be in for it soon!"

And my word, we were! From that moment the weather rapidly deteriorated, and by night-fall the ship was heaving and plunging with all the exuberance of a fairground ride gone riot! Deep laden as we were she'd bury her bows in a wall of water, to then rise in an explosion of spray and sending a Niagara-like cascade tumbling off the fo'c'sle head. It was boisterous and exciting, but it did introduce some inconveniences and anxieties in the various departments of the ship. The cook now had his work cut out keeping pans, and their contents, on his ranges, while the poor galley-boy who bore such culinary arts as were achieved, from the galley aft to the saloon amidships, had the gauntlet-run of the exposed flying bridge to negotiate. There, sweeping seas threatened to carry him off to Davey Jones's locker, and more seriously, our grub with him! Such were inconveniences. Anxieties were more the order of the day in the engine room department. Watching the engine labouring when down below, or feeling her exertions vibrating through the ship when elsewhere, we hoped against hope that the good running she'd shown in our voyage to Hamburg and back, would hold true now. To break down in such bad weather was not just inconvenient, it was dangerous, as the ship would fall off into the trough of the seas, there to roll violently posing many a threat to life and limb.

The 'line storm's' tantrums were fierce, but short-lived. However, although some of the battering went out of the violence, Nature had clearly got her dander up over something, and high winds continued to blow and high seas to run. That this was to be a protracted spell of meteorological bad temper to which the 'line storm' had been merely a prelude, we would discover over the next few weeks. Enduring bad weather was, on the whole, mostly an inconvenience for powered vessels but in the days of sail, ships could experience Nature's moments of drawn-out irritability at enormous cost to them of time and energy. It was particularly true for those windjammers struggling against the prevailing westerlies in the Southern Ocean as they attempted an east to west rounding of Cape Horn, from the South Atlantic, bound for ports on the Pacific sea-board of the Americas. For them, if Nature was in one of her muscle-flexing moods, they could spend endless time tacking back and forth trying to make mileage to windward with a soul destroying lack of success. Then occasionally, so frustrating was the lack of progress it was not unknown for them to abandon the attempt, wear ship, and then run with the westerlies right round the bottom of the world there to be faced with having to make a full crossing of the Pacific to reach their desired ports of call! To do such a thing was a decision not taken lightly for it meant adding many thousands of miles to an already long voyage, not to mention the frustration and hardship of the many more weeks of dragging time it meant for the weary crews.

IN THE SOUTH ATLANTIC; 'OIL AND WATER NEVER MIX'...

Happily of course, we were not taxed with that sort of challenge, and as long as our engines gave us no trouble, all we had to endure was the discomfort and inconvenience of living and working in the endlessly gyrating world of our storm-tossed ship. We enjoyed a few hours respite when we dropped in at Cape Town to take on bunkers, but once they were safely on board we were promptly under way again heading out on the long crossing of the South Atlantic. It was when we were a few days into this stage of the voyage that a long-standing bit of conversational nonsense took a serious turn, but with an amusing outcome.

For some time the occasional, and usually jocular banter, between the navigators and the engineers as to their relative importance on the ship had been getting ever more serious. The significance of it all reflected a problem whose roots lay firmly in maritime history. When steam power, with all its less desirable side effects of dirt from coal, smuts from funnels and stains from oil began to elbow its way into the realm of ship propulsion, an uncomfortable relationship was created between those who practised the old arts of seamanship and navigation, and those committed to the new skills of engineering. That an element of hostility would be established between the old and the new was inevitable when those 'on deck' looked down, literally, as well as figuratively, on those who toiled 'down below', referring to them dismissively as the 'black gang'. Such an uncomfortable relationship between those on deck and those below led to the coining of a well known seafaring adage – 'oil and water never mix!' However, what may have been true (and even justified) in more distant days, had of course become completely outdated as ships lost any vestige of their links with sail, and power, ever more efficient in its development, took over. At that point, the disciplines of seamanship and navigation on the one hand, and engineering craft skills on the other, had to assume a complimentary importance, but nevertheless, the legacy of history persisted and the 'oil and water never mix' tension still knew regular airings of opinion.

There'd been quite a bit of it for several days past, on the Reliance. Everyone knew it was silly of course, but that it happened at all merely reflected the way, when outside stimuli is reduced, which is inevitable on a ship, some things assume an importance out of all proportion to their true reality. For us at that time, the 'debate' was becoming ever more of an argument, drawing something of a boost from the fact that as the weather had closed in even more since leaving Cape Town, the mates didn't really know where we were. They were experiencing great difficulty in getting any reliable sun, or star sights, for navigational purposes, so they were working largely on what is termed 'dead reckoning', basing their calculations of our position on the course being steered, and the distance covered derived from the readings of the rotary log streaming aft in our wake. The engineers were saying that anyone could do that, whereas if the engine ever stopped, the mates wouldn't be able to even start it, let alone repair it!

Things came to a head on a night when it was realised the cloud wrack was showing signs of breaking a little, and the First Mate was hopeful that by the time he went on watch at four am he'd be able to get a decent star sight and thus pin our position down with some accuracy. Accordingly therefore, when he was put 'on the shake' he got his sextant ready in its box, resting it on his bunk while he dressed. As he did so, the ship caught a particularly steep sea and, giving a shudder as she rolled, promptly pitched the boxed sextant off the bunk, sending it in a neat arc to land with a crash on the cabin deck. Fearful of what damage might have been inflicted, the mate was relieved when, as he picked it up a hasty inspection revealed that nothing appeared to be broken. It was not until he'd taken over the watch on the bridge and got the sextant ready to hand for its anticipated sighting work, that he realised it had actually suffered in its cabin mishap. The locking screw on the instrument's quadrant arm was, he found to his dismay, quite badly bent. It being important to get a sight, and loath to disturb any of his off duty colleagues to borrow a sextant from them, he dispatched one of his watch seamen on an errand to the engine room. Thus, to the great surprise of those on watch down below, they found themselves being offered the precious sextant with the polite request to see if they would be so kind as to use their workshop facilities to fix it! And of course, they gladly did so.

It was thus inevitable that at breakfast in the saloon that morning, the 'oil and water never mix' debate now took a serious turn as the engineers made capital out of the fact that such a symbol of the navigator's art as a sextant, had actually needed their craft attention during the night.

Words whizzed back and forth, some like barbed arrows, others with the weight of a thrown punch, until a resounding crash brought the verbal warfare to an abrupt stop.

In a stunned silence, all eyes swung to the point of the noise. There on the deck lay a tray of cutlery. By it were the shiny black shoes on the Chief Steward's feet. He was standing and glaring round the saloon with a face like thunder. With the silence of surprise achieved, he promptly filled it with some words of welcome sanity. "Will you silly sods stop your stupid arguing about importance?" he demanded. "None of you would do anything without your food, and that's my department, so I'm more important than the lot of you put together!"

The silence held as people absorbed the profundity of his words. 'Gosh,' I thought, admiringly, 'Well done Chief Steward.' It was game set and match to him without a doubt. And then, as the business of breakfasting resumed, somebody laughed and we all realised the swollen balloon of the argument had been thankfully burst, exposing its very stupidity. "So you know where we are now, Mr Mate?" somebody asked, jocularly and now reasonably. Jokes about following 'one's star' followed, with gripes expressed about the relentless weather, and, with a snippet or two of the latest radio news of soccer fortunes at home added in for good measure, in no time at all banter's goodwill ruled again.

Inter-departmental harmony was happily restored. And the ship ploughed steadily on, La Plata bound.

We arrived safely and were dismayed to find the wind was not in our favour any more than before, and the meat factory's smells were as nose-twitchingly malodorous as we remembered. However, we consoled ourselves that we wouldn't be in port very long to have to endure them. Smells aside it was revolution news that was of more consequence. We were intrigued to discover that the Agent's prophesying made on our earlier visit, that 'there'd be another revolution soon' had proved to be all too true. The Peron symbols had indeed been readjusted while we'd been away. Of rather more significance however was the jaw-dropping realisation that trembles of revolutionary unrest were actually surfacing again, even at that very moment! Shore-side people coming aboard spoke of political agitation, and revolutionary excitement at fever pitch once more in the country, and we placid 'Brits', accustomed only to the relatively gentle sparring of our democratic two/three party system at home, found Argentinean volatility quite baffling, even, if truth be known, rather entertaining. However, any smiles we were tempted to sport were wiped pretty smartly off our faces when the crackle of gunfire was suddenly heard nearby! "Bloody hell," somebody said, "It's the revolution! It's not 'going' to happen – it IS! And it's actually HERE!" And indeed it was – or some aspect of it at least, for the gunfire was indeed in the refinery complex where we were.

Dashing out on deck we looked around and to our dismay, some distance away, shadowy figures were spotted, flitting amongst the pipes and tanks of the refinery cheerfully taking pot-shots at one another with sub-machine guns! In truth, it seemed scarcely believable. The enormity of the danger was clear to everyone, for a random bullet had only to pierce a pipeline, and a casual spark ignite the leaking oil, and a major problem was guaranteed! And not only that but we were aboard a, by then, part-discharged vessel and were consequently in the most dangerous of situations for a tanker of having holds clear of oil but charged with the residual vapour. As an explosion potential, we ranked second to none, and somebody cracked, that if we 'went up,' then at least 'we'd take the bloody meat factory and its nauseating smell with us!'

Completion of the discharge of cargo was speedily finished, and the eruption of the 'High Noon' gun-slinging activity gave us every incentive to get ready for sea and be off! And we'd noticed how interesting it was that the morning's shore-side visitors, at the first cracks of gunfire, had completed their official business with an astonishing speed, and promptly fled. They'd scuttled off down the gangway like frightened rabbits, seeking the safety of their official cars, and they'd gone with the speed of the bullets they sought to avoid! With the last drop of cargo out, and the hoses disconnected, we quickly made all the preparations to leave. Up on the bridge, I heard later, the 'old man' (the Chief Engineer) had danced a veritable jig in his anxiety to get us cast off and under way. Unfortunately, there was a problem. Several of the crew were absent! A number of our seamen had been ashore the previous night and had apparently got so boisterously tanked up in La Plata's bars on the local brew of anise, that they'd attracted the attention of the police. On their arrival, and having weighed things up, they promptly solved any problem our sailors posed by popping the lot of them in the calaboose. It was simple and effective. Later, they could be delivered back to the ship at some convenient moment, sobered and chastened, after, of course, all the necessary dictates of officialdom had been suitably, and leisurely observed. Then the morning's turn of events with the revolution's gun-slingers had no doubt come as a distraction to the local constabulary and as drunken sailors were not much of a priority, they could be safely left in the calaboose, but to us it meant that their predicament took on every appearance of becoming a most protracted affair. The 'old man' was so beside himself to sail that he was all for leaving them. However, he was prevailed on to wait for them as such an act of abandonment, in the unsettled circumstances of a revolution, could precipitate trouble at political levels that would be far more serious than any simple maritime matter of sailors missing their ship.

WAITING FOR MISSING CREW...

Apparently, one of the morning's hastily departing shore-side visitors had, as he fled, given an assurance he would do something to get our sailors back, and thus we simply had to wait in the hope that whatever string-pulling he could achieve would work. Again, gunfire crackled in the area, sometimes near, then, further away, before coming back again. The atmosphere aboard was now electric as everyone waited for some explosion, or fire, or both to herald our extinction within the refinery! To protect the ship from possible invasion by the roving gunmen, the 'old man' ordered the gangway to be hoisted aboard and the ship to be singled up to just two wires, they being also slackened to allow the ship to come well off the quay. Down below in the engine room, everything was ready for an instant start, and unmooring parties from amongst our remaining seamen were stationed fore and aft ready to get the last two lines aboard, or sacrificed if need be. Thus we waited. We remembered our anxieties of a few weeks earlier when at Port Said armed tribesmen had roamed the ship, but what was happening in La Plata was distinctly worse. It was trouble for real!

Then suddenly, a honking horn and a roaring engine were heard, and a battered blue van careered into view, weaving towards us down the quay. It was bearing our missing sailors, and with the gangway hastily slung ashore they were unceremoniously bundled aboard. That done, we left. The sense of relief was distinctly palpable, and as we got out into the open waters of the great La Plata river and turned to head for the distant sea, an air almost of victory, but certainly salvation, abounded.

Once we were clear of the estuary, and pushing east into the South Atlantic, we soon realised that the grumpy weather of our westerly crossing still held sway – only we were now going with it rather than against it. As we got further out from the lee of the South American land mass, we found ourselves coping with a quartering sea from the south west, driven by the same relentless wind we'd got so used to before. The ship, now only in ballast trim of course, rolled like a well-oiled drunk on a Saturday night. 'Ye'll be seeing her bilge keels if she goes over much more,' somebody said. Later, I went to the starboard boat deck rail to see if you could! I watched as the ship surfed off one giant swell, and then in response to the next, rolled over on her port side exposing a positively indecent amount of her pink underwater hull and, although from the boat deck vantage point it seemed an awesome distance indeed to the thrashing foam round her lowest plates, of the bilge keel fins there was not a glimpse. Perhaps if I'd dared to lean over further…but sense, and remembered safety warnings kept me firmly inboard. After a reflective gaze at the turbulent waters, and a recognition of the truth that if one should, for any reason, happen to fall in, the chances of being rescued were as near nil as made no difference, I made for the dry haven of my cabin.

AN ATTEMPT AT DRUNKEN REVENGE!...

Then the ship's drunken antics found a real life echo on board. On the morning of our second day out I was sat, braced against the rolling of the ship, at our cabin's desk glancing at some company work which Head Office expected apprentices to attend to while at sea. Suddenly, a loud commotion started up in the companionway outside. Going to the cabin door I was amazed to see struggling figures in the dark alleyway, one of whom seemed to be wielding a felling axe of the type found in the fire equipment lockers. He, and a companion who was equally wild (but axe-less!), was trying to get up the internal stairs leading to the Master's cabins, and the bridge, while others were clearly trying to wrest them down. Someone in the *melee*, seeing me shouted, 'Get back in lad – keep out of the way!' and, perplexed, I did so. Later, I discovered what it had all been about. The sailors who'd been returned from chokey in La Plata had got there in the first place because of their over-indulgence in the local hooch of anise.

Back aboard, they'd sobered up but had then fallen victim to a long lasting after-effect of the brew. Once sober they found themselves in possession of a raging thirst, but the drinking of water to ease it had the curious effect of librating the anise still in their systems rendering them instantly as tight as ticks again. Two of them so affected, and having heard that the 'old man' had hinted at leaving them behind, swore to take vengeance on him, hence the fire axe and a truly drink-fuelled aggression. Seemingly the Mate had drawn a revolver from an armoury on the bridge (something I, as a mere apprentice engineer, had no idea existed!) and, stationing himself at the head of the companionway stairs to the bridge deck, he'd readied himself to repel, if not boarders, then at least warring drunks! He must have cut quite a figure, silhouetted at the head of the stairs, and the sight of the gun glinting as he brandished it menacingly, had penetrated the anise-skewed eye of the seaman struggling below him. Realising it carried more weight than his axe, he'd at last given in to those struggling to hold him, and thus the 'old man's' life was spared a gory execution. The offenders were put under lock and key until they really sobered up and restored themselves, shamefacedly and apologetically (especially to the 'old man') to the real world – or as much of it as our nautical speck on the ocean's wastes represented.

THE PROSPECT OF TAKING PASSENGERS...

Then came exciting news! We were going to pick up passengers! Actually it was confirmation of a rumour that had gone round the ship while we'd been in La Plata but which, at the time, most of us had dismissed as being merely 'galley radio' speculation. However, there had been more truth in it than we'd realised. Apparently a doctor and his family had done a stint of duty on the mid-Atlantic isle of Tristan da Cunha, and being now anxious to get off and go home they were, in effect, thumbing a lift on any east-bound ship. Aware of their request, those well informed in the world of shipping movements had picked on us as being a likely candidate to help once we'd be on our return trip – if, that is, no-one else had managed to help first. Now, with our trip to La Plata completed and no other vessel having been able to help, our hitch-hiker pick-up potential was confirmed. More details now emerged. There were supply ship visits from Cape Town but they were few and far between so island traffic depended almost entirely on enlisting the help of passing shipping. This facility was of course dependant on nautical goodwill on the one hand, but far more significantly, on the weather on the other. The basic problem was a geological one for Tristan da Cunha is simply the exposed peak of a mid-ocean volcano rising steeply and directly from the sea bed far below. With no land shelf around it no snug harbour could be built nor a safe anchorage defined, and visiting ships could only therefore stop and lie off while the islanders would come out in their own boats to collect supplies, and conduct any necessary business before the ship would get under way again, and depart. Clearly then, it was the islander's dependence on using boats which was the main problem, for their deployment depended entirely on the weather – and so bad had it been for so long, as we knew only too well, they'd not been able to launch for weeks. It had meant that the poor doctor and his family had become effectively marooned! Many ships had passed of course, all only too delighted to help but, their hospitality was denied fulfilment by the simple fact it was too rough for the island boats to come and meet them. We were now, it seemed, their next transport possibility, and being still several days sailing away, it was hoped that by the time of our arrival the weather might have moderated sufficiently to allow the safe transfer to us of the passengers.

One glance at the storm-driven seas however, over which we reared and rolled, along with a recognition of just how long Nature had been behaving so aggressively, suggested quite the reverse of course. But, such is the effect of romance over reason weather realities could be ignored; ordinary work-a-day tanker that we were, we were, quite simply, going to have the novel pleasure of passenger company! Life aboard brightened distinctly as a consequence. Cabins became noticeably tidier, uniforms smarter, laundry a dash whiter and bright work received some unaccustomed mid-voyage buffing up! Conversation was endlessly about the island, its staggering isolation and therefore the strangeness of the lives of those who'd chosen to live there. Folk aboard were to be seen studying old school atlases they'd brought with them, marvelling over a place whose sheer remoteness rendered it to all intents and purposes as non-existent for one or two of the books examined didn't even mark it! For the poor doctor and his family, champing at the bit to get home to South Africa, every added day must have seemed an eternity, but salvation, we could cheerfully affirm, was on the way. Or was it? We had to wonder. A glance at the weather let the nagging thought surface that we'd probably have to pass them by as so many others had done. Nevertheless, there were a few days left before landfall, and optimism remained high. The course was set directly for the island and the Second Mate, being our navigator, came round looking at our cabin atlases in order to make comparisons of the island's marked position in those whose books showed it, with that on his general South Atlantic chart, so unfamiliar a port of call this was to be for him as much as anybody else.

ARRIVAL AT TRISTAN Da CUNHA AND SAILING BY!...

A day or two later, and that much nearer the island, an ETA was worked out. Such was our position and speed it meant that although we'd pick up sight of land in daylight, arrival at the rendezvous point would be in darkness. This caused some of the engineers to wonder if the passenger pick-up was really anticipated, for if it was, it was felt the bridge would request a reduction in engine revolutions to slow us down a little so that we'd arrive in darkness and effect the embarkation in daylight. No hint of such an arrangement being forthcoming, it was taken as a bad omen; we'd probably be sailing straight past. And indeed, radio traffic confirmed that the sea state around the island remained as bad as it had been for so long. But still we pressed on, cherishing the hope of success!

When finally it came, the sight of the island was dramatic. The word that it was visible went round the ship in a flash and everyone, except those on watch below, sought vantage points to get a good view. There it was! Across the heaving, foam-streaked waves, jutting skywards out of the spume-filled haze, we could see the solitary, shark-toothed shape of the mountain that was Tristan da Cunha. We marvelled at its very loneliness, marvelling too at the manner of its discovery by Portuguese sailors, in 1556. Watching our well-found tanker being 'put through it' by the fierce weather we could only marvel at what life must have been like on the wooden caravels of the sailing adventurers of years before, for the vagaries of sea and storm would have been the same for them as for us. And as they in their exploits were actually *making* ocean charts rather than *following* them as we were, their happening upon this island peak must have been a truly eye-popping experience for them!

As the day wore on and we drew nearer, the peak loomed higher, and the sight, and sound, of the Atlantic seas hitting its windward flanks was awesome. With no sea bed to break them up, the mountainous swells simply hit the rock face, surged on up it in stately slow motion to a height of what must have been a couple of hundred feet or more, then to cascade down in a true Niagara-fall style. We romped steadily on, and darkness began to shroud the scene, indicating ever more clearly that we really were destined to go 'romping on' in the passing-by sense! It was depressing, but some of us still nurtured the hope that in the full lee of the island on its north east flank where we knew the settlement existed,

we might find things to be more favourable than expected. It was not to be. By ten o'clock we were abreast of the settlement, its few lights glinting and shining rather forlornly in the ink black darkness of the night, and after some extra flashing of a signal lamp in response to some message flashed from our bridge, that was it! We were gone!

A great sense of emptiness pervaded the ship the following day. Many aboard lamented that

Approaching Tristan da Cunha

we hadn't even slowed down, let alone stopped, to see if the islanders had wanted to try to get to us, but the Second Mate explained what we all knew and understood at heart. The problem was that although the settlement was on the lee side of the island and therefore sheltered from the direct onslaught of the sea, nevertheless the swells were simply parted by the bulk mass of the peak and promptly rejoined themselves in tumultuous fashion on the lee side – the settlement side. No boat, however well built or expertly crewed stood much of a chance of a safe launch until more moderate weather prevailed. We left the stranded doctor and his family to their fate and headed on, aiming now for the Cape of Good Hope which, once rounded, would take us north to dock at Durban. There, we'd take on bunkers for the run on up to the Gulf again, to load our next cargo.

WORRIES AGAIN ABOUT THE MIDDLE EAST AND SUEZ...

The Gulf! With Tristan now out of our minds, thoughts turned to the Gulf and events in the Middle East. Hostility towards the West had evidently become much more serious, and Colonel Nasser in Egypt, radio news informed us, was playing worrying cat and mouse games with the Suez Canal. Our minds went back to the alarming scenario we'd left in La Plata, and now we were heading towards another, if anything, even more alarming! It seemed the phrase linking frying pan and fire had some relevance! However, the overall attitude aboard was really that it was best to let 'them' – the politicians – look after it all; we had a job to do in getting our ship safely across the ocean, and that was quite enough for us.

One Middle Eastern development of which we knew very little at the time was, we discovered later, to do with the tensions of the Cold War – the 'stand off' which then prevailed between the democratic west and communist Russia. Apparently, Colonel Nasser's aspirations to derive more benefit from the running of the Canal for his people were suddenly given a great incentive through a British misunderstanding over an aspect of the Cold War. Plans were in hand in Egypt for the building of the Aswan Dam as a means of helping Egyptian people, and international help from a number of sources was funding the project. A good deal of it came from Russia, and the British government saw this as something of a threat to world stability, being suspicious as they were, of Russian motives. Colonel Nasser was no communist, nor aspired to embrace that ideology, but at home in Britain our politicians viewed his relations with the Soviet Union, particularly in the matter of armaments, as being very unhealthy and, as a 'punishment,' western help for the dam was withdrawn. Colonel Nasser was outraged, and responded by nationalising the Canal. The political, and commercial consequences of this were considerable, and our government was very worried.

Aboard the ship, with what little we did know, it was enough to get talk buzzing of a possible oil crisis developing at home, and consequently, the 'galley radio' put it out that once we'd loaded, we might be going home! In more ordered times we could have expected another run to La Plata, or to Australia, but they were definitely not ordered times any more. Thus, on our departure from Durban, any anxieties we may have felt about approaching a restless Middle East were greatly relieved by the prospect that we really might be homeward bound. We were therefore astounded when news came that on October 31st, Israeli troops invaded Egypt's Canal zone, followed on November 6th by British airborne forces, all in order to reclaim control of the waterway. Colonel Nasser responded promptly by blocking the Canal completely, trapping several ships then in transit, in the Bitter Lakes region. Thus we were not surprised when orders for home were confirmed – the country now certainly needed our oil! We also knew of course, we'd be in for a very long voyage, effectively all round Africa to get there! At Durban, we'd loaded bunkers and stores to take us up to the Gulf, but with the long voyage back around the Cape ahead of us, the Chief Steward busied himself with preparing increased orders for supplies which we'd take on at our loading port.

A SHOCK OVER OUR STORES...

Entering the Gulf, and approaching our loading port, we wondered what sort of reception we could expect and, rather to our surprise, everything seemed quite normal. Once alongside, cargo loading was efficiently commenced, and we were told we would be allowed to load a maximum capacity of bunkers and fresh water. With our catering supplies however, it was a very different story. We were dismayed to hear that our Chief Steward had been informed that the stores were being withheld! It was not a case of the ordered things not being available. They were available alright, and were even at that very moment, there before our eyes stacked neatly on the jetty. The Chief Steward could be seen talking to Arab shore officials. There was much arm waving and shaking of heads; clearly, he was getting nowhere! They were implacable. It was a case that, yes, we could have our cargo, bunkers too and even fresh water but, stores? No! It was quite extraordinary, and we realised very quickly what a cunning move this was by the Gulf Arabs as a way of showing solidarity with their Egyptian brothers and discomforting the unpopular westerners. Now knowing as they did that we'd have to go the long way home, and denying us obviously important food supplies, they knew that even if we would be able to stop while *en route* we were going to be at least seriously inconvenienced and we might even suffer in the process. In the event, there was much of the former, and quite a bit of the latter!

A LONG VOYAGE ON A DULL DIET!...

The Chief Steward made a thorough assessment of what stores we had aboard, bearing in mind a possible voyage time of six weeks. He revealed that we had ample stocks of potatoes, flour and, oh dear! – corned beef! This information brought wry smiles to our faces as we remembered the disparaging remarks we'd endlessly made about La Plata's meat plant; now, the tins of meat it produced might well save our lives! It was clear then that we would not starve, but the Chief Steward was concerned about the dietary imbalance posed by the lack of fruit and vegetables, the last few of which, taken on at Durban, having been consumed as we arrived in the Gulf. As we sailed, the Chief Steward was busy with the cook working out a menu programme to be as varied as possible within the constraints of the three culinary elements available. It was a task which would have confounded Mrs Beeton! Initially of course, the novelty factor ensured the success of his planning. Corned beef was served fried, as hash, in pies, or in sandwich form and it quickly became a game at mealtimes laying bets on what would appear. Not unexpectedly, the novelty factor soon wore off!

Once we were well clear of the Gulf and our course set for the long haul south, everyone realised what an uncomfortable time lay ahead, surviving as we must on our enforced and monotonous diet. Like all adversity of course, it had the virtue of focusing the mind, and I think we all realised just how important so many of the ordinary things which are so sadly taken for granted, really are. How cheerfully welcome a spoonful of bright green, succulent peas would have looked on a plate of hash, or alongside a slice of pie... I felt sorry for the Chief Steward as he bore our jibes, albeit affectionately made, and I felt sorrier still when sometimes jaunty jibes became serious grumbles. Our plight was not his fault, and everyone knew it but several among the crew did begin to make his position increasingly uncomfortable through their petty grumbling.

Meanwhile, the international news was brimming with comment on the Canal crisis, and apparently the invasion by the Israelis, followed by British and French forces, had attracted a furious response from other countries, particularly America. President Eisenhower's view was so critical that the British government was compelled to withdraw from the venture and, shortly after, it was not surprising to hear that it had all brought about the downfall of our Prime Minister, Anthony Eden. He was obliged to tender his resignation. Of course, such high level goings-on made no difference to the situation by then prevailing in the Canal, which was blocked and was to remain so for some considerable time. (The ships trapped in the Bitter Lakes region, eventually had their crews removed, and the vessels were effectively abandoned!) Nor did the political happenings make any difference to us, now forging south down the East African coast, tucking in with increasing dislike to our diet of corned beef!

People were now beginning to say that we ought to be making arrangements to stop off at somewhere like Durban, or Port Elizabeth for supplies, but although I gathered such views were taken seriously and passed to the company in London, they refused to sanction any such stopping. There was a crisis at home, and getting our cargo there was more important than a grouse or two about corned beef!

So we pressed on, and ports of possible help were passed one by one, until eventually, we rounded the Cape of Good Hope and began the long haul north up the West African coast. By now, several of us were experiencing the effects of vitamin deficiency in the form of coming out in spots, and boils! I had a boil form in my ear – and I found I could attain some relief by placing the affected part close to the sight-hole of one of the boiler furnaces and letting the heat draw the pain! The Donkeyman was initially bemused by such apparently eccentric behaviour, but as visits to the boiler room took on the regularity of one's other usual visits elsewhere to deal with bodily matters, it all simply assumed a new normality. Another boil, which formed on my neck, was lanced by the Chief Steward acting in his other role as our medical officer, and I gather he was getting a dab hand at such procedures, so many of us were affected!

A DOXFORD FEATURE – WATER LEAKS IN THE CRANKCASE...

Happily the main engine ran superbly, and apart from a couple of relatively brief stops for repairs, and not being impeded by bad weather, we made good time towards the equator and the northern hemisphere. The stops we made were to deal with water leaks in the crankcase, and some of those with long experience at sea, and with Doxford engines in particular, remarked that we were very lucky to have so few problems in this respect. Some engines seemed particularly prone to such trouble which meant that those charged with their care found themselves saddled with a very tiresome problem. The trouble stemmed from the fact that the pistons of the engine were cooled by having distilled water constantly circulating through them. To get the cooling water into the six lower pistons as they reciprocated up and down involved passing it through a complex system of jointed, swinging pipes which arced up and down with the action of the pistons. It was at such joints that problems were most likely to occur. The packing around the moving parts would wear to a point when water would start to leak. Besides being a serious loss in itself as it was distilled water rather than the ordinary domestic variety from the tap, it instantly contaminated the lubricating oil present in the crankcase. The engineers on watch would be alerted to the onset of such a problem when water would appear in the sight glasses of the purifiers. These machines were constantly drawing oil from the lubricating system to spin it at high speed in order to remove impurities through centrifugal force. Water was a definite impurity! When water was observed, the bridge would be informed and if the ship was not in danger, or at risk to others, the engine would be stopped. Then, with the inspection doors removed, the position of the leak would be quickly identified. It was then a straightforward task to shut off the supply to that unit and attend to the re-packing of the offending gland, and possibly carry out a re-jointing job between the flanges of the fixed parts of the swinging arms. To say it was a straightforward task is technically correct, but when it is remembered it is done inside an extremely hot crankcase, and everything is covered in slippery oil, it is not always as easy as it sounds. However, from what some of the more experienced chaps had to say about other ships, for us to have so few stops for such trouble meant we were really very fortunate. It could have been a good deal worse.

A FRUITLESS STOP AT SANTA CRUZ...

Thus we pressed on northwards, and although we were making good progress it couldn't be denied that the medical situation resulting from our restricted diet was actually becoming quite serious. In the end, and to our great relief, the company in London relented saying that we could make a stop at Santa Cruz in the Canary Islands, to take on supplies. At this news, life aboard brightened considerably. However, the reality of our visit when it came was a great disappointment. Nearing the island of Tenerife where the capital Santa Cruz is situated, we were reminded of Tristan, for the Canary Islands are also the peaks of undersea mountains, but the fact that there are several of them, and they are all much nearer the land mass of Africa means there is not the same sense of dramatic loneliness which Tristan da Cunha displays.

And there was no loneliness about Santa Cruz itself. It was as busy as a beehive in midsummer swing! Colourful houses in jumbled array, snuggled against the lower slopes of the mountain, and in the docks, where we were worked safely in to a quayside berth, people bustled, crane jibs swung and bobbed, and all around were ships. It was an impressive sight as their colourful funnels and flags added to the exuberance of the scene. And in them, of course, lay the root of our disappointment.

Once alongside, the Chief Steward dashed expectantly ashore only to discover from arm-waving, moustachioed officials that the bland assurances he'd received by radio that stores would be ready and waiting for us, had been merely words – every bit as empty of truth as our pantries were of food! It appeared that as a result of the crisis at Suez, many east-bound ships finding themselves faced with the prospect of the long voyage round the Cape, and being under-provisioned for such an extended excursion, had back-tracked along the Mediterranean and once out in the Atlantic had called at conveniently situated Santa Cruz to obtain more. All that remained for us, by then a relatively late caller coming north, were crates of dark green cabbages and stalks of tightly packed, and very tiny, green bananas! Of the meat, of the beef and lamb variety, our Chief Steward had requested, there was none – although a lorry-load of goats' meat had been made available he was told, should he care to take it. He reluctantly agreed to see it, but when he realised that the lorry pointed out to him parked a hundred yards down the quay was obviously the source of the smell that had caused his nose to twitch defensively ever since he'd stepped ashore, he wisely declined to go near it. Back aboard, we listened sympathetically to his lament that, 'Every damn ship in Christendom's been in an' they've cleaned the place out!' He was upset, and we were disappointed; there'd be no lovely sweet peas, or juicy tomatoes after all. We watched glumly as the distinctly unappealing cabbages and the inedible bananas came aboard, and with them safely on, we were soon under way again. Our country needed us – or our oil at least!

NEARING HOME WITH CHRISTMAS THOUGHTS...

Thus the final leg of our long voyage was entered upon. Our menu remained as before, but with now the addition of servings of cabbage at lunch and dinner. Medically, the vitamins it provided were undoubtedly beneficial for our health, but it could only be said to achieve it on the basis of the old maxim that if it tasted awful, then it must be good! Cabbage is cabbage and few of us, if any, actually had a liking for it, and even less by the time we got home! Our poor cook did his best but enhancing such a vegetable would defy the most talented chef anywhere! And we ruefully reflected yet again on the fact that the staple element of our diet which had kept us alive all the way from the Persian Gulf was the unpopular corned beef, and we felt we had to 'apologise' for the fact that we'd been so ungraciously critical of the factory back in La Plata. We didn't like corned beef but it had 'saved our bacon' so to speak, therefore we did have cause to be grateful for the reality of La Plata's meat plant and others like it, and grateful too to the animals, the workers and the processes which had given us our means of life.

Orders arrived confirming our destination was to be the Isle of Grain in Kent, and finally, as we entered the Western Approaches, the tremors of the 'Channels', that fever of homecoming so familiar to British seafarers nearing the English Channel had us all excitedly in its grip. And there was another tremulous hope gripping many a heart on board. Knowing it was by then December, and as the word was out that after discharge of the cargo at Grain we would in all probability be going for dry-docking at Falmouth, there was just a hope that if all went smoothly we might get home for Christmas! 'Home for Christmas!' What an evocative phrase that is, speaking as it does of reunion with loved ones, in the sanctuary of the home and at a time of Festive joy. The delight in such a thought had of course, to be set against the qualifying phrase, 'if all went smoothly'. The significant word was the tiny one of 'if'. It suddenly seemed a very big word for one of only two letters!

'NO ROOM AT THE INN'...

Soon after passing Dover, and rounding the Kent coast, we picked up the Pilot to take us into the Medway and on into the refinery berths at the isle of Grain. We were nearly there! We'd come such a long way and been through so much, and suddenly the rather depressing thought struck many of us that a mere 16,000 tons of cargo really didn't seem much to have brought! A big power station can burn that much in a single day! Nevertheless, knowing the nation was by then definitely in the grip of petrol rationing so that every gallon was assuming the importance of a good cigarette butt to a tramp, we did feel quite proud to have so successfully completed the long voyage home. Thus nosing triumphantly into the road-stead of Grain, with the refinery ahead in the distance, we really did expect something by way of a welcome. I realised, in my innocence, that I'd so built this moment up in my imagination as to think there'd be the marine equivalent of a red-carpet homecoming for us, in which we'd receive the accolades of dewy-eyed, oil-starved Britons! Binoculars revealed nothing – not even just one flag-waving soul on a distant jetty and, worse still, there was no sign of any tug activity. Again, in my innocence, I'd seen them bustling straight out to meet us to usher us hastily in but, it all looked ominously quiet. Surprisingly too, the place seemed full of ships and, to our astonishment, we realised that after all the urgency of our voyage, now that we'd arrived there was actually no room for us at the berths. It looked as if we were trying to gate-crash an 'At Home' for tankers! The phrase 'no room at the inn' sprang to mind and was curiously apt given the proximity of Christmas and the telling of its famous Nativity story. Joseph's predicament on the doorstep of Bethlehem's Inn received a rare degree of appreciation as we realised we were not going to get in that day and instead we'd have to find if not a stable, then at least an anchorage! We did, and with the hook securely down, we took to studying the shore, speculating wildly on what stores had to be lying there waiting for us, and speculating rather more agonisingly on the chances of our paying off in time for Christmas, Falmouth having been confirmed as our next, and final destination. Speculation focused on the issue of dates, and of what had to be done before a deadline of the evening of the 24th. It was then the 18th, and assuming a berth became free soon allowing us to get in there would be six days left. If the discharge could be achieved speedily we could then leg it down the Channel to Falmouth and all would be well. The 'hopefuls' calculated over and over again that it could just be done!

FOG DIMS OUR CHANCES...

The following morning the signs looked promising. A berth was becoming free as a tanker, now in light condition, was leaving, and preparations were made to weigh anchor and get under way as soon as the departing ship was clear. Thus we were rendered speechless when, just as we were on the point of moving, a fog swept brazenly in from the sea completely immobilizing all shipping! Our dismay knew no bounds. All that day, and the following one, we lay on at anchor, trapped in a damp and chilly prison of fog with the stifling texture of cotton wool. The Pilot, who was trapped with us, was very upset. He had no appetite for our corned beef, and less for our cabbage, and he bleated on about missing his wife's delicious cooking in their cosy little home in Rochester. We were not impressed. Food, as a conversational topic, had long ceased to hold any fascination for us, and all we could think of now was the dire threat the fog was posing to our hope of a Christmas Eve payoff.

ANOTHER DELAY...

The fog lifted on the 21st. We were alongside in a trice, urged on by a Pilot desperate to get away from our voyage cuisine, and once there, discharge commenced quickly. The thud and thump of the big steam cargo pumps resounded through the ship with a vigour that bespoke the urgency we all felt. Clearly, 'Pumps' the pump-man, was getting everything out of them, and he and the mates dashed about setting the tank valves and pipe lines with a frantic zeal. It had the result that they achieved the miracle of the discharge of our cargo in record time, allowing us then to be getting ready for sea on the afternoon of the 23rd! It still seemed just possible that we could make Falmouth on Christmas Eve before it would be too late to get transport out from there towards our homes.

Down in the engine room everything was ready, the place positively hummed and fizzed with life as if the machinery had caught the excitement of the moment and was raring to make the effort to 'get us home'. The Second hovered around the control station, and others of us patrolled fretfully about checking temperatures and pressures, making little adjustments here and there which, if not essential, allowed us to feel we were honing things for a fast departure. We could imagine the activity up on deck as lines, cast off ashore, were being brought in with a cheerful rattle of winches and capstans, and all ears waited for the ringing of the telegraph announcing we were moving. Instead of the telegraph it was the phone that rang. It was the bridge ringing, and I watched the Second talking, noting that his face clouded with annoyance and then took on an expression of resigned disappointment.

Putting the phone back, he called two of us to him. "They're having trouble on the fo'c'sle," he said. "It's the windlass an' they can't get the insurance wire in so we're going to be delayed!" We listened, dumbstruck at such news. It was another turn of the screw of Fate's nerve-tensioner! "Get all the tools you think you might need," the Second was saying, "then get for'ard and fix it – quick!" Then he added with a shout as we sprang for the ladders, "make sure you take everything – it's a bloody long walk back!" And as we scrambled up, he added more advice about putting something warm on over our boilersuits. "It'll be bloody cold up there," I heard him shout through the gratings as we disappeared above, heading for the workshop.

It was cold. Once out on the far-away fo'c'sle, high above the water now the ship was riding light, the air of disembodied remoteness the place always exuded was further emphasised by the gathering dusk of a winter's day and the bitterness of a raw east wind that positively shrivelled the soul. The Mate told us that there was something wrong with the warp drive off the big steam anchor windlass but, because time was of the essence, he was then trying to get the insurance wire in using rope runners led to the smaller deck winch on the forward main deck. The wire had had to be utilised in addition to our normal mooring lines because of the berth position we'd been allocated. It was in fact the end berth on the refinery's frontage, and it therefore exposed the ship to some risk posed by the Medway's powerful river and tidal currents as they swept round the jetty's end. The wire itself was a particularly strong one, kept on board for possible towing duty, or as back-up in dangerous mooring situations such as ours at Grain. On the rare occasions of its use, its recovery usually utilised the power of the big rope warps driven from the actual anchor windlass but, with that giving a little trouble, the Mate had instead, organised the fo'c'sle party of seamen to achieve the recovery using runners and the smaller deck winch. It was to their great credit they achieved it, for with the wire in, the ship could leave. And we did – ignoring the fact that we hadn't actually managed to sort the windlass out! We deduced that the trouble appeared to be a problem with the windlass' clutch drives, and to sail with the matter rather unresolved was to take something of a risk in that if we had to stop for any reason and drop the hook, we could perhaps find ourselves in the rather embarrassing position of not being able to raise it! However, having successfully sailed, it was agreed to leave the windlass problem until it could be better assessed in daylight the following morning, as some dismantling was envisaged, and so we left the deck crowd tidying their mooring ropes, and headed back to the warmth of the engine room.

OUR 'CHANNEL DASH'...

Shortly after, once the Pilot had been safely dropped, 'Full Away' came ringing cheerfully down. This was our cue. The main engine controls were now gradually eased up, the fuel valve setting lever going notch by notch to its usual running position and then, slowly to the next, and the next. Everyone watched the quivering needles of the gauges and indicators of the instruments at the control station. In films, to show the drama and tension of pressure and speed, needles are often shown spinning round their respective dials like demented merry-go-rounds! There was no such silliness on our gauge board! A mere glance of the eye at needles quivering at positions a little further on than usual spoke volumes of the urgency of the moment! The revolutions built up steadily; the counter ticking away with the exuberance of a meadow cricket on a summer morn, but it was the revolution indicator itself that mattered, its big dial holding our riveted attention. Normally, its needle showing our engine revolutions hovered around the figure of 105 per minute, but under the extra encouragement of more fuel it had crept round to 110 and on, to 112. This, more than anything, told its own story of our engine now working more and more like a racehorse approaching the final furlong! We were going to make a 'Channel dash' that night, and no mistake. Such was our enthusiasm we felt our 'dash' would put the famous wartime one of February 1942, of the German warships Scharnhorst, Gneisnenau and Prinz Eugen really in the shade! They had been tucked away in harbour on the French Atlantic coast posing an enormous threat to our war-time shipping and Prime Minister Churchill had said that they *must* be 'dealt' with. However, while action was being planned, the German ships, knowing the danger they were in, slipped secretly out of their French haven one dark night and made a furtive dash eastwards, right through the English Channel. They were making for the relative safety of the fiords of enemy-occupied Norway, and that they achieved it successfully, slipping through under our very noses so to speak, unseen and unchallenged, enraged Churchill greatly; but such were the fickle fortunes of war. Our 'Channel dash' was westwards, and like the German sailors in the war we held nothing back, going flat out through the night, and all the following day, fairly romping along the south coast until, with bated breath, we slid into Falmouth harbour, there coming to anchor at just after six in the evening of Christmas Eve!

PAYING OFF, AND A MAD RACE FOR HOME...

During the afternoon, thought had been given to what would be done in the event of paying off arrangements being possible. Some hands would be required to stay aboard to act as a docking crew of course, but others would be free to get ashore if it proved possible in the time available. We apprentices were among the lucky ones to have that prospect but I had to say that as the day wore on I reckoned our chances steadily diminished. I was therefore astonished to find when we'd anchored and were stood down from duty that paying off was indeed going to happen. We raced to finish our packing! Shore officials arrived very promptly, and the paying off formalities went surprisingly smoothly, and we were informed that a launch would be available to take us into the dock area of Falmouth itself. Once there, we were told that there was a local train running out of Falmouth later in the evening which would connect at Truro with the night express from Penzance to Paddington. The express was due at Truro at 9:30 pm; watches were studied and calculations made, and it was reckoned we could indeed 'make it'! It was a very frantic evening, and for me at least the fact that it was dark proved an advantage. One bit of news shore visitors had brought told us that also in the harbour, and anchored very nearby us was the big four-masted barque, Pamir. As one long fascinated by the great windjammers of earlier years I would have loved to have seen such a famous ship, but the blackness of the night rendered her completely invisible. She had once been part of the famous Flying 'P' line of the German owner Mr Laeisz, and then later owned and managed by another well known name in sailing ship circles, Gustaf Erikson of Finland. By 1956, she had reverted once more to German ownership and had become a sailing school ship. I was sad not to see her. (And I was to be sadder still when, not that long after, news broke that she'd been lost with all hands in a terrible storm in the Southern Ocean). At any rate, as the night precluded maritime gawping I got on with my final sorting and packing. Then, with much chivvying from the launch men we bade a hasty goodbye to the ship, and chugged off towards the beckoning lights of Falmouth.

Once ashore, we discovered that we'd missed the last local train out from the town; an earlier group of those who'd been paid off had managed to catch it, but we were just a fraction too late – it had gone. However, local advice suggested all was not necessarily lost. A fast taxi, we were assured, could yet make Truro in time to catch the express, and thus, with haste, we found a cab, piled in and urged the driver to drive as he'd never driven before! He caught the excitement of the moment as we told him something of our story of the 'Channel dash' to get to Falmouth, and he grew ever more determined to play his part and get us, not 'to the Church' but to the station 'on time!' Happily, traffic being light in those days, his rally driving speeds on the twisty Cornish roads were not too big a risk, with the result that we screeched to a stop at the portals of Truro station just in time. As we paid him off with profuse thanks for his efforts, the express was grinding to a huffing, puffing stop on the up platform. It was a mad scramble to get ourselves and our luggage over the connecting bridge but with the same huffing and puffing as the engine had made when it arrived, we tumbled aboard and with a slamming of doors and a blowing of whistles, we were off!

The express eased out of Truro and, rapidly gathering speed, thundered off eastwards. We were leaving the deep 'south west', with all the images of summer holidays the name suggests, and we were being borne away to places where an even more significant holiday awaited – Christmas at home! I was due to change trains at Bristol Temple Mead, picking another up there for Gloucester. Some others off the ship had far longer journeys ahead of them, but the spirit of the moment carried all before it; nothing mattered, we were all going home. I sat back and relaxed.

At Bristol, sometime in the small hours, I left the train, bidding hasty farewells to those shipmates who were travelling on, and then, from a platform phone I rang home. I spoke to the firewoman on duty in the watch room of the fire station by which we lived, and she assured me she'd let my father (the then still relatively new Chief Officer of the City of Gloucester Fire Brigade) know of journey times and my expected arrival time. On the station at Bristol, early on a Christmas morning though it may have been, the railways were working superbly, and station staff were cheerfully helpful, thus when the Gloucester-bound train puffed merrily in I was excitedly helped aboard with all my kit for the last lap, borne on a tide of true Christmas goodwill! Not long after, just as dawn was breaking, I found the train rattling over Gloucester's well known Barton Street crossing, and easing in to a stop at the city's Eastgate Station. Getting off the train, I caught sight of my father waving an excited greeting. As he hastened up to help with my kit we fell into an arm clasp of welcome, and I found myself marvelling at the unique joy of those priceless moments of family reunion; how very precious they are! Then, as we lugged my gear along the platform, Dad said, "You're a surprise and a half today, and no mistake. And Mum doesn't know yet. She thinks I'm out checking on a fire call we had during the night." Then he added, with a twinkle in his eye, "If you're a surprise to us today, there's one for you, outside!" And there, parked outside the station entrance, I was stunned to see a gleaming Sunbeam Mark III. Dad let me drink in the sight as he knew how fond I was of Sunbeam cars, and then he dropped the bombshell. It was his new staff car; so it was ours to go home in! I was ecstatic.

ON SUNBEAM CARS AND RALLY THOUGHTS...

Ever since we'd lived in a flat above the appliance room of Bournemouth Central Fire Station before moving to Gloucester, the flat overlooking the big Rootes Group Agency garage of George Hartwell, I'd been obsessed with the Sunbeam cars which were one of their principal sales lines. George Hartwell and his staff were enterprising rallyists, always entering the Monte Carlo and the Alpine Rallies and they had developed some fascinating features on the vehicles, primarily Sunbeams, which they raced. In addition they had used a Sunbeam Talbot saloon car and developed a beautiful two-seater coupe model especially for the Alpine Rallies. Their 'Hartwell Coupe' was then developed commercially by the Rootes Group itself being marketed as the Sunbeam Alpine Sports car. As a schoolboy, I'd absorbed all this avidly, always cherishing the hope that I might one day have a more tangible link with these wonderful cars as I regarded them, rather then being a mere show-

A Christmas morning surprise; my father's new Fire Brigade staff car.

room window gazer. And there I was, safely home on Christmas morning, now being driven home in a car of my dreams!

It was a home-coming and a half! Once home in our house by the fire station, my mother suffered the shock of my surprise arrival with a confused mix of gasps of amazement and cries of delight, and then promptly set to work in her beloved kitchen knocking up a stunning version of her family-famed fried breakfasts.

I was home indeed!

TRAVEL STORIES, AND MEMORIES OF EARLIER ONES ON THE 'BARON'...

At home, people were fascinated by the story of our 'Channel Dash' and of the nail-biting delays we'd experienced, not least in respect to the trouble we'd known in recovering the insurance wire at the Isle of Grain. Talking over the event, and mentioning one of the wire's potential uses for towing duty

The MV British Baron on which I served my first trip to sea.   www.fotoflite.com

reminded me that the first ship I'd served on had actually been equipped with a full-blown towing winch with an enormous cable drum of wire – and what's more we'd used it! That the use was only brief, and we'd actually felt cheated by the circumstances that took the tow we'd found off us, didn't alter the fact that it had been properly used, and was something well worth 'logging' in the memory bank of experience – especially from the point of view of us first-trip apprentices.

It had been explained to us that with the very extensive range of the British Tanker Fleet the company had decided to equip two of them as 'towing vessels' on the basis that if a company ship ever required a tow, it would be more economic to do it on an 'in house' basis, than pay the full whack of specialist salvage firms! The MV British Baron, on which I was then serving, was one of the two official towing vessels, and the other was her sister ship, the MV British Duke.

Our towing adventure took place at the southern end of the Gulf of Suez. Having cleared Suez one sunny morning, we were heading south for the Red Sea where we would then round Arabia in order to enter the Persian Gulf for our loading port. 'Full Away' had long since been rung down so to hear the sudden strident ringing of the telegraph came as a surprise. I'd dropped things

on the bench in the 'tween decks workshop where I'd been busy, and dashed for a point on the galleries where I could see down to the control station. There, I'd quite expected to see the Fourth engineer who had the watch at that moment, looking after whatever it was that had

Above: On the top platform of a four cylinder Doxford similar to the one that powered the British Baron.

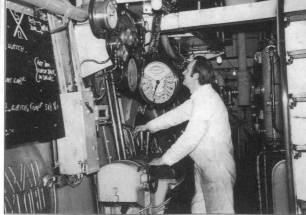

Right: Stood by the controls of a four cylinder Doxford.

74

happened. There was no-one there! I'd been puzzled and, being only a first-tripper, unsure of what to do. When on passage, the ringing of the telegraph was invariably the bridge responding to information from the engineers of a need to reduce speed, or even stop for repairs, but the very emptiness of the control station proclaimed that no-one had rung to give them anything to answer! They must therefore, have been ringing us, and I realised I'd better investigate more closely. I'd slid down the ladders and stared up at the great dial of the telegraph. The handle we used, with its shiny brass pointer, registered importantly, 'Full Ahead', but the centre pointer from the bridge now stood, somewhat dismayingly I'd thought, at 'Stand By'! I'd looked up through the maze of gratings and ladders hoping to see the white boiler-suited figure of the Fourth coming to take charge, but he was not to be seen. Staring back at the pointer I'd been tempted to swing our handle round and answer it, but I'd stopped as the implications had dawned on me. If I'd rung an answering 'Stand By' they would assume that we were then indeed 'stood by' when we were not! Other orders might then have come, and I'd have been in a difficult position for as yet I'd had no experience of the mighty levers of the engine controls. I'd looked round feverishly for the Fourth but he was obviously oblivious to the summons wherever he was, and suspecting that to be the boiler room, I'd been on the point of turning to fly there when the bridge pointer had suddenly trembled, and then moved in sweeping arcs back and forth to the accompaniment of the electrifying ringing of the bell to come to rest again at 'Stand By'! 'Heavens,' I'd thought, 'I must do something!' and with urgency lending wings to my feet I'd flown up the ladders to the boiler room.

Inside, the Donkeyman, busy with his burners but guessing what I wanted, pointed to the claustrophobic tunnel formed by the bellies of the two great Scotch boilers. There, under the plates, I'd found the Fourth wrestling with a difficult changeover flap valve. He'd looked up in surprise as my shout had penetrated the din and blinking the sweat out of his eyes in the suffocating heat he'd come closer to get my message. I'd no sooner mentioned 'Stand By' and he'd scrambled out and was gone. Down below he'd taken control, answering the telegraph with a flourish, and sending me to get the starting air back on the main engine. Then he'd grabbed the phone and rung the bridge to find out what was happening.

The drama, for drama there was, had been interesting. Ahead of us lay a

The stricken British Lancer, stopped in the Red Sea. After three days she was making a last attempt to start. This column of black smoke revealed that it failed and she was taken in tow.

broken-down tanker of our own fleet, the MV British Lancer. I'd heard about the ship as she was one with a bad reputation for being broken-down. Many in the company, especially among engineers held to the view that she was a jinxed ship; she was powered I'd been told with a Werkspoor diesel engine, normally a reliable product of a continental design, but the word was that the Lancer's machinery had been a ship-yard 'tea-break' effort! Apparently she had been drifting for three days while her engineers had struggled to achieve a repair, but with the set of the currents taking her more and more towards Sinai's mountainous coast, concern for her safety had been growing. Her engineers were going to make one last effort to start her engines by late that morning and, if it failed and knowing that we were one of the company's towing vessels, they were asking us to take her in tow at least as far as Suez. So – it was SALVAGE we were into! It had been exciting news for it meant to some degree, extra money all round!

By mid-day we'd closed the stricken ship and lunch had been forgotten as we'd lined the rails to watch her. All had been absolutely still, and the heat intense, with the sun high overhead glazing the Red Sea's placid waters. Then, a signal had come. They were going to attempt a start. We had watched, agog; the engineers among us trying to visualize the scene in the Lancer's engine room. Then, across the narrow divide, we'd heard the faint chuffing of compressed air as her engines had been turned. It had been instantly followed by the appearance from her funnel of a column of thick black smoke. The sounds had died away, and all had been as still as before. There had been no thrashing of white water at her stern nor any jubilant signals of success. 'Well, we've got a tow,' someone had said, but even as it was uttered, any elation we might have felt had been tempered by a sobering sight. Many of us had had binoculars trained on her and thus we'd all seen the incredible sight of some black figures emerge, one by one, clearly from her engine room, to collapse limply on her deck. We'd stared, aghast, and someone had summed it up with a dry, but very feeling, 'The poor buggers!' They had been, literally, black from head to foot, and we'd gathered their problem had been something to do with their engine's scavenge system which admitted air to the engine. Clearly, they'd had serious oil contamination problems with their system, hence the sticky blackness revealed in their weary figures. We'd been pulled back from our reflections on what nightmare experiences they'd endured by the shouts and orders which had told of the readying of the towing wire on our big winch at the stern. The Fourth had been dispatched to get a new brass roller turned up on the workshop lathe, to fit the towing wire fairlead. Everyone had worked with a will and, as dusk had fallen, we'd got the casualty safely in tow about four hundred yards astern, her lights, especially her two red not-under-command ones, jewelling the deep violet of a summer night's gloaming in the Red Sea. And then, we'd been the victim of one of those strange ironies which only life in its most bizarre moments, could throw up.

Our sister ship, the British Duke, the other company towing vessel, had been even at that moment, romping up the Red Sea, loaded and, homeward bound! She could have been on the other side of the world – and it was just our rotten luck that she was not! On company orders we'd had to hand our 'prize' over, and they'd gleefully received her for they knew they'd not just take her to Suez, but all the way home. And they did! We got a few pounds extra for our bit of salvage work, but the lads on the Duke did a great deal better, and no doubt said of us, just as dryly and just as feelingly, what we'd said of the Lancer's engineers: 'the poor buggers.'!

ANOTHER MEMORY FROM THE 'BARON' – ONE OF REMEMBRANCE...

Another memory from my first ship was a very sobering one. Near the big towing winch on her after deck, I'd spotted some curious footings, and when I'd asked about them I'd been told they were what remained of the guns that the ship, in common with many in the Merchant Navy, had been equipped as a gesture of defence and protection when she'd sailed in the war years. I'd found that information very sobering. The ship I was privileged to be serving on had, I realised, sailed in times of enormous danger, especially so considering her role as a tanker! I'd looked around her and wondered just what had it been like to be on such a ship when the dangers of war had been so appallingly real.

There was one at least, who knew, first hand. It was the Third engineer.

His hair was a crown of brilliant white, and I'd been warned in the course of a conversation with others, never to ask him about it. 'He'll tell you about it if he wants to,' I'd been told. I'd been intrigued, and then, one night when I was sharing his watch, he did tell me. It was a most astonishing, and humbling tale. He'd been a Junior engineer during the war, and he'd actually been torpedoed twice, and survived! One of the incidents was an amazing story. On one tanker, he'd been in the engine room on the starboard side of the main engine where the controls were, when a torpedo had hit the ship on the port side of the engine. The resulting explosion had lifted the main engine off its mountings, causing it to crash over, fracturing pipes and smashing gratings and ladders, but the engine's mass had shielded the engineers from direct death. Then they'd found themselves being swept up on the inrushing sea water, and they'd floated and scrambled through the fractured metal work, with spraying oil and blasting steam adding to the hell of it all, and they'd found themselves at the engine room skylights. They'd managed to get out into the sea, much of it by then ablaze with burning oil and swimming clear as the ship had gone down, they'd been astonished to find themselves being picked up by another ship of the convoy, and they'd survived! The shock of the whole experience had caused a young man's hair to turn white! I had listened to the tale in stunned awe and amazement. It had made me realise that it was not only the Fallen who should be remembered at Remembrance-tide, but all those who had faced death, literally in the face, yet had survived. The dividing line is so fine a one it can seem barely discernible!

Such indeed, is the stuff of real Remembrance!

There was now of course, the final year of my apprenticeship looming up, and I made the most of my Christmas holiday, and voyage leave, readying myself then for a year or so in heavy industry.

Part Two

FROM HARLAND AND WOLFF TO ORDINATION!

A sizeable package arrived in the post.

It contained instructions for me to report to Harland and Wolff's Marine Engineering Works in Glasgow and also the necessary travel documents.

This was the final year of the apprenticeship I'd taken up with the British Tanker Company and it was designed to give all cadets a good experience of heavy industry somewhere in the country.

And in those days there was plenty of scope for shipping companies to choose from. Shipyards and engine builders were active all over the country and Glasgow was no exception. It positively thrummed with the creative life of industry and the River Clyde was a ship spotter's paradise.

Harland's three enormous factory blocks on Glasgow's cobbled Anderston Quay produced an astonishing range of engines from the relatively small auxiliary type to enormous main engines, all under the name of Burmister and Wain of Denmark, the engines being built under licence. The main engines, and one was under test when I was given my first look round the factory blocks, were truly impressive. In some respects there was something similar to the Doxford design I'd become familiar with. The B & W design however was distinctly more massive. Like Doxfords, the B & W featured the opposed piston principle but there was an important point of difference. In the case of the Doxford where the upper piston acting as an exhaust valve also served to contribute to the drive of the shaft through its connection to the cranks on each side of the main one, with the B & W, the upper piston acted solely as an exhaust valve being driven from the crankshaft by truly enormous eccentrics. These were connected by four side rods to a chunky yoke holding the piston and these, as with the Doxford, made an impressive sight of dancing movement when the engine was running. Once tested, the engines were dismantled in unit sections and then, starting with bed plates and crankshafts, they were loaded on great low-loader railway trucks and taken out along tracks set in the cobbles. A little way along the quay was situated a mighty hammerhead crane affectionately known I was informed, as the 'Finieston Cran', Finieston being the area name of that part of the city.

The crane then lifted the engine parts, swinging them high and out to be lowered with care into the cavernous spaces of the engine rooms of new ships built and launched at yards down the river and towed up to receive their sources of life. It was an absorbing place and, once

A typical example of a Harland and Wolff-built Burmister and Wain opposed piston marine engine.

settled in, I enjoyed working there in the great machine shops where giant lathes were in use turning the crankshaft journals and pins of the biggest engines. In other areas enormous radial drills were endlessly at work, and other machine bays and fitting shops, for pipe and valve work provided an endless stream of experience. As a shipping company apprentice and therefore a 'guest' in the factory, I was pleased to follow the firm's guidance as they moved me and the few other marine cadets who were also there, from one department to another.

In one section I was moved to, something that was to prove quite remarkable happened. It was the section where much work was carried out on the giant eccentric straps of the biggest engines and, as the section workers were assembling for a new day's work the foreman, in his brown coat and black bowler, presented me as one to join them for a while. He introduced the men to me and of one he said something which I thought seemed a bit odd. "An' this," he said, pointing to a strikingly tall lad, "is 'Big Hughie'; ye'll need to watch him. He goes to church!" Some laughter rippled through the group, but then we settled to our work and the Gaffer's warning slipped to the back of my mind. However, some might say I should have kept myself more aware

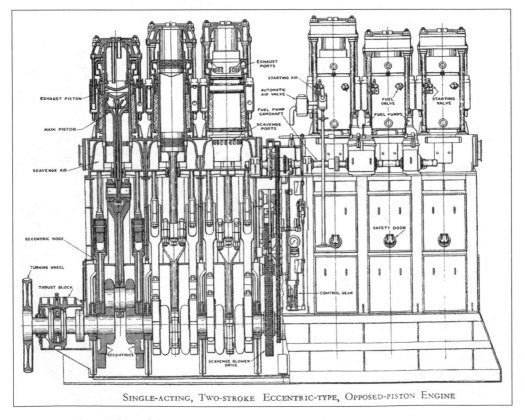

SINGLE-ACTING, TWO-STROKE ECCENTRIC-TYPE, OPPOSED-PISTON ENGINE

A cross-sectional view of the engine shown on the previous page.

of it for not long after something was to happen that was to be the trigger of life-changing events the scale of which I could never have imagined in my wildest dreams.

The inevitable happened. One day I was put to work with 'Big Hughie' on our own and, as was his way, he tub-thumped into a discussion about religion. Evidently he attended what was known as the Argyle Street Mission, a place it seemed of fervent salvation. As one who'd never gone to Church apart from my scout group Church Parades, I was all at sea with vociferous Hughie and, in desperation, I resorted to falling back on the very simple defence that everyone was a Christian as we lived in a Christian Society. 'Big Hughie', well worked up by now and almost beside himself with frustration yelled "Och, ye're wrong, ye have it all wrong! There's a difference between being, *a* Christian, and being Christian-like" and to emphasise the profundity of his words, he clipped the mighty casting we were working on with a hammer. The sound rang in my ears for hours after. We worked on in silence after that, and although I stayed in the section for a little longer before being moved, to my relief I was not in much contact with 'Big Hughie' again.

I was moved next to a valve fitting section, working on the valves great and small that went in the multitude of service lines serving the engines. Like everything else it was varied and absorbing work but now I was carrying an intrusive burden in my mind. 'Big Hughie's' hammer-endorsed words kept

Installing a massive crankshaft in Harland's factory.

surfacing over and over again in my mind despite whatever distractions of work, study or play I could put in their way. What had he meant I wondered? Was there something about this Christian faith business that, as I knew absolutely nothing about it, it might be interesting to discover? And if one wanted to learn where would one go? 'Big Hughie's' Mission Hall had sounded so terrifying it held no attraction, so perhaps I might just go to a Church and ask someone.

I found myself starting to look at Churches. Many of them seemed so big; a big one was in fact just round the corner from my lodgings and I felt I wanted one that suggested I might enjoy a degree of anonymity. I spotted one one day that spoke anonymity partly because it was itself both small and, partly hidden by virtue of being tucked in a corner of a lane between two of the enormous buildings in Renfield Street in the city. A notice gave times of services and I thought a Sunday evening one would be the best. I could scarcely believe what was happening but a die seemed in the process of being cast! Having got this far I would have to give it a go.

A Sunday came, and went. I'd chickened out! It would be the next I said, firmly.

Then another problem loomed. What would others think? By that time I'd moved into a large boarding house with quite a host of students and apprentices, and on Sundays Mrs Watts, our landlady, used to deposit big platters of sandwiches, cakes and a good supply of tea in a sort of common room and we'd all congregate to enjoy both the goodies and, each other's company. On the fateful Sunday of my Church foray decision I thought it might be circumspect to give tea a miss. I heard Mrs Watts's call ring out that 'tea was up,' and there was the clatter of eager steps as others dashed down. I hung back; but I was hungry! Then a shout echoed up the stairs, "Keith, where are you?" In the end I gave in and slunk down hoping that some at least might have finished and gone. They were all there of course and I took their chiding about being late in good part. Then came the inevitable question: "Are you coming down the George tonight?" With pubs shut in those days in Scotland anyone wishing to get a drink on a Sunday could go to a hotel and claim bone fide traveller status. We often did this but, on this occasion I said, "Er, no. I won't be coming tonight." Why not? I was asked, while another said, "Come on – what's her name then?" And if I'd had my wits about me I'd have plucked a name out of thin air and made a story up. Instead, I blurted out that I was going to Church.

A stunned silence gripped the room, broken only when someone said, "Bloody hell – he's gone mad!" I felt terrible; there I was getting it in the neck and I hadn't even gone at that point! It determined one thing of course. I now had to do it!

Slipping off Renfield Street into the anonymity of the lane, I approached the Church door and paused. Then I extended my hand to the handle with all the timidity of one offering a pork chop to a tiger. Pushing the door, I went in. A figure at a table inside, looked round and promptly took a 'double take' when he realised I was a stranger. He straightened up and eyed me suspiciously. "Hello," I said, brightly. "I thought I'd come to Church tonight." He was a tiny man with parchment skin drawn tightly over skull-like features and as he gave me a book he pointed with a bony finger to an inner door.

I went through into a dark, wood panelled room with high, enclosed bench seats. It had a distinctly Dickensian air about it, and it was astonishingly bare – and quiet. There was no music playing, and of things like candles, pictures, ornaments or flowers, all things dim recollections from past brief experience suggested a Church might have, there was nothing. Scattered around were a few head-bowed people.

Then, a black-gowned man suddenly appeared, taking a high tiered seat facing us, and the cadaverous man from the door entered and took a seat below him. After a few moments of silence, I was taken aback when a strangled caterwauling of a strange chant began, which was echoed by the people. It seemed to go on for ages, and it was all incomprehensible. Spoken, or read moments, seemed little better, although I did register that there seemed to be a great many references to the Pope in, I thought, a pretty derogatory way. Clearly he was not popular here whoever he was! After it was all over I tumbled outside feeling absolutely flummoxed. The problem was however, that the question I'd really gone with namely, to find out about the Christian faith, hadn't actually been asked, so I knew I was going to have to go back.

Fortunately, the distractions of the start of another busy week meant that the interest of my friends in my Church adventure was short-lived and I was relieved, for I felt that if they learnt how awful it had been, their opinion of my mental state would have been confirmed! On the following Sunday then, I went again. The cadaverous man with the books was very surprised to see me return for a second helping, and he was even more surprised when after the service he realised I was still there, as he stacked away the books of the departing people.

Once they'd all gone I approached him to have a word. He flinched as if I was going to bite him but relaxed when I asked if it might be possible to have a word with the minister. He thought for a moment. Clearly he didn't get many requests like that. Pursing his lips he said, "Weell, ye'll be coming this way," and beckoning with his bony finger he led me through the Church to a wooden stair leading to an office. The black-gowned man was sat stonily at a desk and examined me coldly while the cadaverous man whispered in his ear.

He departed leaving me standing like an army squaddie on the mat before the CO. Taking the silence as a cue I brought my question out.

"Excuse me sir," I said, "but I would like to find out about the Christian faith".

The minister ignored that and instead began asking questions of his own. It was turning into an interrogation! Where was I from? What was I doing in Glasgow? Where was I working? Where was I living? He considered all my answers and then leaning back reflectively in his chair he said that as I was from south of the border he felt I'd really be much better advised to take my question to somewhere like Saint Mary's Church which, he said, I'd probably find would be more like anything I might be familiar with, however vaguely, for it was the equivalent of the English Church in Scotland. Saint Mary's was in fact the big Church near my digs and which seemed daunting by its very size but emboldened now by my new experience I thought that indeed, I would take the advice given and have a go.

Bidding him goodnight I set off back to my digs, pausing on the way to have a closer look at Saint Mary's. It didn't seem too daunting really so that's where I'd go on the following Sunday.

I went to Evensong, as the notice board had proclaimed it. The place was distinctly more user-friendly than the Church I'd tried. Saint Mary's was light and airy, full of life and colour and there were lots of people who actually smiled at you and even said Hello!

The service meant very little but it seemed a good deal happier than that in the Church in the lane. A tall man spoke from a pulpit and, after the service I saw him stood near the door speaking to people as they left. He was now dressed in a purple robe and he was leaning I noticed, on a curly topped staff. I went and hovered nearby and eventually he noticed me and guessed I wanted to say something. I went closer and said "excuse me sir, I'd like to learn something about Christianity."

He looked down at me quizzically for a moment and then said, "I think you'd better go and talk to Father George." He pointed to a man behind me dressed in a black robe who was talking to people in the Church.

I was a bit puzzled by the 'Father' bit, but I pressed on with my cause. Eventually the man in black turned to me and asked if he could help. I explained what I was seeking and, to my surprise, he seemed genuinely interested.

As we talked he suggested that I might like to join him and some young people who were meeting in his house on a weekly basis. They were thinking about confirmation but he said that needn't bother me; just being there would be an opportunity to ask the sort of questions which, in their answers, I might find the help I was looking for. He asked me who had suggested I spoke to him and I pointed out the tall man in purple at the back. George laughed and said it was the bishop, but that didn't mean a lot to me. Then I told him of my experience at the Church off Renfield Street and how there,

I'd been advised to try Saint Mary's. As I told him how different it was to my new experience he asked me more closely about where it was. As I explained he suddenly burst out in a roar of laughter. It was no wonder I found Saint Mary's different he said. Where I'd been was a 'Wee Free' Church and, he laughed, they were more 'Presbie' than the Presbyterians themselves. I didn't really understand that but I took it to mean I'd found myself among some particularly dour and strict people of faith. George was still laughing. I liked George. We'd get on well I felt, and indeed we did.

I went along to the meeting he'd suggested and, straight away I felt at home. George was talking about life and creation saying that Christians believe it is not merely a matter of random chance but that it is the work of a creator who, having created, loves his creation – just like you love your marine engines that you're creating down at Harland's he added, nodding at me. He said I should count it a privilege to be able to be extending God's creation through the things I and all the other workers were doing in the great factories of Clydeside. All this appealed to me.

Another B&W engine, which Father George suggested was, in its making, an extension of God's creation.

I began to realise that having a thing called a faith was not some burden one had to tack on to life but rather that faith and life went quite easily hand in hand, thus 'Big Hughie' had been quite right in saying there was a difference between being a Christian and being Christian-like.

Most people, and I'd been among them, thought if anything, that Christianity was simply associated with leading a reasonably well behaved life. This, the majority would maintain, they tried to do as a matter of course and therefore must be Christian, but in truth, as I was now discovering, Christianity had everything to do with something called faith and very little to do with morals and behaviour.

The figure of Christ through His earthly life, had brought an awareness to the world that God actually wants to share the human life experience with *all* people, sharing it in all its richness and diversity, along with its woes and its joys. Thus believing in God as one sharing your life experience therefore also meant that you could view the world and what went on in it through His 'eyes' as well as your own.

Realising then how God might be seeing things leads naturally to thinking what He might expect, and hope for from His created people; and that He must want the best we can offer has to be, I thought, surely obvious. That being so, I realised one would wish to care about life, the world and one's behaviour in a responsible way quite naturally, knowing that to do so is His wish. I realised too, that this happily dispels completely the notion so many people hold that to think of having a faith, and attending a Church, is going to invite being burdened with tiresome rules and forbidding laws that take all the fun out of life.

I don't know what 'Big Hughie' and his fervent friends would have made of that. They seemed to have taken the finding of faith to terrifying lengths under the baffling heading of being 'saved', and they spoke of nothing else. I never understood what that meant and I much preferred the life-affirming normality of the faith I found expressed in Saint Mary's where I was encouraged to see that the God I 'met' in Church on Sunday, quite simply, then came with me to the factory on Monday, the theatre on Friday and the George for a drink on a Sunday night!

Clearly then, 'Big Hughie's' ideas, and now mine on finding a faith, were clearly very different, but I did have to gratefully concede that I owed it to him for getting me started on thinking about it all!

I was feeling increasingly 'at home' in Saint Mary's but one question needed clearing up. I'd accepted it as part of the Church's life but I wanted to know about the use of the title 'Father' when referring to the clergy there. George explained that it was not in any way an apeing of the Roman Catholic Church but simply a recognition of God's fatherly care of His people through the pastoral ministry of His priests. When later, through a tram window I caught a glimpse of it actually happening as I shall relate later, I understood. The title seemed to be exactly the right one. Being now so 'at home' it came as no surprise therefore when the matter of the confirmation, which the others in the group were aiming at, was put to me. George suggested that it might be a wonderful thing to have my growing sense of faith 'confirmed' by the Lord Himself through the ancient custom of the laying on of hands by the bishop. The Lord had laid His hands on His disciples, and they in turn had laid theirs on those who succeeded them and so it had gone on down the centuries through the bishops of the Church. That too appealed to my practical, and poetic senses, and I was happy to agree. And for me it really was a significant thing for my mind went back a few years to the day when as a schoolboy of thirteen I'd chanced to overhear my parents talking about me when they thought I was out of our house. I was alarmed to hear them saying that perhaps it was time they got me confirmed. My first thought was that it was something to do with the doctor! All that day I kept imagining some dreadful injection and with the passing hours the needle got bigger and bigger! That evening my father had suddenly put his newspaper down and the anticipated father to son chat was upon me. The needle went up another inch! Dad spoke about the matter and, when I asked what it was about and he mumbled something about the Church, my relief knew no bounds! I said no, I didn't want to go through such a thing and the matter was dropped. It was raised again the following year when I was fourteen and by then of course, a number of my school friends had gone through it without any enthusiasm so, once again, I declined, and the whole thing was never mentioned again. How strange then, that now in Glasgow, I was choosing it for myself. My parents were of course, very surprised!

Thus I was duly confirmed, rather amusingly I thought, by the purple-robed bishop who was the one I'd first approached at Saint Mary's, unaware then of who, or what he was. Thinking back over the weeks from the moment of 'Big Hughie's' remark, to my confirmation, it did seem the most surprising of developments, but if I thought that surprising there was more to come! Shortly after, returning from a study day at the Technical College, I was on a tram rattling along Great Western Road. It was a dull day with a hint of drizzle that made the cobblestones glint and glisten. The tram came to a stop and I noticed through the window a group of people chatting on the pavement, one of them being, I was intrigued to see, the cassocked figure of Father George. (I now knew that those purple and black robes I'd seen on my first visit to Saint Mary's, were cassocks!). With smiles and waves the group broke up and, just as the tram moved off again, I caught sight of George's figure turning into the black maw of a tenement entrance and I realised he was out and about on parish visiting. And then a startling realisation hit me. In few moments I'd just witnessed a profound endorsement to the truth I'd already begun to grasp that religion, and life, were a reality together; that God was as much at home in Harland and Wolff's as he was in Saint Mary's or even, I had to suppose, in 'Big Hughie's' mission hall or the 'Wee Free' church for all its forbidding coldness. Christianity took its true life from the life of Christ, and though He'd gone regularly to the churches of His day He'd actually spent most of His time out amongst the people. And that was it. In the little scene I'd just chanced to see from the tram, of the 'fatherly' priest out among the people, I'd seen Christ out among the people in the streets of Galilee! And a voice like a whisper seemed to say 'You'll do that one day'. As quickly as the thought had come I dismissed it. It was ridiculous, and as my stop was approaching, I gathered up my tech note books and stepped out into the bustle and drizzle of Glasgow and thought of Mrs Watts's dinner waiting for me, and a visit to La Bohemme at the theatre that night.

COCKINESS GETS A COMEUPPANCE...

It was a mere couple of weeks later before something else happened that drew the whispered voice heard on the tram back to mind. It was a Sunday morning and I'd attended the morning Service in Saint Mary's. The Provost of the Cathedral had been the preacher that morning and now, as one feeling very much at home in the place, I really tried to take in what he had to say. However, it seemed remarkably difficult and I felt a sense of disappointment. After the Service we'd gathered for coffee in the adjacent hall, and seeing George coming towards me I thought I'd dare to be critical of the sermon. It was both cheeky and unfair of course, for I should have spoken to the Provost, but youth and familiarity encourage a woeful spirit of cockiness.

"Father George," I said, "I didn't think much of the Provost's sermon this morning. It was way over our heads."

To my surprise he neither agreed nor disagreed but after a pause for thought he looked at me over his coffee cup and said simply,

"Look lad, if you think you can do any better you'd better get in and do it!"

I was stunned, and though we went on to talk amiably about other things his words went ringing round in my head. The memory of the 'voice' on the tram came back and was now linked with a challenge! Days later it was all still there. I kept thinking of it all in the context of where I was working and of the people I was so involved with in the great world of industry. I felt sure I was right that if any of them had been with me in Church that fateful morning what they would have heard would have meant little or nothing to them and the confounded thing was I began to feel that I might just try to do things differently! It was all ridiculous of course, and I dismissed it as fast as I thought about it but, the thought and the feeling simply would not go away. Perhaps I, as an ordinary working chap in the world who'd found a practical sense of faith, could help others relate to it too without feeling brow-beaten in the manner of 'Big Hughie's' way, or heavily rule-burdened as was assumed going to Church meant! It was a challenge! Furthermore, it was one that I increasingly felt I could take on. In the end I went to talk to Father George about it. I really thought he'd send me packing but, to my great surprise, he listened very carefully to the muddled story of my thoughts and, after a long reflective moment he said, "D'you know, I think you're going to be a priest!" I could scarcely believe my ears.

"Don't worry," George said. "If God wants you He'll make it clear. Say your prayers, and think about it carefully and we'll see how it all develops."

The notions did indeed persist and, rather to my surprise considering their earlier reactions, my friends in the digs, and in Harlands, although somewhat bemused did try to be supportive. When he heard how things were going George suggested that perhaps I ought to go and see the bishop. I baulked a bit at that but he was insistent and he set about arranging it for me. The bishop said when I attended as arranged, "Ah – it's you again!" clearly remembering my impulsive request to him to know about the faith. And again, to my astonishment, when I fully expected to be shown the door, the bishop was in fact most interested and fully supportive. I found this baffling. At every turn where I'd expected to be laughed away the very opposite was happening! The bishop said that there was an ordinand's selection conference coming up soon and he'd get me on it. The conference was to be held at Kelham somewhere down near Newark towards the east coast and, said the bishop, it's a monastic community and they have a theological college attached to them. Then on reflection, he thought I probably wouldn't go there. I might be considered a bit too worldly for such a place! A much better idea he said would be for him to get me a place at Coates Hall theological college in Edinburgh, but first there was the selection conference to get through. I duly attended. Kelham was impressive. In between the interview sessions with clergy and important looking lay people, we attended services in the community's beautiful chapel. With its shiny black marble floor and atmospheric lighting, together with the haunting loveliness of Gregorian chants which the monks sang so beautifully, the place exuded a rich spirituality. It was a fascinating weekend but looking round at other candidates I felt sure I was now going to be exposed as a fake and put back in place where I belonged in the world. Thus again I found myself absolutely astonished when I was informed that I'd been successful and that I was being recommended for ordination training. Reporting back to the bishop in Glasgow he was delighted, and said that he'd get me a place in Coates Hall as soon as possible. I was beginning to feel a bit alarmed at the speed with which all this was happening, and I tried to explain that I wouldn't be able to start all that soon as even though the end of my apprenticeship was drawing near I was bound to my shipping company to serve a two year contract with them as some recompense for their having spent a good deal of money on my training. The bishop felt that as it was the Church that was laying a claim to my attention and not that I wanted to change to another shipping firm, the company would be sympathetic to a request to be released from my contract. The only way to find out was to go and talk to them in London. A meeting was duly set up, and my father came up from Gloucester to join me and we went together to BP's offices of Britannic House in Finsbury Circus in London.

A FATEFUL DECISION...

My poor parents were of course quite bowled over by this turn of events in my life and they must have been a little dismayed to say the least at the thought that having got their son safely established on a lifetime career, he was now in fact threatening to be falling back on them again for the duration of theological college time, if not longer! However, bricks that they were, even if they didn't really understand what had happened they backed me to the hilt. We were met at Britannic House by Mr D G Alcock, the superintendent in charge of the apprentice training division and he listened carefully as I related all the things that had happened and indeed, as the bishop had thought, he was very sympathetic. His considered reaction however was that as clearly everything had happened very quickly some slowing down might not be a bad idea. His advice was that I should stay and fulfil my contract, and the two years involved would allow me to get enough sea time in to complete a qualification already begun through my first two years at technical college. And more importantly, he said, it would give me time to really assess the truth of the sense of vocation I was experiencing for the Church. After all, he said, the Church won't be going away! However, he then said that if I really did feel ready to move in a Church direction the company would be prepared to release me. Dad and I came away feeling that we'd received really gentlemanly treatment, and the decision was clear; I'd stay and do my contract.

I returned to Glasgow and reported it all back to the bishop. Rather to my surprise, not to say dismay, he picked up on the fact that the company had said they would actually be prepared to let me go. I protested, but he was cheerfully insistent, assuring me that all would be well and he would get me into Coates Hall that same year in the September intake of students. I was beginning to feel really confused. By then it was January and my time at Harland and Wolff was ending and the final two months of my apprenticeship saw me making a move to G & J Wiers of Cathcart in Glasgow, makers of steam auxiliaries such as feed pumps and evaporators. This, like Harlands, was another fascinating place, but somehow, being now so confused about my life, I got little enjoyment out of my time there. The bishop, admittedly in the nicest of ways, kept the pressure on for me to make the decision to leave and, in the end, I sat down and wrote the fateful letter.

The company accepted it without any further comment, and I didn't know what to think. I felt sand-bagged on the one hand and like a man who'd walked off a known path into a fog-bound forest and was lost, on the other. For his part the bishop was delighted and set about making arrangements for me to be able to start at Coates Hall in Edinburgh that September as he'd promised. A visit to the college was arranged to give me some idea of what and where I would be going but even as I went and found it very interesting I realised I was carrying a powerful sense of guilt that I'd broken my contract. I didn't feel the wrong decision had been made, only that perhaps it had been made too soon. I felt a bit like the person going to buy a car only to find that he ends up being sold one, which really is quite different! He's happy enough with what he gets but it wasn't actually what he'd meant to get! And besides, there was another issue to face. It was only March when I put myself 'on the beach' and September therefore was a long way ahead, so there was a good part of a year to fill with some sort of gainful employment.

OFF TO DUBLIN...

The bishop came up with the suggestion of my taking a position with the Missions to Seamen as a 'Student Helper'. Enquiries were duly made and, soon afterwards, I found myself appointed in that capacity to the Flying Angel premises of the Missions to Seamen on Quayside in Dublin. It proved a very difficult time. The sense of a burden of guilt persisted, and the very nature of what we did in the Mission brought me into daily contact with ships which was very unsettling. I was now part of marine life without actually being engaged in it. However, I tried very hard to identify with this new role.

I began taking services in the Mission chapel and helping in all the social activities the place afforded visiting seafarers, and I found I got on very well with the chaplain, the Reverend Don Lewin. He had a great sense of humour and we would have many a laugh in the course of ship visiting but, for me, it persisted in being an unsettling time. I found it particularly so one day when I was down in the dock area and I saw a big Brocklebank liner coming in. We'd heard about her coming and she'd been scheduled we'd been told, for a night tide arrival. However, here she was coming in on the earlier afternoon tide instead. I watched her docking, hearing the distant clamour of telegraphs and the sounds of her engines being manoeuvred. Once she was secured and the gangway was down, I went aboard. I made my way to the engine room and stepped inside to look down on the machinery. It was a truly impressive sight and I felt my heart-strings being tugged unmercifully! It was very hot and a slight haze of scavenge smoke was in the air speaking volumes of the exertions of the main engine. It was a big Burmister and Wain opposed piston engine and she'd obviously been pushed hard in order for the ship to make the afternoon tide. The engine was simmering from its work, looking like a racehorse steaming in the paddock after a hard race. Far below through the gratings I could see a couple of her engineers dashing about as they shut 'the job' down, and I simply ached to be with them. This sort of thing was doing my sense of equanimity no good of course, and for sanity's sake I turned and made my way ashore. Emotionally, things were really quite difficult, and I didn't seem to have anyone to talk to about them. The only thing was to press on with the work I'd undertaken and, it had to be said, there were of course, plenty of pleasant and amusing moments in it.

DIPLOMATIC FOOTBALL...

One came one day when a Danish freighter docked, fresh in from the Tropics. I went with the chaplain to visit her and while chatting with the crew Don asked if there was anything they'd like him to arrange for them while they were in port. They said excitedly that as they were very keen on football they'd love it if he could arrange a match for them. It was duly set up. A local youth club agreed to field a team, and we went down to the docks with a coach to pick up the Danes. And my word, they made an impressive sight. Massive of physique and bronzed by tropic sun, the blonde Danes trooped impressively down the ship's gangway with a clatter of studded boots, and resplendent in their own team 'strip'; they really were keen! Then, at the field of play in a local park, as the Danes warmed up with a kick-about, the local team watched them with an air of disbelief; tiny of stature and wan of colour, they looked like lambs lining up for the slaughter and the chaplain clearly feared for their safety. However, there was no need to worry. Marshalling the teams, the referee blew his whistle and the game was on and, within a matter of minutes we knew it was the Danes we had to worry about, not our Dublin lads. The Danes' muscles, good at coping with the ladders and companionways of a ship and bracing against its rolling and pitching, were not up to sprinting around a soccer ground! The Irish lads, wiry and match-fit, ran rings around the poor Danes who lumbered about like ships in a Biscay storm. At half time, with an embarrassing score line of twelve nil to the home team, the chaplain decided he'd better have a diplomatic word. "Now listen lads," he said as our boys gathered in an orange-sucking huddle, "for my sake, the Danish Ambassador's sake, not to mention God's sake, let 'em get some goals in!" The sight of the Danes lying puffing, like stranded whales, touched some chords of pity in their Irish hearts and, as the referee called for the second half, they took to the field in a spirit of diplomatic compassion. The weary Danes, clearly wishing it was time to go back to their ship kicked off, but suddenly found new heart as their striker, to everyone's surprise, not least his own, got a goal home in the Irish net. As the Danes danced and clapped the Irish winked knowingly at one another and, in the end, the match had a score line at 18 goals to 7 that reflected the appropriate talent involved but good sportsmanship too. The Danes went back to their ship having had a wonderful time, and we in the Mission chapel that evening, winked at the Lord in true Don Camillo style, in recognition of His help in another quiet success of Christian action!

SOME BLACK MARKETEERING!...

Another of my Dublin experiences was also amusing and came as a revelation to me as one naively innocent in the world of underhand commerce. A regular caller in Dublin's docks were a couple of Bristol Steam Navigation Company's coasters, the motor vessels Pluto and Juno. I got very friendly with the crew of the Pluto and one day I popped aboard for a sociable chat. I knocked on the Second Mate's cabin door and as I went in I was surprised to see him looking very pleased as he held a bulky envelope in his hand. "Look at this," he said, with an air of conspiracy. He held the envelope open and I was astonished to see it full of bank notes. "Won the pools?" I asked, innocently. "Nah," he said, "it's our takings." "What from?" I asked, and was stunned by his answer of 'condoms.' I had no idea of what had been going on, for ages it seemed, all as a result of the strict ruling of the Catholic Church in Southern Ireland forbidding the use of such things. Human nature being what it is someone had realised that whether the Church forbade the use of condoms or not people wanted them, and the lads on the Pluto hearing of the need undertook to buy in bulk at home and, once in Dublin, they could be fed onto the black market for a handsome profit! I had to confess that I was very impressed by such business enterprise!

My time in Dublin was coming to an end. I found myself saying farewell to many new friends whose company I'd come to value during my stay but, it was time to go for I'd be travelling soon to Edinburgh to start a very new phase of life at theological college. I hitched a lift to Bristol on the Pluto, and travelled home to Gloucester. There, my still somewhat bemused parents helped me get ready to go north to commence what was going to be a truly new experience.

WITH THE CANON MISSIONER; A DEPRESSING MEETING...

There was one formality which had to be attended to before leaving and that was to meet the Canon Missioner – a priest responsible for the care of ordinands at Gloucester. It had been agreed by the Church authorities that while my vocation had begun in Scotland and through the good offices of the Bishop of Glasgow I had been given a place in the theological college of the Scottish Episcopal Church, once I had been successful (assuming I was!) in passing the General Ordination Examination, I would actually be ordained in my home diocese of Gloucester. Accordingly then, I was required to make myself known to Canon Daven Thomas, one of the residentiary Canons of the Cathedral and who also had the responsibility of the care of those from the

The MV Pluto, a regular visitor to Dublin. Kegged Guiness went home but it was the 'secret' cargo that came in from England which made a few small fortunes!   www.fotoflite.com

diocese who were training for the ministry. My father came with me for what was to be a depressing meeting. The Canon, bless him, couldn't relate to my background in engineering, or the way my thoughts of the Church had really arisen. He waffled a lot about the need for the most dedicated application to my forthcoming studies. He dwelt at length on the fact that I must not allow myself to get distracted by worldly thoughts, adding darkly, that this should put all thoughts of girlfriends and such things right out of the picture! And as for marriage, well! Such a thing was unthinkable! I could not help but contrast the Canon's dreamy way with the down-to-earth, practical words of Mr Alcock in his care of his apprentices and their sea careers! It went on and on and, in the end, after giving me a slightly bemused expression of his best wishes, he showed us out into the dark of Miller's Green, tucked in the embrace of some of the lovely old buildings within the precincts of Gloucester's historic Cathedral. I was in no mood to appreciate them or their history however. I wondered what on earth I was letting myself in for, and Dad, sensing my mood of dejection, put his arm round my shoulder and said, "Well son, that's the price for leaving the navy." I wasn't sure whether this was said in pure sympathy or whether it carried a touch of cynicism for I knew he felt at heart that it would have been wiser to have taken BP's advice and stayed on to finish my contract. However, the die was cast, and whatever Dad really thought he kept to himself, assuring me instead of his, and my mother's, loyal and constant support.

TO THEOLOGICAL COLLEGE...

Once again then, I travelled north and, arriving in Edinburgh, I took a cab out to the college situated in the Haymarket area of the city. The college was an attractive house of some onetime importance as the private residence of a significant Edinburgh family. It was set in pleasant grounds occupying an area right at the end of two imposing crescents of city buildings with a park area in the middle and, at the other end of the crescent stood the majestic bulk, with its three landmark spires, of Saint Mary's Episcopal Cathedral. I was allocated a room in what was a building the college had acquired for expansion purposes, it being the end house of the crescent which abutted the college grounds. I began the process of settling in but it looked to be a difficult job to make it feel in any way homely; the room was big and bare, furnished in very spartan style and boasted a little electric two-bar fire with an ominous meter standing hungrily by in a prominent place on the wall. I could see some chilly experiences looming when winter would get Edinburgh in its grip! Once I'd unpacked it was time to meet some of other students. Over in the main college house there were several having tea in the common room. Some of course, were students in their second or third years while one or two were new first year entrants like me. I hadn't been there five minutes when I sensed I must be something of a misfit before we'd really started! I was asked at which university I'd been, and what degree I had come with, and there were looks of surprise from some and even disdain from others when I said I'd come from the Merchant Navy. (I was to get a very similar reaction but in reverse when a few years later I would be back aboard a ship. My shipmates then were to be stunned when it was revealed that my previous ship was not a ship but a Church!) To my dismay I discovered that apart from one student who'd been doing National Service in the RAF and another who had been some sort of shoe salesman in Falkirk all the others had come from universities and were very much at home in the academic atmosphere of the theological college. I made friends with the chap from the RAF well enough but he was a very quiet and independent sort with a gift for photography and in truth we really shared little in common. The others, even those of the new intake fresh from university, were all very much more at home, wearing the academic gowns we were required to put on over our jackets with accustomed ease. And of the endless lists of books which we were told about and advised to try to acquire for our own libraries, many of the students already had them or knew all about them. I felt rather at sea in all the academic whirl, but I struggled manfully to keep my head above water. I was going to make a go of it all, of that I was determined!

COLLEGE LIFE – AND ILLNESS...

College life had a well established routine. The day began with a service in the chapel followed by breakfast, the rest of the morning being devoted to lectures. A midday service was followed by lunch and then the afternoons were free-time. Late afternoon lectures, or personal study, led to an evening service in chapel after which dinner was served. Thereafter, study time took us to the night service of compline at 9 pm after which silence was observed until after chapel the next day. It was very different to anything I'd experienced before but, I adapted well enough although I found the tone and style of some of the lectures pretty heavy going.

The Principal, Canon Wimbush, lectured in Church doctrine (what the Church believes). He was clearly a very scholarly man but he had a depressing air of weariness about him, walking with his head always listing to starboard in an apprehensive way, and his lecture technique had in consequence, a wooden quality about it which I found very difficult to engage with. The Vice-Principal, Canon Donald Nicholson, affectionately known as Father Nick, had a very different personality. He lectured in worship (the meaning and conduct of Services) and practical pastoralia (the work of the priest in parish life) doing so in lively style, and I took to him very quickly. He had a cheerful impishness about him with eyes that twinkled with alertness and humour. His shiny bald pate and rotund figure added to his image of one who would be a jolly good friend and guide, and he was certainly to prove so to me. From early on in our relationship he seemed to be one at least who genuinely understood me, and I was to value it enormously. The Chaplain, an elderly and amiable priest in charge of the Chapel and Service arrangements, lectured in Biblical studies and New Testament Greek. This latter subject was to be my permanent *bete noire!* One other lecturer came on certain days, from a parish in far away Dumbarton on the Clyde. His name was Canon Goldie and he lectured in Church history. His style was as dry as blown saw dust which only served to endorse the boyhood impressions formed at school which said history as a subject was boringly dead. It would be several years before it would really spark into life when I found myself appointed as the Rector of a lovely, and historic Church!

I settled slowly and unsurely into college life and I kept trying to remember the things whose inspiration had pointed me along this way. I tried to keep the tram-window vision of God's priest out in the streets among God's people, as Christ had once been in the streets of Galilee, as a beacon in front of my mind, together with the forceful nudge of Father George to find a way to be a communicator of the simple faith to ordinary people. In this latter ideal I was to find that I'd got a ready inspiration in Father Nick. Already I'd sensed he was a brilliant exponent of the art of communication in a way I felt instantly at home with, and I knew I was to learn a great deal from him.

Keeping these basic things afloat in my mind despite the dragging effect of the weight of sterile academic study was to be an abiding struggle but, as I strove to cope, I realised there was a bonus in where it was happening. It was in Edinburgh after all, and the city which I took to exploring with growing fascination and delight, endeared itself to me and I to it! There was another bonus too. I quickly found that only a short bus ride away was Leith, at that time a busy and thriving port, with its own active ship-building yard of Henry Robb's as an added star feature! I found endless pleasure in mooching around the docks savouring the constant pageant of shipping, but equally, I had to be honest, there was a down-side to the experience. It was doing nothing but keeping the wound of my early departure from the navy, raw and wide open. In truth, I was unhappy and I knew it. I nursed an abiding sense of guilt over the broken contract with BP, and a nostalgia for the practical world of engineering which I'd abandoned. The result was that I became ill.

One day, when visiting the 'topos' (the Greek word for 'place' and used as student slang for the lavatory) I was dismayed to find it full of blood! A hasty visit to the college doctor was followed by an even hastier one as an out-patient in the gastro clinic of Edinburgh's Great Western Hospital. There I was told to kneel on an examination couch like a crashed aircraft – on my knees with my nose on the couch leaving my 'tail' end stuck in ungainly fashion in the air. Something was draped over me and a flexible examination light inserted in my 'stern tube'. Then I heard a doctor's voice call out to a colleague in a neighbouring cubicle, "I say Charles, do come and look at this!" I felt like exhibit 'A' in some sort of freak-show! And besides, I was exceedingly uncomfortable! Eventually I was told to relax and get up, and I was informed in a casual way that I'd got a 'granulation of the proctitis' – a chronic inflammation with consequent bleeding in the bowel. It was often associated with worry or anxiety I was told, so if I was worried about anything then stop worrying and it would probably clear up! That I thought was easier said than done – if that is, it was my anxieties about how my life was so mixed up were the culprit, as I felt sure they were. To help me, I was prescribed steroid drugs together with steroid enemas which I had to insert at night to try and combat the inflammation. I could scarcely believe what was happening but, like any new eventuality, it had to be taken on board and coped with.

Time passed. I got through my first year at college successfully, passing

An atmospheric photograph taken in Leith docks by one of my fellow students, Philip Blomfield. He, having been in the RAF, like me found college life in Edinburgh 'difficult' at times, and likewise too, he found a 'haven' in the docks only for him it was not ships but photography which was his saving forte.

(with the exception of Greek!) the end-of-year examinations, and having coped tolerably well with my emotional and, now the medical problems, bouts of illness being dealt with through sessions of the undignified enema treatments, I could now seek some holiday respite. For the long summer vacation I took a job as a beach-hand, working off the picturesque little bay known as Maidencombe Cove, near Torquay. There I gained, beside a remarkable tan, some restoration of health, for bowel trouble actually abated, in the face it seemed of the physical demands work on the beach called for! Coping with sheer physical work was perhaps indeed a very good way of putting emotional stresses on the 'back burner' for a while!

AN ACT OF REBELLION...

My second year at college then began, and I found the emotional problems once again exerted a powerful influence on my life. By then I'd absorbed the college routines, and become as well, fully involved in much of the social life on the folk song and jazz scene in clubs down Edinburgh's famous Royal Mile. However, it was during this second year that emotional feelings came at one point to something of a serious head. Coping with some of the lectures was still, I found, a constant struggle, and this was particularly so with the Principal's doctrine contributions. One morning we assembled in one of the college's richly book-lined rooms and Canon Wimbush entered in his distracted fashion to deliver a lecture on the subject of angeology. I think I was in a particularly rebellious mood that day but the subject itself made me seethe. After a bit I gave up trying to take notes. I listened with a growing sense of amazement and disbelief. The lecture seemed to me to be just an unending flow of unbelievable drivel. With growing impatience I fretted in my seat. Not that far away in other parts of the city, other students were sitting in on lectures dealing with aspects of medicine, engineering, geology, art and hosts of other important subjects, and there we were in Coates Hall listening to nebulous ideas about angels! Something within me that morning finally snapped. As soon as the lecture was over I stormed off to my room, a plan forming in my mind. I was going to leave – but I'd have lunch first!

DRAMA AND STRESS DOWN AT THE DOCKS...

I ate my lunch in the tight-lipped manner of one determined on a very particular, almost daring action. Lunch over, I walked out of college and took a bus straight down to Leith. Walking out to the docks I stood and savoured the scene, and then had a quiet stroll round as if to fully check the action I was about to take. Across the dock I could see some buildings, one of which I knew I was about to enter. In most dock areas, certainly the bigger and busier ones there were offices known as 'The Pool' or, more accurately the Shipping Federation. They were where seafarers who may not have been company men but were happy to take employment on a whole variety of ships could go in search of work. Squaring my shoulders I walked back round the dock and approached the offices. There were a number of entrances for different categories of service and I went of course in the one for engineers. A helpful clerk listened to my rehearsed tale that I'd been at sea and then been 'ashore' for a bit, and that I was now looking to get back to sea; had he therefore got any jobs on his books? Opening a big ledger he ran his finger down a list of entries. There was a need for a fourth engineer on a tanker due out to Mexico, or there was a need for engineers with a small company running ships in and out of the Baltic and across the North Sea. He mentioned several others but I thought the North Sea and the Baltic might be a good way of getting the feel of things again, and the clerk said brightly that that was good because the company actually had an office there in Leith. He'd give them a ring he said, and I could walk down to meet them and find out more about what was involved.

Leaving the office I turned to the long line of buildings along the shore side of the road along the dock-side and as I walked in the direction the clerk had said to go I was surprised to see a man appear from a doorway, looking expectantly in my direction and then when he saw me, he waved in a cheerful fashion. I was most surprised. Greeting me at the door he ushered me in to an inner sanctum and offered a welcoming cup of tea. He said he was delighted to have had a phone call from the Pool and then he began asking a bit about my past experience, and about what sort of kit I could provide. I was feeling there was something slightly odd about it all but I couldn't put a finger on what! I said I did have engine room clothing and I could even come with oilskins but surely I said, it was summer and it couldn't be that bad in the North Sea. It was the man's turn to look puzzled. He said by kit he meant cold climate gear! It went on for a little longer but gradually we both realised we were totally at cross purposes. He began to sound rather annoyed at having his time wasted for, he said, he was busy as an agent on behalf of Salvessons of Norway. He was, he explained, preparing a whale factory ship which was currently lying in dock in Dundee, for a two year Antarctic expedition, and for which he was desperate for engineers! I was appalled. The Pool clerk had clearly rung the wrong office number, and this particular job he'd not bothered to mention from his ledger list as he'd realised from what I'd said that it wouldn't be my cup of tea at that moment. Indeed it wasn't, then, or at any moment! I was not going on any such venture (I didn't approve of whaling anyway!) and the kind man who'd welcomed me in, realising he hadn't got an engineer after all, now curtly asked me to depart forthwith! I stumbled out into the street, catching sight of a clock on the wall as I did so, and realising the Pool would now be closed I knew I couldn't go back there. I stood outside feeling utterly deflated. I'd got no job after all. The Pool had closed. I'd 'left' my college, and home at Gloucester seemed a very long way away. My life at that moment seemed to be in ruins and I think I could almost have gone to the dock edge and jumped in by way of solving it all. In the end I did the only thing I could do, and that was to slink back to the vague sanctuary of my room in the college. I managed to slip in without being seen and I went to ground in my room, missing chapel, evening dinner and ignoring lectures. I sat in a fog of bewilderment wondering what I should do next. I realised I'd had a lucky escape from the whaling venture, but what on earth was I going to do I wondered.

HELPFUL ADVICE...

Then, late in the evening there was a gentle knock at my door. I said 'come in' and as the door opened the bald pate of Father Nick appeared. Looking across the room he just said quietly, with deep understanding, "What's up?"! I was so relieved to be able at last to speak to someone that I started burbling it all out, but Father Nick stopped me and suggested we went to the greater comfort of his rooms downstairs where there was the added attraction of a soothing glass of sherry! Down we went, and once settled I poured the saga of my confused life out in full. Like the good priest he was he just listened, letting me get it all off my chest. Finally it was his turn to offer some considered advice, and I in turn, listened to him. I could go back to the Pool of course he said on the following morning and pick up the thread of the action to leave that I'd begun, but the fact that it had gone wrong that afternoon might be a sign it wasn't really the right thing to be doing. In coming to college whether it was the right time to have come or not I had, he said, 'put my hand on the plough' and to leave what I'd begun there, as I'd left the navy with unfinished business, would only compound the problem. Besides which he felt sure that I did have something to offer the Church by way of a ministry; it may not be fully clear what it was then but he was sure God would reveal it in His own good time. We sipped our sherry, and I felt emotionally that things were coming back to an even keel. Thanking him for his compassion and time, and feeling utterly drained by the day's events, I went to get some restorative sleep.

I stayed in college! It was as well that with Father Nick's help I pulled myself together because in the second year there was the challenge looming up of sitting the Luscombe Scholarship Examination. This was an external examination, managed through the college but quite independent of the college's principal purpose of preparing students for the General Ordination

Examinations of the Church. The Scholarship was unique to Coates Hall having been established by a distinguished past student and it was marked quite independently of any college involvement. It required the writing of a very extensive essay cum thesis on a subject revealed at a specific time prior to submission of the work thus precluding any unfair preparation, and the final result, if it was awarded a pass, was deemed of sufficient academic calibre to justify the right to the wearing of an academic hood. For those students who hadn't already acquired one by virtue of an existing degree qualification, this was an attractive encouragement to sit the 'Luscombe'. I was quite determined to have a go!

The day of the announcement of the subject of the essay/thesis came and it was posted up on the notice board. It read: 'Are all the Canonical Scriptures Given of God or are they Merely a Human Record of Divine Acts?' I got to grips with forming my considered response to that, seeking inspiration down at Leith docks as much as in the college library! I duly handed in my effort and was pleased to be awarded a 'pass' being given 145 marks out of a possible 200. I even passed the end of year examinations successfully (with the exception of Greek!) and thus my third and final year loomed up – with Ordination to come at the end of it!

BACK ON A SHIP...

But there was the long summer vacation to fill with gainful work first and, with my brush with the Pool in mind I tried again looking this time, to see if there was any work for relief engineers. Indeed there was and, to my delight, I got a position as a relief engineer on the Houlder Brothers tanker MV Newbury, lying very conveniently for me considering my parental home was at Gloucester, in Barry docks in nearby South Wales. Travelling home for a brief visit with my still bemused parents, I gathered my nautical kit together and went on to join the Newbury. I was delighted to find she too had a Doxford main engine, a five cylinder, centre scavenge type, so I felt quite at home very

Right: Serving as a relief engineer on the MV Newbury, one of the ships in the fleet of Houlder Brothers. (I am on the left).

quickly. Her Scotch boiler system however although similar to many of the ships of that era, suffered for some reason from a weak Howden forced draught system with the result that we frequently kippered the residents of Barry with thick black smoke when an onshore wind blew up the Bristol Channel! I enjoyed my experience on the Newbury even if it included indulging in some underwater swimming in order to clear blocked bilge strums when we had a flood in the engine room from a serious leak at the stern gland around the propeller shaft. The vacation time passed in a flash when spent like that, and all too soon it was time for me to be travelling back to Edinburgh for my third and final year at theological college.

THE FINAL YEAR...

Once back in Edinburgh I thought of the year's forthcoming two main elements of experience. One was the daunting task of preaching a sermon before the student body and staff of the college! The second feature of the year, and which would come near its end, was of course the sitting of the finals of the General Ordination Examinations themselves. Clearly, it was going to be a year of some heavy-going!

ON PREACHING...

The first challenge was the matter of preaching to the college. This was something dreaded by all students and I suffered particular agonies because so many of the efforts preceding mine had reminded me of the Provost's sermon of years before which had gone 'over my head'. I had to try very hard to avoid that being said of my effort when it would come to my standing up to deliver it. The trouble was of course that the academic atmosphere and ethos of the college seemed quite naturally to influence sermon construction along 'lecture' style lines. I felt strongly that this was wrong and, remembering Father George's challenge, I was determined to avoid what I saw as an error. One ready inspiration to do better, which I was ever more conscious of, was in Father Nick's address and preaching technique, and I observed, and listened to him with ever greater care. He was frequently erudite and 'technical' but always in a user-friendly way that carried the listener with him. One evening at the end of a Chapel Service he was on duty to address us. He came slowly down and took his place sitting in a chair at the chancel step and, once settled and relaxed, he delivered an absolutely brilliant address. I noticed that occasionally he glanced at something hidden in his cupped hands resting in his lap and I guessed he must have some notes there. I listened to him spell-bound, and afterwards over coffee in the common room I offered a word of praise and thanks. His eyes twinkled and he asked if I wanted to see his notes, and when I said yes he delved in his cassock pocket and produced a slightly battered cigarette packet down a clear side of which he'd put some key words and a phrase or two! I was impressed. Father Nick gave me much good advice, a key piece of which was to have something you really 'want to say' and then say it, don't read it! He advised keeping things as simple as possible, avoiding big words and phrases, and always, he said, do *look* at those to whom you are privileged to be talking. This was particularly sound advice for when I thought of some of the clergy whose preaching I had experienced they often looked at the ceiling rather than the people thus adding to the sense that their words were over everyone's heads! And, added Father Nick, prepare well, and rehearse as frequently as you can in your mind, especially the key things you do want to say. You'll be fine, he said, winking encouragingly.

The day was drawing ever nearer when I would have to stand in the 'hot spot' and I kept wondering on what I would preach. Inspiration came in the form of a reading heard in Chapel about that time. It was the account of the entry of Jesus into Jerusalem at what would be the first Easter. The reading is normally associated with Palm Sunday but it had come up in another context. As I heard it again, and registered the story's detail of how the crowd made a great fuss

Fan trouble with the boilers! When the wind was on-shore, we 'kippered' the poor residents of Barry!

of welcome of Him, and how some in the throng expressed surprise, asking just who this chap was, it was in the answer that was given that my sermon inspiration lay. The question drew the answer that the figure arriving on the donkey was, 'Jesus, the prophet from Nazareth.' That's it, I thought – there was my sermon! If our faith is right it wasn't Jesus, a prophet arriving, but God Himself, riding in ready to die for His people. It was a mistake then, in Bible times, and I knew it still was. I knew that if I'd asked many of those I'd known in industry, or at sea or anywhere else in our society, what they thought about Jesus Christ, they would be likely to say, "Jesus? Oh yes, He was a great teacher (prophet!)." Thus to point out in a sermon the error made by those in the story carried a present day relevance too! Remembering all the advice I'd received I prepared my address, putting with it a separate sheet bearing word pointers. The great day came and I joined the students and staff seated in a wide arc in a big lecture room with a lectern standing expectantly in the middle. The Principal kicked proceedings off, announcing that it was me having the duty that day of addressing everyone, and then he called me forth to the 'hot spot.' Stepping up as casually as I could, I arranged my notes on the stand, paused, and looked around. Then I preached my sermon. Once it was done the Principal took command again and invited comments from my fellow students. Someone was quickly critical of the fact that I hadn't said anything about the 'doctrine of the atonement.' Another said he thought the address lacked Biblical quotations, and so it went on, until to my great surprise Father Nick, who had sat quietly throughout the 'onslaught', interjected and said, "Gentlemen, whatever faults there may have been we have at least heard a sermon this morning…" There was an absolute silence. For my part, I knew an inner thrill; perhaps indeed, I'd actually succeeded. Afterwards, I knew that the decision about Ordination, and meeting Father George's challenge, had been the right one even if the timing was bad – and it certainly was for the 'pull' of the sea was still there and the sense of guilt over the broken contract was not one whit less. However, we'd cope with that when I'd finished at college.

ORDINATION…

With the preaching done it just left the GOE finals themselves to face. These duly came of course, and again I managed to pass – with the exception of Greek! That really was a dead end to me. I was told that the examining board would like me to attempt a re-sit so my Ordination which was due to take place in Gloucester Cathedral in September was put back. I did attempt a re-sit. I still failed! It was all Greek to me! What then took place behind the scenes, among those in authority in the Church, I had no idea of, but the upshot was that I was to be given a 'dispensation' from the subject and that my Ordination would be carried out by the Bishop of Gloucester privately, in his personal Chapel in his Palace House residence. It was to be done on Monday, the first of November 1961 in the presence of my family and a few close friends. I was dreadfully nervous, and very uptight. This seemed to be such an enormous step. The weekend of the end of that October was one of intense political stress on the international scene becoming known popularly then, and since, as 'The Berlin Crisis', and there was even talk of the possibility of war being declared, it was that serious. To my shame I found myself almost hoping that there would be as I felt it would be like a last minute reprieve. It would I thought let me justify going back to sea in order to serve my country, and Ordination could be avoided with some degree of dignity at least. There was no declaration of war of course, and early on that Monday morning I walked into Gloucester to attend to the legal preliminaries before assembling later, in the presence of my family and friends, for the Ordination itself. By lunchtime that day, the deed was done. Now, as the Reverend Keith Corless we enjoyed a family lunch, and then that evening I presented myself at All Saints Church in Cheltenham where I was to serve my Curacy as a Deacon.

PARISH LIFE BEGINS...

The people of All Saints had put on a 'bun-fight' in the parish school and there, guided by Father Wood the parish priest, I was taken round to meet and shake hands with an astonishing variety of people who made up the body of the Church congregation. It was all bewildering but, I was there and I was determined to do my best and make a good 'go' of my new role. The 'pull' of the navy however, was still there too, together with a gnawing sense of guilt about that broken contract! And things got off to a strange start. Father Wood, a quiet and saintly priest who was to prove a masterly tutor for me in a very unflustered way, suggested that I might spend my initial days in the parish just walking out and about to get the hang of the geography and, of course, to get to know some of the people. I was in a sense in 'digs' in my own house at that moment since not being married I had no need of a whole property and the Curate's house had been rented out before I came, to the Barrett family. They offered to give me rooms, and they stayed on as tenants, which was a sensible arrangement for everyone.

On my first morning in the parish then, after breakfast with the Barretts, I set off following Father Wood's advice, to take a walk around to see, and be seen! I set off along All Saints road and as I approached a corner a very imposing lady appeared walking towards me. She was very smartly dressed, topped with a big hat and wielding a fierce looking walking stick which made resounding tapping noises on the footpath. As we neared she stopped and held out her stick across the path. I facetiously expected her to come out with 'Stand and Deliver' but I took it that she simply wanted to chat. However, she got in first before I could even say 'Good Morning' properly. In querulous tones and with a very big plum in her mouth she said, "I imagine you must be the new Curate here?" I agreed but before I could enlarge, she went on in a lofty and superior manner, "I hear you have come from the sea!" She made it sound as if I was something not very nice which had been washed up by the tide! "Good morning," she barked and, tapping her stick even more fiercely she strode off along the road. 'Crumbs,' I thought, that was all a bit rum. Clearly I'd met my first example of one of Cheltenham's famed upper class, retired 'gentlewomen.' However, there were of course many more ordinary people around and I settled happily into the life and routines of the parish. I found Father Wood a great encourager of one of the two main factors which had influenced my thinking about the Church namely, the importance of being out and about among the people. Whatever was happening in the parish the priest, said Father Wood, should show both an interest and a presence however brief. This applied likewise to our local school, and most especially to the hospitals, regular visits to which were always to be regarded as a top priority. In those days clergy had access to hospital admission information and Father Wood said that I had to check for all addresses within the parish and visit those concerned whoever they were and whatever their belief may be. The Church of England priest he said, had a care of *all* the souls within his parish, and this was training I was to put into practice throughout my ministry when it would develop in the years ahead.

NOSTALGIA, AND AN OMEN...

I immersed myself in the life of the parish and, to ease the emotional pain of my nautical nostalgia and guilt, I responded to an advertisement in an edition of the monthly magazine 'Sea Breezes' which revealed one could buy job lots of photographs of ships taken by Skyfotos of Kent (now known as fotoflite). I knew this firm from my own days at sea as they flew out from Lympne Airport in Kent to photograph shipping in the English Channel, and often a representative of the firm would then visit ships to sell the pictures which had been taken. I had an excellent such shot of the first ship I'd been on, the MV British Baron, and the thought of just having a general collection of the firm's work was very appealing. Many of the pictures that came in such 'job lots' were overprinted in the corner with the word 'proof' but it in no way detracted from the pleasure of viewing the ships portrayed. Many on the other hand were free of the word and one of them was a truly magnificent shot of a striking looking tanker named the MV Border Keep. It became one of my favourites and, strangely, it was to prove almost like an omen!

The enjoyment of my growing collection was however a rather conditioned one! The emotional stresses were never far beneath the surface and I would

The MV Border Keep: this photograph came like an omen on the future.

www.fotoflite.com

suffer recurring bouts of colitis in the bowel which proved distressing while they lasted. The loss of blood was itself debilitating, and although I kept going in parish life there were times when I truly did not feel well. On one such occasion I was in a queue of people in the Hewlett Road post office when I heard a chap behind me say, "Good morning, Keith. How are you today?" I turned to see a chap I'd got to know in the parish and I said, "Oh, hello. Well, since you ask, pretty lousy really." "Good Lord," he said, "what's a young man like you saying a thing like that for?" Ah! I thought. If only you knew!

My first year as a deacon passed, and I was then made a priest, the Ordinations that year being carried out in the beautiful Abbey of Tewkesbury. Thereafter, I returned to All Saints, now a fully fledged priest and I pitched into everything as enthusiastically as I could.

A TURNING POINT...

Then came a surprise. I had a call from my old shipping company of BP in London, enquiring if I might be interested in exploring the idea of appointing a chaplain or even chaplains within their, at that time, very extensive fleet of ships. Apparently the idea had been floated by the Reverend Tubby Clayton (of Toc H fame in the years after the First World War) as he was always a champion of the idea of linking the Church more closely with the Services, and also to industry. What his link with BP was I never discovered, but although I did indeed help him with an exploration of the chaplaincy idea, I knew, as did everyone else involved, it was really a non-starter. Besides, it would certainly have been no good for me to try as it would only have put me so close to the engineering which I was missing but without being able to practise it! The idea was dropped but unfortunately it had only served to open my emotional wounds more widely again! I tried to close my mind to them, busying myself in parish life and, as my second year at All Saints passed into the third, I received a call from the Bishop of Gloucester.

"GO BACK TO SEA..."

I went to see him and, as we settled in his study I weighed him up. He was quite new in the diocese at that moment having been appointed after my priesting so we'd never actually met before at all. He was quite business-like but in a friendly way and I felt confident that we would get on. He explained that he'd called me in because a parish was falling vacant in the diocese and as I'd now served my curacy I would be eligible to make a move. The parish in question was Sharpness and, said the bishop, as it was a small but active seaport on the Bristol Channel, and as I'd been to sea before, he thought I might like to consider moving there to be the parish priest. I was flattered. Very often a curate such as I'd been at All Saints would be expected to serve a second curacy in a different and possibly bigger parish before being offered one in his own right. It was a tempting offer indeed! However, the surging emotions of the last few years still being so active I thought the opportunity which our meeting presented, of speaking about them with one in authority like the new bishop, was too good a one to miss. I thanked him for his offer and for the confidence he had expressed in me, but I explained that before I could give him an answer about Sharpness there was something I'd very much like to talk to him about first. As if realising a demanding moment was coming, the bishop sat back to listen. (Afterwards I realised what a debt of thanks I owed him for his patience because, poor man, busy as he must surely have been, he was to give me his absolutely undivided attention).

I poured my story out, telling of the speed with which ideas of ordination had developed, and my shipping company's urging of me to stay to complete my contract, and of the Bishop of Glasgow's persuasion to leave, and of going to college and feeling the burden of guilt and of my abiding unhappiness

Outside Tewkesbury's beautiful Abbey Church, on the occasion of my priesting in 1962. (I am on the left.)

about it all, despite the privileged reality of my now being ordained....

The bishop listened, most attentively I thought and, when I'd finished, he sat back reflectively in his chair, his fingers steepled together and resting on his chin. He thought for what seemed an age and then, to my astonishment, he looked at me and said kindly but firmly, "Keith, go back to sea and sort yourself out!" 'GO BACK TO SEA!' I could have kissed him! Then, business-like again, the bishop said he'd get round my departure, in official circles, by saying he was 'seconding me for special duties,' and when I felt I'd got things sorted out in my mind properly, then to report back to him and we'd go from there. It had been an amazing meeting and no mistake!

THREADS BEGIN TO BE PICKED UP...

I left him with my mind in a whirl, but it was a mix now of relief and, anticipation! I got in touch straight away with my old superintendent, Mr Alcock at BP. He was both very sympathetic and helpful. The company would love to have me back he said, but I might find it difficult should I meet any of my peer group of apprentices as many of them by that time were moving up the seniority ladder of experience. What he could do he said, was to get me a position with a subsidiary company of BP's and that would get me back 'in', in a way which would avoid any possible embarrassment with other ex apprentices. In the meantime Mr Alcock advised, I should arrange for a new Seamen's Identity Card to be issued to me from a Mercantile Marine Office. Happily, Gloucester, with its old dock complex, still had just such an establishment so there was no delay in getting things organised. The card required the provision of a passport type photograph and I dashed into town from All Saints to get one to put with my application. Unthinkingly I went as I was, wearing my white clerical collar. That was to prove something of a mistake!

Shortly afterwards, Mr Alcock was in touch again to say he'd secured a position for me as a Junior Engineer with the Lowland Tanker Company, owned and managed by Common Brothers of Newcastle. They had their own fleet of ships he said, but as a subsidiary of BP they carried that emblem on their funnels as an addition to their own company funnel colours. The ship I was to join he said was then in dry dock at Smith's Docks in North Shields. She was, he said, the MV Border Keep. 'Border Keep!' It was the ship in my Skyfotos collection which had caught my eye most, and I got the picture out to study it with an altogether different spirit of appreciation. I would be going to sea on it soon! Truly, I could scarcely believe it. My poor parents, bemused even more by the topsy-turvy events of their son's life, could do no more than they'd always done, and give me every encouragement, but I did sense that my father was secretly pleased for I knew he'd much regretted my hasty departure from BP leaving things so unfinished. Now it could be put right.

Part Three

THE MV BORDER KEEP, AND OTHER SHIPS

I had said my farewells to the lovely parishioners of All Saints who, bless their hearts, couldn't really grasp their curate's antics but who nevertheless expressed their good wishes to me most warmly in my new venture.

Once back at home in Gloucester, I sorted out my kit, and packed ready to leave for Newcastle on Tyne.

The night before I was to catch the train north was a sleepless one! I thought over all the events of the last five years or so, coming back time and again to the moment when I heard the bishop say 'Go back to sea…'

I was going. This was it at last!

On a chill February day, waving farewell to my family, I left Gloucester to travel to what I was sure would be an even chillier North East to join the tanker MV Border Keep then lying as I'd been told, in one of the dry docks of Smith's Dock, in North Shields. The journey was a long one and I arrived in Newcastle tired and hungry but although the station buffet looked very tempting I really wanted to get the whole journey over by getting out to Shields as soon as I could. I took a taxi and the driver, a cheerful Geordie, realising I was joining a ship enjoyed himself making cracks about me sailing off to sunnier climes while leaving him to endure the winter. Cheerful as I tried to be in response however, such banter was not at that moment readily appreciated. I was tired, and I kept wondering what the ship would be like and who I'd meet – and whether when I got there there'd be anything to have as a meal!

In the event, all went surprisingly well. The taxi was waved through the dock gates as if it contained royalty, driving on down a steep hill lined with the shadowy bulks of workshops, and past heaps of the inevitable dockyard clutter. It pulled up finally near the gangway of what looked to be a fine ship indeed. She was sat solidly yet very gracefully in a dry dock and she looked every bit as good as the Skyfotos picture had suggested. In the dockyard lights her white upper-works and chequer-banded funnel with a BP shield on, looked very impressive. Having paid off the taxi I stood for a while looking at the scene and drinking in the atmosphere. Forgetting my hunger I left my kit by the gangway and strolled to the

Smith's Dock, North Shields. The MV Border Keep was in dry dock (bottom left) and one of the busy shuttle ferries running North and South Shields arriving at the pier.

dock's entrance off the river. The smell of the Tyne tugged at my nostrils. It was a unique blend of muddy water with a dash or two of oil, and I listened, as chivvied by the breeze it lapped at the piles of the jetties and, in the deep shadow of the dock entrance, caused an accumulation of flotsam to bounce gently against the great gates. Out on the river a pageant of lights moving slowly against the amber necklaces of the street lights of South Shields, declared the passage of a ship with its attendant tugs, heading for the sea.

MEETING JON, AND HEARING OF OTHER SHIPMATES...

Coming back to the gangway and my pile of kit, it was time to get aboard. Nobody seemed to be about and I guessed that those who were would be in the accommodation. Humping my gear aboard I carried it around open tank tops and over deck pipes to the midship house. In the starboard alley the sound of a radio suggested life and I knocked on a door with the legend 5th Engineer above it. And there I met Jon Barsdell. He was living aboard although his parental home was not far away in Whitley Bay, and I was very glad he was for he made me very welcome. I liked him immediately. He had an impish grin, and a cheeky sense of humour which I found very cheering. Jon was to be a wonderful friend and I was to find him to be one of the most inventive and creative of people. He'd 'served his time' in the Tyne's famous Swan Hunter's shipyard, and his engineering skills were, in consequence, second to none. He said another junior had joined, a first tripper whose name was Maurice and he was berthed in a cabin on the port side so Jon took me to what would be my cabin as the remaining one for the engineers and I registered the designation over the door of '7th Engineer'. I felt pleased. I was back on a ship and I was starting right at the 'bottom' which I felt was quite appropriate under the circumstances. Leaving me to unpack a bit, Jon went off and found one of the engineers' stewards and to my delight and surprise, 'Lofty,' a tall and cheerful Indian from Goa came and rustled up a meal for me.

Afterwards, I sat with Jon and he told me he'd been with Common Brothers for a while and had already done two trips on the 'Reiver' and a couple on the 'Keep'. All the Border Boats were very similar in design and indeed there was quite an extensive fleet of them all having a 'border' name reflecting the area's proximity to the border with Scotland. Jon reeled off some more of the names and they had a splendid ring to them: Border Lass; Border Minstrel; Border Regiment; Border Laird and many more. I asked him about the crew and he told me about those with whom I'd be shipmates. Mr Mayne, who'd been Chief Engineer on the last trip was still aboard but he would be handing over to bustling Joe Beasley from Newcastle for the next voyage. The Second engineer was a Mr Graham, a portly and somewhat dour Scot from Glasgow but his dourness could be understood when it was realised he'd survived weeks in an open boat after being torpedoed in the war. 'Wally' Laimens was the Third engineer, a round little man from Latvia and I sensed there was a wartime story behind his presence here but I was never to get it. He was off the ship at that moment visiting relatives in distant Cardiff to which place apparently, he'd drive at any opportunity in big hired cars. Ken, a cheerful South Shielder was the Fourth; Maurice I'd heard about, and Ernie Wood was the ship's electrician. Jon said I would be on the Third's watch which traditionally was the '12 to 4.' He himself was with the Second on the '4 to 8,' while Ken would be having Maurice on the '8 to 12.' We chatted on but it was getting late and before I put my head down I felt I had to have a look in the engine room. Wending my way aft I entered the starboard alley and stepped over the high sill into the dimly lit engine room.

Jon had told me that the ship was powered with a Doxford engine, and I was pleased at that for familiar memories, even if now coming back after a span of years, were surely going to be useful. Jon's information was confirmed by the sight of Doxford side rods jutting up like a row of soldiers' pike one on each side of a gaping black hole. The holes proclaimed the fact that the engine's pistons were all ashore being overhauled there. I recalled the troubles we'd known some years before on the British Reliance after her dockyard overhaul at Falmouth and I hoped we could be more confident in the ministrations of the fitters at Smiths. I felt sure that we could be, for I was already aware of there being quite a 'family' feel to being on a ship, built, owned, managed and cared for, in a very comprehensive North Eastern context! I worked my way down to the bottom plates as there was one last thing I wanted to savour before turning in that night, and it was to admire the engine's crankshaft. At floor level, through the open inspection doors, and despite the gloom, there I could see it. The main crank webs had a lovely figure of eight, profiled shape which, together with the smaller side cranks, attendant massive bearings and connecting rods was all very aesthetically pleasing to the eye. There was however, another reason for my wanting to take a look, for the crank is in many senses the heart of the machine. It is through the crank that reciprocating motion is converted to rotary, and it was the sight of my first crank in operation which had sparked what was to be a lifetime love of engineering, and all things mechanical.

It had happened when I was a schoolboy in Bournemouth. My father had been appointed as the Deputy Chief Fire Officer of the town's Fire Brigade, and we lived in a flat at the Central Fire Station. I had developed a great devotion to the Fire Service but, and perhaps oddly, I'd become increasingly besotted with the sea, and ships – provided that is, it had anything to do with sail. I'd read every book in our local library on square-rigged sail, and I revelled in the activities of the few schooners and ketches that worked out of what was then, the very busy seaport of Poole. The fact that at the quays there, Poole hosted quite a summer fleet of paddle steamers that ran regular excursion trips along the coast, was a matter of complete indifference to me. It came as a shock therefore, when my father announced one afternoon that I was to be going on a steamer trip that evening, to Poole via Swanage. Apparently one of Dad's fellow officers, Mr Harry Cutts, had been at sea before joining the Fire Service. He had served as a Radio Officer on a number of ships during the war and immediate post-war years, and hearing about my love of the sea he'd said to my Dad he'd be pleased to take me on an evening steamer trip and he'd be able to point out with the authority of his own experience, some of the important features of ships. I protested. I did not want to go on any smokey steamer. Dad however, told me in no uncertain terms, not to be so churlish. Mr Cutts had made a very kind offer, and I would accept it, graciously.

After our evening meal, I joined Harry and we walked to the pier with, for my part, dragging feet. Once aboard, Harry was soon busy pointing out marine features of interest, not least those to do with his former craft of a serving 'Sparks.' Once the steamer was well under way and romping towards Swanage, having exhausted deck features to study, we went below. At the bottom of a wide companionway, we turned to walk aft and I was suddenly bowled over –almost literally! As I'd turned I was facing a window and a huge shining object was launching itself directly at me, only to disappear, then reappear… I was intrigued. Moving closer, through other windows along the side of this area in the ship, the incredible sight of a great working steam engine was laid out before us, and I found myself enthralled. Here alas, poor Harry was now out of his depth. He'd mumbled something about it all being visible because it was a paddle steamer we were on, and the working axis of the wheel shaft was therefore across the ship and above the water line. I was utterly mesmerised, and watched with absorbed delight the whirling cranks of the engine, realising it was the sight of one of them 'head on' as it were, which had so startled me as we'd turned at the foot of the companionway from the deck. I felt sorry for Harry. I sensed he was dismayed that the gift of his trip, and the enthusiasms he'd wanted to share with me, had turned out rather differently to the vision he'd set out with. The one thing that had brought me most to life, was the thing he knew least about! However, I was truly deeply grateful to him that night for, unwittingly perhaps, he'd opened a whole new and exciting world to me, and furthermore, it was one which was accessible. After all, there were precious few ways of spending a lifetime romancing about 'sail'!

From that moment, I'd added a power dimension to my love of the sea and ships, and every time I saw a crankshaft I thought of Harry and his 'steamer trip'. Looking now at the great shaft in the engine of the Border Keep, Harry seemed very near, and I 'thanked' him mentally for what he'd triggered. Straightening up, I shivered, realising how cold the engine room actually was, and what a depressing mess everything was in with all the clutter of the dockyard workers. However, looking around as I climbed the ladders, a little imagination enabled me to 'see' it as it would one day be again, clean, hot and, above all, alive. And hot was perhaps the word to dwell on for the first crank I'd seen in action knew the sociable warmth of the big steam engine of which it was a part, and Doxford diesels could, as I well knew, build up their own store of heat. Jon had said with a chuckle, that the Keep's engine room was one of the hottest in the Border Boat fleet but I doubted that for all engine rooms are hot, especially those in tankers sailing for the Gulf ports in the summer months.

I left the engine room and went to my cabin to get turned in. I was back aboard ship, and now, I'd work that broken contract out at last!

A REVELATION...

After a few days aboard and steadily getting to know others in the crew, as well as getting the feel of boiler-suit life back, I became lulled into a false sense of security. I had known that at some point details of my ordained state were bound to come out and I had anticipated that to reply to the question 'What was your last ship?' by saying, 'well, actually, it wasn't a ship but a

40 02 27 41. Page 3

BRITISH PERSONAL

All particulars to be in BLOCK CAPITALS

Surname .... CORLESS

Other Names ...... KEITH RONALD

Birth (a) Date ..3-1-37.. (b) Place ..STOCKPORT

Colour of (a) Eyes ...... BLUE

(b) Hair ...... FAIR

Complexion ..FRESH.. Height ...5.. ft. ..10.. ins.

Distinguishing Marks (if any) ......

Discharge Book No. ...... R 62575 4

Nationality ...... BRITISH

Home Address ..HIGHFIELD HOUSE ..EASTERN AVE, GLOUCESTER

Name and Address of Next-of-Kin ..H. C. CORLESS-FATHER.. AS ABOVE. JEAN. HELEN - WIFE

MNOPF No 174718.

Page 4

SEAMAN'S CARD PARTICULARS

Serial No. **110643 A**

National Insurance No. ZS 70 43 91 A

Union or Society No. ......

Photograph of Holder

M.M.O. Embossing Stamp

Signature of Holder
(or, if Holder is unable to sign, his left Thumbprint and the signature of a witness)

Keith R Corless

My newly issued seaman's identity card.

church' was going to be tricky! I'd planned to have a sensible answer ready but somehow one hadn't formed, and I'd found that, initially at least, it hadn't been as necessary as I'd expected. People had indeed asked, and I'd simply said the name of the British Reliance without letting on it had been some five years before! I did let on that I had 'been ashore' for a while but that was simply taken to mean it had been in some engineering context. Time slipped by and I felt I was quite accepted, so I thought I'd cope with revealing and explaining about the Church at some future date. Such a notion was, as I say, a false security.

One morning, an edict came round that any of us who had to have inoculations brought up to date were to report to the Medical Officer at the nearby Marine Office in North Shields. Near the appointed time we assembled to walk up together, and most of us simply put on a reefer jacket over our boiler suits, stuffing our 'papers' handily in our pockets. Once the 'jabs' were done we made our way back to the docks, deciding on the way to give ourselves the treat of enjoying a 'swift half' for medicinal purposes! Thus we went into the unprepossessing but well frequented tavern known to seamen the world over as 'The Jungle Bar'. It was situated right on the quay, adjacent to the dock gates of Smiths on one side, and on the other the terminal of the busy North/South Shields passenger ferries. Once inside, sat at a table with Newcastle Browns to hand, we relaxed. My jacket had fallen open as I sat back and suddenly, one of my shipmates spotted the bright red cover of my newly issued Identity Card. Too late I realised what he was about to do. He leaned across the table and seized the book from my boiler suit breast pocket in order to indulge in that time-honoured amusement of travellers the world over namely, to study the owner's photograph. Putting his glass down and leaning back, he prepared to open it up. My mind had gone an absolute blank and I waited for the discovery of my priestly role like a Stalag escaper having his dodgy documents closely examined by a zealous SS guard. Opening it up my shipmate found the picture immediately, and his eyes grew round with wonder as he found himself gazing at a young man sporting a white clerical dog collar and dressed in a suit of priestly black. He stared, stunned for a moment, and then said, "A bloody vicar!" Others grabbed the book in order to see for themselves, and four pairs of incredulous eyes fixed themselves on me. My stomach had sunk like a crash-dived U boat having had its bottom spanked by a flurry of depth charges. An explanation was clearly demanded but, caught so unprepared one was not forthcoming. I mumbled a confirmation that indeed I was a priest, and I rambled on about being anxious to get back to sea in order to fulfil the unfinished business of a broken contract. Their expressions however made it very plain that they thought it all bafflingly odd, and I wondered how the news would be received amongst the rest of the crew for I knew it would now be round the ship faster than the news of a pay rise or a fire!

A clergyman on a merchant ship is not entirely so remarkable a thing when one thinks of the stalwart work of the chaplains of the Missions to Seamen going about their work of ship visiting, as I could vouch from my own Dublin experience, but the situation on the Keep was quite different. I was not there on behalf of the Mission but simply as an ordinary working member of the crew, of an ordinary working ship. My comrades were finding this very difficult to relate to, and my mind went back to my introduction to life at theological college when I'd met similar incredulity from the more academic students that an artisan type had entered their midst! I could sense some of the questions racing through the minds of my shipmates as they stared again and again at the photograph and then at me. Had they uncovered a sinister 'fifth column' of the Church? Or were they now hob-nobbing with a priest of such notoriety that he'd been, what was it – unfrocked? Or even was it a case that the chap before them was on the run from the law? Silence reigned, while thoughts raced! Then at last someone glanced at his watch and said, "Hey! We'd better get back aboard. They'll be wondering what the hell we're doing."

Finishing our drinks, we left the bar and, rather silently now I thought, walked back through the docks to our ship. I went to my cabin and slumped disconsolately in my newspaper covered chair. I was upset. The manner of the bar room revelation had stirred a hornet's nest of apprehensions in my mind. It was indeed a long time since I'd actually been at sea, and now I knew I was going to be an object of very close scrutiny not only as one who'd been 'out of it' for quite a while but because as a 'vicar' everyone would now be wondering if I was really capable of doing the job at all! Scrutiny on that scale was I knew going to be painfully penetrating. It was not helped when moments later a loud bang at my cabin door proclaimed a visitor and before I could say 'Come in' I was astonished when the captain burst in with battleship indifference to formality. "Is that right you're a vicar?" he demanded. When I confirmed it he glared at me uncomprehendingly for a moment, and then promptly stormed out as fiercely as he'd come, clearly wondering what was happening to his ship. From that moment I found myself being treated with a strange sense of caution and reserve by my shipmates, with thankfully, the exception of Jon who although as bemused as the others never let it come between us. It was to be several weeks before something happened that was to prove the way of my being fully accepted again.

A MISHAP...

I tried to put the bar room revelation aside, together with the air of bemused curiosity that, as I say, now followed me wherever I went or whatever I did, and I simply got on with the job. Dockyard work proceeded steadily and we arrived at the point of filling our two big Scotch boilers and performing the slow process of warming them through in readiness to start raising steam.

The furnaces were to be flashed at intervals, and so our boiler oil fuel pumps were brought into use, running of course using shore steam of erratic pressure supplied from a boiler installation in the dockyard. Warming up, and the running of pumps now demanded the start of some watch-keeping and rotas were worked out to be observed by the three junior engineers. At an early stage in this procedure when I happened to have the watch I went to have a chat with the Donkeyman, and see how he was getting on with his burners. After watching the flickering light from the sight holes of the burners he'd lit I thought I'd better check the oil pumps now wheezing and jerking arthritically below in the engine room. Sliding down the ladders I registered the fact that with some aspects of watch-keeping starting the quicker the shore workers finished their tinkerings in the bilges and got some of our floor plates back in position, the safer we'd all be. Plates were up in the vicinity of the oil pumps, with planks spanning the gaps, and I balanced on them watching the pumps' hesitant and jerky action. They were of the well known Weir design having their strange but amazingly dependable steam shuttle valve feature, but with the erratic pressure of the shore supply they groaned painfully in their strivings and seemed in constant danger of stopping. Indeed, even as I watched, one did, with an alarming air of finality. One could almost hear it say as a rebellious slave might for whom consequences mattered no more, 'enough is enough!' However, the pump had to be kept going for my eye registered the fact that the pressure gauge on the discharge side was wilting like a tulip in a drought and the poor Donkeyman would be fretting about his spluttering burners. Thankfully I remembered the slotted bar spanner, unique to Weir's steam pumps which often saved the day in crises of the sort I faced. I unhooked it and positioned it on the lugs of the valve chest stay and the valve rod itself and gave it a heave. 'Chung – pause – clunk,' went the pump, and order was restored.

It was at about the fourth visit I made to the pumps to ginger them up that mischief befell me. Balancing on the plank over the gap in the floor plates and reaching across to do things to the wretched pump, my foot whose insecure grip was rendered even more so by the film of oil that seemed to be everywhere, promptly slipped. Teetering on the edge it was one of those ghastly moments when one knows something awful is about to happen, that it cannot be stopped and there's actually time in hand to dwell on it! The teetering done and the fall commenced, my flailing arm made contact with the pump's filter assembly and I seized a projection on it with the grip of a Blackpool day tripper on the last deck chair of the day. This saved my head from damage on floor frames and pipe flanges but it gave my shoulder a dreadful wrench. There was no one about and I wasn't sure whether to be glad at the saving of my embarrassment or sorry for the lack of sympathetic help. I struggled out of the hole and stood leaning on a nearby rail alongside the propeller shaft, feeling the pain in my shoulder begin its inevitable throbbing. I wondered if I'd done anything serious and if so, what would happen. With my good arm I managed to bash the pumps into life in a way that I felt sure would frighten them into behaving themselves properly and I went up on deck. I did feel a need to tell someone of my misadventure and I was drawn amidships where I knew there would be a body or two still up.

Slipping my shoes off at the sill I stepped into the starboard alleyway and heard the murmur of voices through Ken's cabin door. A knock produced a cheery hail, "Awa in." A little party was in progress, and cans of ale were in abundance with empties dotted about like yesterday's confetti. "Have a beer?" said a kindly voice, and a can was proffered. I took it, wondering in passing what the effect of ale on shock might be. "How's the kettle doing?" enquired Ken, clearly wondering if my presence was to report on some problem or other down below. I reported that things were going well, but I had a grumble about the oil pumps. We chatted on about the inadequacy of the shore steam supplies and other problems of dockyard life while I searched for an opening to say something about my accident without sounding either foolish on the one hand or that I was making a fuss on the other. It was Ken's wife who realised something was wrong, not down below but with me. She'd put two and two together from my obviously pale face and limply hanging arm. "Are you alright?" she asked, with a concern I could have hugged her for. "Oh fine really," I said with the affected nonchalance deemed for reasons I can never understand, so necessary on such occasions. "I fell through the bloody floor plates by the pumps and I've wrenched my shoulder a bit that's all."

A declaration of war on our little group couldn't have produced a more instantaneous effect! I warmed to the flood of criticisms of the dockers for not roping off their working areas properly and I basked in the expressions of concern everyone kept making. Were it not for the throbbing getting worse I might have felt quite better! As it was I found myself being urged to pop ashore and seek the counsel of the dockyard first-aider who I knew inhabited a grimy hut adorned with an even grimier red cross.

Ken waved me ashore saying they'd keep an eye on 'the kettles' and I went off to knock the first aid man up. The little cloth-capped man inside had I think been having a nap for he seemed a trifle resentful at my disturbing him, and he listened to my tale of woe defensively. I thought that a bit odd because medically-interested lay people, which he must have been numbered amongst to be where he was, usually can scarcely be restrained when there's a chance to show their worth! On the other hand perhaps the more visual delights of hammered thumbs were his forte rather than the obscure complexities of distorted muscles!

"Ah canna do much for ye here, lad," he kept saying as he gingerly prodded the throbbing limb, but my obvious pain won his compassion and soon he was fussing about rigging me up in a sling, and tinkering with his telephone to arrange for me to be seen at the local hospital.

"Ye'll only need a sittin' ambulance," he kept saying and, to my great surprise, shortly afterwards one arrived. It was a sort of utility bus with a foreshortened appearance as if it had recently come off second best in a collision with a wall. A dour driver sat broodingly at the wheel, and as we drove off out of the docks I discovered he had no conversation in him at all. This only added to my depression and as we trundled through the night I had a growing sense of it all being a completely futile exercise. I was right.

At the hospital I found myself ushered to what appeared to be the one remaining seat in a waiting room which, astonishingly, considering it was the middle of the night, was packed with people. Not a soul spoke. Everyone looked either thoroughly dejected or truly miserable, or both. There was an air such as one might have found in a room full of convicts on the eve of their transportation! Eventually I was seen by an exhausted doctor who prodded my shoulder, jerked my arm and wiggled my fingers and then suggested I report back later in the day to have an X-ray. Leaving an equally exhausted nurse to strap my arm, he passed wearily on to his next patient. I eventually stumbled out into the night to find a cab to get back to the ship. I had no intention of returning, and indeed, later that morning having a go at opening cargo tank valves out on the main deck seemed to work a healing magic of its own.

The MV Border Keep, out of dry dock and berthed at the neighbouring wharf for completion of work prior to sailing. Alongside, the MV British Reliance has been moored prior to entering the dry dock. Since my time aboard her the funnel marking pattern has undergone a change.

SAILING DAY DRAWS NEAR...

The day came when the ship was moved out of the dry dock and moored by the adjacent quay for the finishing touches to be done in her overhaul schedule. There were ships everywhere and I was very pleasantly surprised when on turning out one morning I found another tanker had been secured alongside, it being my old ship of my apprenticeship days, the MV British Reliance. It seemed like an omen and I went aboard and roamed her engine room, hearing an inner voice saying as the memories were stirred, 'You're going to finish that contract!' Soon afterwards for us it was time to test the main engines. Extra mooring lines were passed ashore and made fast and with everything running down below the engines were started up with the usual dramatic whooshing of compressed air. It was interesting to see that the crowds of dock workers who were still aboard were not really at home anymore once things were running and everything was warming up. They were to be seen tucking themselves safely away behind the oil storage tanks in the 'tween decks peering out apprehensively at all the action. Clearly they preferred the engine room cold and quiet, while for us it was beginning to feel more and more as a proper engine room should. The trials were duly completed and the entry was made in the log book 'Main engine trials satisfactory.' Sailing day was drawing near!

SAILING DAY...

The tugs nuzzled alongside like well fed piglets with their sow, and so discreet were they in movement, that it was only the fact that they actually were tugs which gave any suggestion at all that for us, something of a mildly dramatic moment had arrived. They looked more as if they'd come for a cuddle than to engage in the sterner work of turning us round and sending us packing off to sea.

On the starboard side, I looked down at the quay, and at the water faintly glinting as it moved sullenly in the dark shadow of the ship still snug against the wall. I rather wanted to catch the moment when that gap would suddenly begin to open – a tangible indication that our voyage had begun.

This business of sailing seemed to be something that just happened, rather than being the fruit of ordered thought. Ordered thought was there of course but in the way it is in the process which sees the transition of a chrysalis into a butterfly; a twitch here, a jerk there and hey presto, one thing suddenly becomes another. So with our ship, the moment of sailing 'emerged' from a cocoon of apparent aimlessness.

Up on the bridge a trilbyed head glanced idly down. It was the pilot. A hand gave a casual signal and away along the quay some wharf men materialised from the grimy anonymity of sheds and cranes to indulge in a moment of exercise. They heaved the great ropes and wires mooring the ship, off the shore bollards, and a rattle of winches and capstans indicated the hauling of them aboard.

Then, joining the rattling chorus of the winches there came from down aft another noise, and a ghastly one at that. It was like an Agatha Christie's victim getting the silk stocking treatment round the throat! I saw that the funnel was wreathed in a fog of swirling steam and the source of the noise of murder most foul was the steam whistle which had been actuated from the bridge. There was clearly a bit of condensate in the way which the steam was busy dissipating in all directions, but this done, the sounds of strangulation gave way to a rich and sonorous blast causing the gulls to leap in alarm off shed roofs, mewing protestations, and dockers here and there to turn a head in our direction.

The blast was answered by a cheerful tooting from the river, and out on the port side I noticed that two of the tugs had moved, and were now out in the stream with propellers churning and wires twanging as they took the strain of the ship.

And then, there it was. The gap between the ship and the quay was suddenly,

Sailing day for the 'Keep'; the tugs are turning her in the river.

perceptibly, beginning to widen! I felt a tiny tremor of excitement. Our voyage had actually begun.

There was another blast on our steam whistle, and as the din subsided I heard a rasping noise on the bridge which was the audible response on the wheelhouse telegraph to an order signalled below to the engine room. On the instant there came too, from the distant engine room the busy whooshing and hissing of air blasting into the main engine. As it died away I could visualise Maurice dashing along the middles' platform shutting the indicator cocks on the cylinders and, while he did this, Ken at the controls would be priming the fuel system to about 5000 lbs on the gauge. Then, more subdued, there came the sound of the air again followed by a deep throated chuffing from the funnel uptakes proclaiming that the engine had started. Under the stern, the turgid water of the Tyne began to swirl in great coffee-coloured eddies as the propeller blades turned over, and the tremor of vibration which spoke so feelingly of the ship coming alive at last was distinctly felt.

We were now well clear of the quay, with our bows swinging out in a steady arc across the river. Soon we would be turned and headed for the sea. I looked back at the quay vaguely expecting to see a small gathering of shore folk moved at least with a silent admiration for this handful of their fellow beings now committed to departure on a year's voyage round the world. There was scarcely a soul to be seen! There was none of the flag waving and streamer

The upper pistons of the Border Keep's Doxford main engine.

hurling of passenger ship departures. There were no tears of despair, or throaty cheers. Not even a cloth cap was raised in a wave. I felt sure Walter Raleigh, or the Merchant Venturers must have had better send offs in their day but then, I had to admit, our voyage was a very pedestrian venture of purely commercial enterprise, and ranked no more highly than any of the host of similar departures of ships from the Tyne, or any other port for that matter.

Before long the turning operation was completed, and the ship with her own main engine working steadily, began to nose slowly toward the sea. Now, out in the stream, well clear of the quays we had a fine panorama of the Smith's Dock complex spread along the waterfront like the equivalent for ships of a tourist's bed and breakfast strip. Behind lay the township of North Shields, carpeting the rising land of the North Bank like a grimy axminster. On the flatter South Bank, spread equally snugly was the carpet of South Shields, no less grimy than the North, and frilled at that point by the great ship yard of John Readhead's. The fussing steam ferry that plied so cheerfully and tirelessly between the two Shields, slowed on one of its traverses of the river, and politely bowed us through. The tugs, their duty of turning us done, had relaxed a little but gambolled vigilantly alongside ready to assist in case something went wrong requiring us to stop our engines, thus putting the ship in hazard in the restricted waters of the river.

It was gone 11:30 am and I was due below at 12 noon. The steward kept worriedly reminding me that the '7 bell' lunch for the 12-4 watch keepers was serving so I made a move for the saloon, taking another quick glance forward over the bows to where the great Tynemouth piers could now be seen looming closer, and proclaiming the presence of the sea beyond.

AT SEA, AT LAST...

Lunch was eaten quickly, and I hurried aft to get below. I felt seriously anxious to get to grips with the job on its real terms for the first time since I'd joined instead of being a ship's engineer in the engine room of a vessel tied securely to the dock wall. As I turned into the after accommodation entrance, I could see that we were well clear of the piers and that the Pilot Boat was heading busily back to her station clearly signifying that we were now on our own – which in turn of course, meant we were therefore actually 'at sea'. I felt the excitement of that magic phrase, and noted too the subtle play of emotions created by the blending of, on the one hand, the sheer romance of the sea, and on the other, that this was no joy ride of adventure but the beginning of what would undoubtedly be, a long, sweaty, hard-working and very demanding exercise. And, as if to give a hint of heat to come the sun suddenly came out, looking rather peaky, with a winter wanness about the gills, but out and shining for all that.

I quickly donned a boiler suit and stepped into the engine room, and what a significant step that seemed, the first of many such steps which would commence a good many watches in the weeks and months lying ahead.

The view was magnificent.

I stood for a moment looking down on the top of the engine experiencing that eye popping, just-look-at-that sensation, great machinery always arouses, in this case by the compelling sight of our engine's six massive transverse beams leaping up and down. Our mighty engine was alive and free at last after her dockyard tinkerings and she looked as if she was enjoying her liberty. It was like watching a horse joyfully flexing its muscles after a stable lay off! It was a stirring sight and one I would never tire of.

Yesterday's sailor must have known the same feeling of excitement when from the deck of his windjammer fresh out of port, he could gaze aloft at towering masts curvaceously clad in straining canvas speaking eloquently of power beautifully harnessed. Doubtless too, such a view would speak volumes about desperate and dangerous hours to be spent aloft on bucking yards in storm and tempest, suffering the miseries of frozen limbs and bloodied hands. But, those who sailed such ships, unashamedly responded to the romance of sail. Likewise too, the romance of a great engine at work cannot be entirely lost even when as one gazes starry-eyed at it, there is leering over ones shoulder, the spectre of the reality of some gruelling toil to come.

I hurried below to see what toils would in fact lay claim to my energies on this, my first watch back at sea. It was a minute to noon. Ken was standing by the control station, beads of perspiration riming his forehead a testimony to the strain of our so recent departure, but the twinkle of humour was in his eyes proclaiming that the burden of responsibility was relaxing a little now that we were safely out of the river. "Where are we?" he hailed., "Well out now," I said waving a hand expressively in a seaward direction, "and the Pilot's away." "Aye" said Ken, "they'll be giving us Full Away then in a tick," and he nodded at the telegraph. As if it had heard him the telegraph suddenly rang out and the pointer swung madly back and forth round the dial, coming to rest again against the sector marked 'Full Ahead'. Maurice, tight-lipped, and looking as harassed as a hostess, the collapse of whose soufflés had coincided with her guest's arrival, leapt to answer it. "Get the revs," shouted Ken. I bent to scan the revolution counter's figures, and then mentally rehearsing them I turned to enter them in the movement book. Thus it was that at noon on the 8th of March 1964, with the engine counter noted at 0059120 we were Full Ahead and on passage and the year's voyage had begun. To be in keeping with any of the romance of our now being 'at sea' we should of course have been heading out for the fabled Orient or, at the very least, the New World, and the fact that we were only scheduled to saunter down to the Isle of Grain in Kent appeared to be a bit out of character with the moment. It seemed as silly as if Columbus setting off from Palos bound for the Indies and discovery had stopped off at Cadiz just down the coast and put his feet up for a couple of days!

However there was an evident wisdom in breaking into the trip by degrees. A bit of coasting allowed the engines to run in after the surgical disturbances of the dockyard overhaul, and if anything was found to be unsatisfactory, repairs could be carried out on home ground, with the ship even brought back to Smith's Dock on the Tyne if really necessary without too much trouble.

So, to Kent we were bound; an easy first leg run down the North Sea.

Ken and Maurice were now free to go off watch and the prospect brought a cheeriness to their countenances so that even Maurice relaxed his now familiar cragginess and made some jest about a 'life on the ocean wave'. The 'Full Away' ringing of the telegraph had brought Wally round from his generators and he appeared at the fore end of the engine wiping his hands on some rags and peering inquisitively at the engine's cooling returns as he passed. Ken was saying words about shutting the compressors down and watching the engine temperatures, and he had a word with Wally about the setting of the engine controls; evidently we weren't going to be opening her up wide for a bit. This done, he and Maurice departed and wended their way up the ladders to the deck and the fresh air.

"Get the air shut down," instructed Wally, and I went forward, glancing at the circulating returns in passing – how instinctive a thing this was to become. I don't think I ever saw an engineer pass these sight glasses and their thermometers without looking at them. I swung the main air valve to the engine shut, and then with rag and wheel spanner in hand, I advanced, a trifle cautiously, on the compressors vibrating as arrogantly as a couple of blustering thugs full of huff and puff. I'm bound to say I found these machines of Weir's construction rather intimidating with their top heavy appearance, and all of a dither with their steam powered exertions to pack air away in the big reservoirs in the 'tween decks above. Squeezing between them and feeling the heat of their vibrating bodies, I reached for the underslung steam valves and eased them shut, watching the machines lose their posturing life and come to rest. With the steam exhaust valves shut and likewise the air delivery and cooling water valves, and all the drains open I nipped up to the 'tween decks and shut the air bottles down.

SOME 'TEETHING' TROUBLES...

The next job was to get the main engine temperatures sorted out and I got back below to see what the thermometers revealed. The cooling water being circulated through the pistons and around the cylinder jackets, in separate pipe systems, was passing through the tube banks of big vertical coolers. There, sea water being circulated round the tubes, extracted some of the heat imparted by our now hard working Doxford. By adjusting the sea water inlet valves to regulate the quantity of water passing through, the temperature of the engine water could be controlled and Wally squeaked into my ear as I went past "ve keep ze jackets at 150 and ze pistons about 160". "OK" I shouted and went to have a go.

Skill at this adjustment business was soon acquired but initially it was predictable that the mercury in the thermometers would appear to do something of a jig as a result of the sea valves on the coolers getting too generous a degree of attention. The balance between the flow and temperature was so fine that only a nudge of the big sea valve wheels was often all that was needed to effect an adjustment of the engine readings.

The same principle of cooling was applied in the other primary engine circuit namely that of the lubricating oil. The oil which was being pumped by the combined efforts of an electric powered screw pump and its bed fellow a steam driven bucket pump, picked up a lot of heat en route through the tortuous passages of the engine bearings, and a sea water cooler enabled this to be controlled.

Busy then about settling our engine down to steady running, with even pressures and temperatures prevailing, and at the same time keeping an eye on the boilers and everything else now going in earnest, Wally and I found ourselves fully occupied.

The first bang therefore, came as something of an intrusive shock. I was somewhere up near the boiler room and Wally was round on the port side at the back of the engine, but by the third bang we were both at the control station, our eyes raking over the gauge board instruments.

"Relief valve – fuel valve stuck" bawled Wally as he pulled the control lever back and wound off the fuel pumps, "Ring to Stop". As I swung the telegraph handle round and brought it to rest at 'Stop', Wally had the controls at zero and the engine was running down. The banging ceased. Glancing up through the gratings I noticed engineers sliding down the ladders to see what all the excitement was about – the banging had clearly been heard amidships. The bridge responded to our signal on the telegraph, their pointer swinging round to come to rest with ours on 'Stop' and I visualised John the Second Mate, and the Seacunnies (Indian seamen serving as Quartermasters – the ship's helmsmen) breaking out the two black painted baskets kept on the monkey island over the wheelhouse, to haul them up one above the other as an indication to other shipping that we were broken down. "Log the time and shut the coolers down" said Wally. I logged 1242 hours and dashed forward to shut down those things I had just so painstakingly adjusted. When I got back I found Wally up with the Chief on the middles' platform prodding at the innards of a fuel valve with a forked lever, a device designed to straddle the spindle and by levering against the cam arm push the spindle and thus the needle of the valve tight against it's seating. This was a move necessitated by the fact that occasionally they would seize in the open position thus allowing fuel to pass to the cylinder unchecked.

"OK, now" said Wally importantly, brandishing his lever. I must confess I felt his confidence to be over optimistic. Sticking fuel valves as I recalled, seemed on the whole to keep sticking, and the only answer was to change for a spare, enabling the offending one to be dismembered at leisure and encouraged by a bit of lapping to be more co-operative. However, Wally's optimism carried the moment and I was dispatched to open up the air to the engine. We rang 'Full Ahead' on the telegraph, and it was a moment or two before it was answered from the bridge, due no doubt, I thought, to our call catching John still up on the monkey island messing about with the signal balls, then at 12:54, with a happy whoosh of air we started up again.

Under way once more we got things settled down, but we went about our duties now on the tip toes of expectancy, ears waiting to wince at more bangs. However none came and the tranquillity of ordered noise re-established itself. At 3 o'clock the Tailwallah (an Indian engine room rating) materialised like an Indian Jeeves with afternoon tea, and this touch of domesticity further endorsed our sense of well being. In this world of steel and heat, oil and noise, 'afternoon tea' had an incongruous ring about it, yet on the other hand it certainly humanised the place, rendering down the mechanical sterility with a touch of homeliness. Thus, mug in hand, I leaned comfortably on the control desk watching with a sense of satisfaction the working of our great engine and visualising the great crankshaft and rods whirling and swinging behind the crankcase doors. I had a feeling my first sea watch was drawing to a successful close and I had a word with Wally about making up the log book. "Go round" he said into my ear "viz a piece of paper and make a note of all ze readings. I'll fill up some of these from down below".

MORE 'TEETHING' TROUBLES!...

Obediently I set off up the ladders to get the exhaust temperatures from the middles' platform and check the condenser, boiler room and 'fridge room' readings. Humming a merry air, I'd nearly reached the middles when the bangs we'd forgotten we'd been waiting for, suddenly burst forth again. They really were ear-splitting, but quickly died away as Wally, all arms, operating the telegraph and controls simultaneously, brought her to a stop. It was 15:30 hours and after shutting the coolers down I joined the gathering on the middles' platform under the exhaust trunking (for it was a back fuel valve which was giving us trouble) where the Chief was deciding what to do.

"Whip the bugger off" said Joe, and set to with a will himself, and in no time at all we'd got the offending fuel valve off. Other engineers who had come down were waved cheerily away as we had the job well in hand, and the sweat glistened on our brows as we worked. It was warm under the great

134

exhaust trunking and I thought of doing this sort of job in the heat we would be experiencing in the not too distant future. That we'd work a bit slower would be sure! The Chief pitched in like a beaver but with a joke or two as well and in only a little under twenty minutes we had a replacement one on and we were starting up again.

We were still settling her down at four o'clock when the Second and Jon came below to take the watch, and I was spared the chore of filling in the log book, being advised to simply enter the legend 'pressures and temperatures normal'. However, the Second had several jobs in mind to be done, and told me to bear a hand with Jon for a bit before I knocked off. Thus it was that I was neatly to hand in the 'tween decks, messing about with some of our spare gear, when the deafening symphony of banging relief valves struck up again. This time we were stopped for an hour, and besides some fuel valves being changed, the relief valve which had lifted most was also changed as it was thought it's mighty spring might be a little tired after such unaccustomed activity, rendering it more apt to allow the valve to operate at cylinder pressures below those of real danger.

By half past five we were under way again, and I was thankful to get changed for dinner which I found myself anticipating with all the relish only honest toil can create. The meal was good, and the saloon atmosphere not a bit impaired by jests from the mates about the engines 'falling to bits' or needing 'new elastic', or that they could do with 'winding up a bit more'. But it was clear afterwards as I leaned on the rail, that they did have genuine misgivings about the ability of the machinery to keep us moving as the absence of any sight of lights on the land suggested they'd put us on a course well out to sea – a prudent move of course, for it would indeed be embarrassing to endure a breakdown of such duration as would see us drifting in-gloriously onto the rocky fastness of the East Coast! A ship's progress fresh out of dockyard hands was always viewed a little indulgently of course, and some stops to sort out teething troubles were expected. This was as well because we were obliged to stop again just after seven o'clock for another hour, and, now in darkness, the ship lay rolling slowly on the cold North Sea swells with the two red lights which had replaced the daytime black signal balls, swinging in long arcs against the sky. However, soon after eight bells at eight o'clock, when Ken had Maurice officially took the watch, the engines were started up again, and at last the new trip tantrums seemed to be sorted out, because by the time I got below at midnight the engine was running like a ballerina with her teeth well into 'Swan Lake'.

Appreciation of our engine's new found zeal was, at that witching hour of midnight, rather slow in coming forward. I found the business of stirring the grey cells be-numbed by the sleep of the just, at the moment they were being really successful in getting the most out of unconsciousness, really a bit of an ordeal. It would clearly take some getting used to but, on this occasion the stirring process was aided by the novelty of it being my first night watch back at sea, and indeed, it passed surprisingly quickly. Wally and I found plenty to do in the engine room, and it didn't seem long before we took a break for a heartening pot of tea brought to us by our watch Tailwallah and a munch at some of the lucky dip surprises in the supper box furnished by the stewards for the benefit of those on watch during the night hours.

At 3am, the tannoy burped a signal and the Second Mate's voice issued forth to tell us that our ETA (expected time of arrival) at Grain, provided, he commented a trifle darkly, the engines held together, would be about 0700 hours. Wally scribbled it on the board for the benefit of the next watch.

This provision of ETA's by the mates for the engineers was a perfectly standard drill of course, but something in the manner of its coming from John, suggested he was a deck officer with a slight difference in this respect. Communications from the bridge were accepted as being pretty sparse, and on the whole confined to bare essentials, but occasionally one met a mate who seemed to appreciate the plight of the men below who, while being so intimately concerned with the progression of the ship, were exceedingly cut off from the knowledge of how the progression was actually getting along. This was especially so when something of interest was at hand; then it was like being on a scenic excursion tour in a bus with no windows, and a word from a communicative chap on the bridge was really appreciated. Something about John's manner on the tannoy as he gave us the ETA, suggested he was just such a chap.

AT THE ISLE OF GRAIN...

We ignored his jibing witticism about the engine, and indeed she held together splendidly throughout our watch, and the next, so that when I was dragged forth from sleep again, at eight am, it was to find that we had arrived at the Isle of Grain, and were peacefully at anchor some way off the oil refinery berths. Looking at the view, I remembered the occasion some years before when I'd arrived at this same spot on the British Reliance, and we'd fretted as to whether we'd make it home for Christmas. Many of us had and I thought that had been a voyage with a real fairy tale ending! Now before me again were the towers and tanks of the refinery under the grey sky of late winter's day; a view to be savoured now in the grey atmosphere of a voyage's start, not the technicolour excitement of its ending!

The morning passed idly and the greyness eventually gave place to a little wan sunlight which glassed the grey brown waters of the estuary with a sheen of silver. Shortly after lunch, some tugs moved towards us with all the eagerness of swans spotting a likely picnic benefactor. They ranged alongside but, once secured, they promptly seemed to go to sleep! Wally and I got the engines ready for moving, and at three fifteen we got under way for the oil berths securing up after nearly two hours manoeuvring. Clearly they didn't rush things at Grain – unless it was Christmas.

The Second decreed that we juniors would maintain sea watches while the seniors would go on day work and at first I thought of staying aboard ship to get some rest before my watch at midnight. During dinner however I changed my mind, the exercise of a walk, even if only through the refinery would do no harm. and I could get back for a bit of shut-eye at least. Thus it was that after dinner I set off and trudged the monotony of the refinery circuit road, past the dark shapes of tankers lying at the piers of the other berths. Eventually, far out it seemed from the refinery itself I bought myself a drink in a comfortable little pub whose cheerfully lit windows beckoned the wanderer in from the dark. It was clearly a place used by seamen, being the nearest to the refinery and in consequence it had gathered a few trappings of nautical décor on the walls, a photograph (framed in black like an obituary one!) of some tanker or other, and a shipping company badge or two. But it crossed my mind as I sipped my beer that it was a place to call in at when out for a walk, not one to walk to just for a drink – such was the isolation of the place. It was another instance of the remoteness of the seamen's life, especially tankermen, who really were cut off from the little things that make up what is thought of as the normality of life for shore-dwellers.

With the vague thought in mind that I'd better get back to the ship if I was to get any rest before midnight, I finished my beer and sallied forth into the night and eventually back into the eeriness of the refinery complex. Refineries are curious places in that although it is human beings that bring the oil they need, those same people seem as insignificant in the process as the work of hop-pickers might do at a beer festival! The public at large only have an interest in the end product! I walked past seemingly miles of great silver pipes some of which cracked and pinged disconcertingly in the darkness, and I looked with awe at the towering shapes of the towers, bedecked with dozens of starry lights so that from a distance the whole place had an air of fairy land unreality about it. One would scarcely have raised an eyebrow if one had bumped into a little green man with pointed ears and a pair of stalk-mounted eyes. But there were no such diversions, just the sense of the great emptiness of the whole area under the black vault of the heavens and it was good, when the ship was finally reached, to savour the cosiness of one's cabin. It was just gone ten and there was time for a wink or two of sleep.

COMING TO TERMS WITH DISTURBED SLEEP!...

However, when I felt myself being dragooned into wakefulness just before midnight it was a miserable experience. When you are awake you can cheerfully talk about having a 'short nap' to 'keep you going' but then you invariably neglect to take into account the fact that by definition a 'short nap' is one which is going to be terminated early and the termination process is bound to be painful!

Once up, I went dozily aft down the flying bridge chewing a cud of mixed vows. I would not indulge in short 'kips' any more; I would not go ashore when I was due on watch soon after, and I would simply stay on my feet preferring the general ache of tiredness to the battering required to get the body into action again after but a short taste of sweet oblivion. What I had yet to realise in this whole matter of broken sleep, whether it was for the general watch routines, or going ashore, was that the body can be trained to do almost anything. In the course of the voyage to come I would learn to do with a lot less sleep than I was normally accustomed to ashore – and getting it in very small consignments of only a few hours at a time, at that!

The bright lights of the engine room, the noise and heat, and a note on the desk with a list of jobs to be done, all conspired to help me achieve a proper sense of wakefulness. The Tailwallah's appearance with a pot of tea capped the waking process nicely and, with the tissues restored I reflected on the list of jobs. There was a steam pipe for one of the auxiliaries in need of re-jointing. Several valve glands were listed as needing checking with a view to re-packing or adjustment, and some spare gear was in need of more permanent stowage space. The pipe flange was clearly the most important job, and with some planks to perch on atop the general service pump's steam chest and wedged conveniently among other pipes, I set to with spanners, a hammer, chisels and ropes to get the pipe section out. Considering the feats of contortion such jobs usually were, this one was not too bad, and with the flanges cleaned up, new joints cut and pasted liberally with a savoury mix of black oil and graphite, re-assembly followed speedily. As I worked, I noted a trickle of sweat running down my back, and I knew this sort of job in a few weeks time, would be a really hot experience; but then what wouldn't be, I thought, looking round the packed confines of the engine room!

We were at Grain for three days loading a two-part cargo of fuel oil for delivery to Jarrow and Sunderland respectively. Most of us had been ashore during our stay, going more on principle than for the pleasure of it. We were all mindful of the fact that in some of the long hauls we'd soon be doing we would have none of the relief of a run on dry land. It was a sort of enjoy-it-while-you've-got-it principle. For my part, mindful of the first night ashore, I confined my excursions to the early evening, and going only as far as the refinery works' canteen. There, besides the refreshments available, a shop facility existed where odds and ends useful to chaps like us whose domesticity was of a mobile character could be purchased. As a facility it was greatly valued.

When our loading was complete, the pre-sailing routine of 'testing the gear' was undertaken. Jon and I leaned on the rail of the accommodation, looking over the main deck, and listening to the blasting of the whistle and the distant clamour of the telegraph proclaiming that the testing was in full swing. It also included of course, the steering gear, and an engineer was required to have opened the steam to the hydraulic pump's engine and, if it had been shut down for any length of time, to have drained its crankcase sump of condensate. Sometimes this was so much that a man would get the distinct feeling he'd tapped an artesian well instead of an oil sump! Once the steam engine was running sweetly the bridge would then operate the steering telemotor in the wheelhouse, and the engineer in the steering gear flat would watch the action of the big rams as they moved the massive rudder stock hard over from one side to the other.

CARGO TANK HEATING, AND AN ILL-TEMPERED RETURNS' TANK...

Evidently Ken and Maurice found all to be satisfactory, and the main engines were then made ready for sea. Thus when Wally and I went below at noon Ken was able to shout cheerfully above the noise of the running pumps, "She's all yours!" He and Maurice disappeared up the ladders to their off watch liberty and Wally and I took stock. All was indeed ready for sailing but there was still one other job to be done in respect to the cargo now aboard. We'd all noticed how cold the weather had become during our stay at Grain, and it had been decided that the cargo tank heating coils had to be opened up before we actually left. These coils, fed by steam, would help to keep the viscosity of the cargo such as would enable us to then pump it out at our ports of call. It would be something of an embarrassment to arrive at a discharge port and have the recipients ashore look expectantly for their oil like waifs with dinner pails ready, only to be unable to fulfil their desires due to the oil being so thickened by the cold it would not go through the pumps! To avoid such red-faced moments heating coils are designed to solve the problem. They used a lot of steam of course, and in order to produce it larger burners had to be used in the boiler furnaces. Wally sent me off to tell the Donkeyman, and I watched, as having changed the tips, he fired up, and the firelight beaming from the sight holes, danced a flashing tattoo on his swarthy face. Steam was thus well maintained for its delivery to the deck range, but there was its return to consider as well. Because of possible contamination through any defects in the pipes in the cargo tanks, the return was led to a special 'returns tank' separate from the condenser to allow its condition to be monitored visually. Such monitoring was made easily possible by the fact that the steam tended to condense itself in the immense length of the pipe circuits, returning as exceedingly hot water. This decanted into the returns tank and heavy glass portholes enabled a watch to be kept for any oil coming back with it. The unit was situated in the port 'tween deck, near the condenser and just for'ard of the boiler room, and what a beastly and ill-tempered thing it was. It clearly nursed a grudge at having missed a vocation as one of Merlin's spell pots, and even as I moved towards it on what would become one of many such checking visits, it hissed venomously. There it sat, high on stout steel stools, brooding malevolently through the wide, yellow coloured eyes of its sight ports, waiting to catch unsuspecting passers by when it would invariable then have a fit of indigestion and burp scalding water over them! We learnt to scurry past this monster when it was in use, with a protectively hunched shoulder! I now approached it with caution, noted the fact that the water, bubbling well already, was not showing any signs of oil-well aspirations, and I left it to its own surly devices for a bit. There was the task of working the ship out now to be done, and 'Stand By' had been rung down.

COASTING EXPERINCES – AND AN EVENT TO MY ADVANTAGE...

Some three hours later, when the Pilot had been dropped, and we were 'Full Away' bound for exotic Jarrow, I came up on deck to find us well out in the cold, grey anonymity of the North Sea with the Thames estuary falling astern. After Jarrow and Sunderland, we might well be coming back to Grain of course, as part of our initial coastal port-hopping prior to going deep sea, and I entertained the hope we might be sent to some of the continental ports for a change. And indeed, that proved to be the case.

We found ourselves visiting an interesting assortment of continental ports such as Malmo, Wilhelmshaven and Antwerp – interesting in name even we didn't physically see much of many of them, time always being so short. It was in the course of such calls that a situation arose which was to help me greatly. I wanted to be accepted simply as one of the engineers on the ship, without having the curiosity factor of being a 'Vicar' as well, always hanging over me. The solving of a problem with one of the cargo pumps was to provide the very means for this to happen. Our frequent port arrivals and consequent cargo discharge requirements put a lot of strain on the big steam pumps and, with one in particular, we experienced a real problem. A hefty rod which straddled the steam end of one of the pumps, and which was rotated back and forth by links from the piston rod in order to open and close the slide valves, sheared in two. A spare rod was available and this was brought into use, but later, when the ship was in Antwerp discharging a cargo of fuel oil, the new rod sheared like the first. Not having another spare, and with the time factor, not to mention the likely cost to the company in mind, the idea of having one made ashore was abandoned in favour of making one ourselves. While some of us would be doing that, others could get to work to open the valve chest in order to check the accuracy of the 'D' valve settings. The first shear had been put down to metal fatigue, but two aroused suspicions that a more fundamental problem existed, most probably with the actual setting of the valves.

The Second had a meeting to plan it all. As he outlined the situation he looked across at me and asked if I was alright using the lathe. As I was to be on at midnight I was to start the work and Jon, when he came on at six, could hopefully finish it off. 'Crumbs,' I thought. 'I haven't touched a lathe for over five years!' but this was not a moment for indecision. I affirmed to the Second that I'd be fine, but I could sense the 'wondering' in the minds of the others. The 'Vicar' was about to be tested! In the event, all went well and, when Jon appeared at six he was able to take over as planned so that, by breakfast we had a new shaft made. The valve settings had by then been checked and indeed a fault in their setting had been identified and corrected. Thus with the newly made shaft installed, and the pump able to run again, it was all counted as a pretty successful job. And I detected a new attitude to me!

It was all to do, I knew, with the problem of stereotype images. Most lay people have little idea of what clergy are like, or do, but curiously they often have very set images in their minds, images which usually lean to the view that the dog-collar wearer is rather unworldly, or a do-gooder or even a 'bible-basher.' That clergy are rarely like that, and most have their feet firmly on the ground of the 'real' world, sometimes therefore has to be proved. This can be achieved through demonstrating a secular work skill as I'd just done, or through a hobby or sport interest, and sometimes simply through the ability to laugh and joke. This was to be proved by a young lady I would meet in the future when I was by then back in parish life as a full-time priest. She had been with her fiancé to plan their wedding, and she said as they were leaving my Rectory, 'You're not like a proper vicar!' 'Good heavens,' I said. 'Why ever not?' 'Because you laugh!' she said. Poor girl! I wondered whatever ghastly stereotype image of the priest she'd been harbouring, probably for years, but at least I'd managed to break it down for her. Apparently that was just what I'd achieved on the ship! At last, I was no longer a curiosity piece!

A CHANGE OF ORDERS...

Our coastal voyaging had brought us to Grangemouth with a cargo of clean oil from the Isle of Grain. Once it was discharged we were due to go back to Grain again. A sailing time was posted. We were to leave at three pm on an afternoon tide, and I went below at twelve with orders to make everything ready for sea. As I went aft down the flying bridge, savouring the afternoon sunshine, I looked out over the rolling countryside of Fife, responding well to the call of spring, and I thought we shouldn't be seeing many more views like it in the UK as the coasting honeymoon must surely be coming to its end. However, it wasn't over yet for indeed we were then only faced with a nice little 'jog' down the North Sea back to Kent. And perhaps, after that, another continental port.

I got changed, slid down the ladders to the top platform and walked aft to the boiler room. The Donkeyman stood beaming in the doorway. "OK, Donkeyman?" I asked. "Ok, Sahib," came his answer in its usual expressive manner – a beaming smile, a shake of the head and an energetic semaphoring of the arms. I found this response quite fascinating. Our Indian donkeymen were always burning to please and always anxious to assure you that all was well and that they were in complete control – provided, that is, that you were around as well! "Yes," said the smile, all is well. "No," said the shake of the head, it isn't. "See for yourself," said the arms! All in all, they covered themselves rather well I thought.

I did see for myself, and all was indeed well. Water levels and steam pressure registered as they should, so I went on down below to busy myself getting the 'job' ready for sea. After a while, Wally came down and bustled about as well, and by half past two we were ready. I leaned on the desk, wiping my hands and, through the gratings above I spotted Jon coming down for his stand by watch. Above the din of the machinery he gave us the news that the tugs were alongside and shortly after the telegraph rang out with its querulous tones announcing 'Stand By'. Air was put on the main engine, and Jon went up to the middles to deal with the indicator cocks. Wally twiddled with the fuel pump control wheel and I stood by the telegraph, with the movement book ready on the desk, at the same time keeping an eye on the steam lubricating oil pump jerking arthritically up and down by its side.

Thus we stood, expectantly waiting for the first order to come ringing down. We stood, and stood. Experience told us that the time from 'Stand By' to the first order was always a variable factor, but generally the bridge managed to get things moving in about ten minutes. Ten minutes became fifteen. "They've dropped the bloody gangway in the drink," I said. "And the mate too perhaps," responded Wally. The waiting was beginning to get on our nerves. Wally fidgeted about, periodically wiping the sweat out of his little eyes as he stared up at the gauge board. "Blooty mates," he said. "Vat ze 'ell are they playing at?"

Up on the middles Jon had visibly wilted and was now draped over the rail like an old bath towel as he stared down at us. The instant alertness of 'stand by' had been dissipated by such immobility as we were experiencing, like morning mist by the sun. We stared at the clock whose hands crept round with an infuriating indifference. We stared back at the telegraph; would it ring, or would it not? Through the multitude of sounds I could hear the compressors throbbing away, and pumps whining tremulously, all doing their best to buoy up what was fast becoming a state of stupefied anti-climax.

Wally stumped backwards and forwards, muttering imprecations about the mates. "Tese blooty mates," he said, again and again. "No blooty good!"

Actually of course, whatever it was that was happening on deck was probably nothing at all to do with the mates; they were merely a convenient peg on which to hang our expressions of frustration caused by our ignorance of developments. This sort of frustration through ignorance of events was often a real problem for ships' engineers, but anyone can suffer it of course. A parent can suffer agonies not knowing what an absent child is doing, or a noise in the dark announcing unseen activity can be frightening. Even if the world were to blow apart at the seams to see it doing so would not be so bad as being in a position of knowing it was happening but not knowing how it was getting along in the process! Thus for us in the engine room, alone with our frustrations, we stood and speculated wildly as to whether the ship had sunk where she lay, received a visitation of the plague or whether a coach load of dancing girls had appeared on the quay causing a mass desertion of all hands!

The time had come for action.

"I'll ring the bridge," I said. Taking the phone in one hand I leaned on the call button with a stabbing finger of the other. Eventually, a surprised voice issued from the tannoy. "Er... bridge here." "What the hell's going on?" I bellowed. "We're standing around like dreams down here!" "Oh...Oh dear!" announced the voice. "Er.. we're not going. Didn't we tell you?" " No you damn well didn't," I said, slamming the phone down.

The telegraph suddenly came to life, its strident clanging making us all jump like startled grouse. 'Finished With Engines' it now proclaimed. So there it was, now at last, we knew something definite!

Wally, scowling with disgust, hurled a fist full of rag on the plates, and we set about shutting the 'job' down. Thereafter, we hastened on deck, agog to find out the cause of this strange turn of events.

Gradually, we pieced the story together. Sailing drill had apparently been proceeding in the normal fashion, and the ship had been singled up to her last two wires. The tugs had taken station at bow and stern, ready to swing the ship in the basin and, just as the order to 'Let go' was about to be called, all had been dramatically changed by the precipitous arrival of the ship's Agent. Seemingly he'd dashed madly to the docks with a change of orders for us, and leaping from his car, his papers fluttering in his hand, he'd arrested our departure. Then, when he'd scrambled aboard, he'd announced that we were no longer to sail for Grain in Kent but that we were to be going deep sea at last. We were, he instructed, to stay alongside until the next tide and, in the meantime and with all haste, take on maximum quantities of fuel, water and extra stores. When we then would leave we would be bound, he said, for the Persian Gulf!

This news was not well received. A static of tension now crackled through the accommodation, and with a wailing and gnashing of teeth the wives who'd been coasting with us had to hastily pack their gear. There was much coming and going to the quayside telephone as train times were sorted out and taxis ordered to get people into Edinburgh. Hoses were coupled up and, as fuel and water gurgled into their various tanks, beverages of a variety of sorts gurgled down the throats of those who sought something of an anaesthetic to ease the pain of our departure. Dinner that evening was eaten in a rather restrained atmosphere. There was no quibbling with the orders of course. We'd all expected them sooner or later, and we were aboard for the very purpose of fulfilling them, but even so, there's something about them when they come that causes the mildest of flutters in the digestive system! There were only spasmodic attempts at any conversation.

"Well, we'll soon be on 'East of Suez bonus,'" said one voice in an attempt at some cheerfulness. "Aye – but we'll make it to the Gulf just as it warms up nicely!" said another, gloomily. It was one of the engineers who'd said it, and he was clearly thinking of the Gulf's summer temperatures and their effect on the sweaty sauna, which by then our engine room would have become!

But in truth, we were too full of our own private thoughts to chatter lightly, and the meal was eaten absent-mindedly as each person's thoughts flitted from scenes of cosy domesticity in the homes we were leaving to ones we could expect to see in the year ahead as we would stomp round the faraway oceans of the world.

Down aft, on the other hand, in the crew's mess rooms, a different atmosphere prevailed! There, the news of the orders was received with glee because, for the Indians of our crew, it meant they were about to be heading in a homeward direction. Once the ship was east of Suez it would only be a matter of time, and a few ports of call, before a stop would be arranged at Bombay to change the crew. They at least, were well pleased, and wide smiles blossomed like exhibition roses in high summer. This matter of changing crews was a well established one with a number of shipping companies, not least Common Brothers. The policy of using home-grown officer talent from, essentially, the UK, and using Indian ratings for general duties in order to keep wage costs down, was a well established one, and many of them became in effect regular company men. The stewards seemed to come mainly from Goa, while deck and engine room staff were drawn from the many, mainly coastal villages, around Bombay. The policy of the company to work their ships on a year long trip basis enabled the officers to be changed at the annual dry-docking at home, while the ratings, who by then had been aboard for some six months, were changed over, some six months later. Thus at Grangemouth that day, our Indians were very happy; they were 'homeward bound.'

To avoid the gloom and despondency amidships, I retired to my cabin to read a book, deciding as well that an early nap would probably be a good thing as clearly the night was to be a busy one. And as if in sympathy with our mood, the weather changed, going gloomy, and flexing its muscles for a blow. Thus by the time I was turned out, towards midnight, a cold wind and driving rain were chasing madly up the Firth of Forth from the North Sea. I hastened aft down the bleak flying bridge to seek the warmer sanctuary of the engine room. Our now imminent night-departure with the gloom of our leaving home accentuated by the night itself, contrasted badly with the atmosphere of the afternoon's departure with its simple trip-around-the-bay-back-in-time-for-tea air of the run to the Isle of Grain. Our work was now beginning in earnest!

A PROPELLER INCIDENT...

I had to get things ready for sea, and even the machinery itself seemed to have an added air of urgency now the voyage was really beginning. Wally hastened down, a bit unsteadily I thought, and he went to stare abstractedly at his generators, returning eventually to the control station where he stared fixedly at the gauge board. There was no messing about this time. 'Stand By' rang out imperiously, and was soon followed by the first order, 'Dead Slow Astern'. Wally came to life thrusting the air lever over, while Jon did his bit with the indicator cocks. The engine stirred, and kept turning on air until Wally realised how prodigal he was being with it! He started her up properly, and we were off. Not however, very successfully! After a few movements, just

The Second Mate, in charge of the after deck mooring party.

as we were getting our teeth into the departure routine, there was a most tremendous, and alarming thump! The ship rocked sluggishly, and grabbing the movement book I entered the legend 'Bump' and logged with it the precise time. Clearly we'd hit something, and we were instantly alert for something of a flap. Had we sunk a tug, or, worse, taken a lock gate out!? For a moment we had an alarming vision of the waters of the dock pouring into the Forth and our ship stuck with her bow poking forlornly out of the entrance! However, neither the telegraph nor the tannoy gave an indication of anything untoward. We relaxed, and from the nature and duration of the continuing movements we guessed at our progress through the locks and out, into the Forth. There, the tugs having done their duty, would leave us, and we were bound out to sea at last.

My watch was now over, and I thankfully left the engine room. It had been a busy, and emotive watch, and I was anxious to get changed and turned in. Stepping out of the after accommodation door, the wind struck savagely. It was chillingly cold after the warmth of the engine room and I dashed along the flying bridge giving only a cursory glance at the shore lights There was no point in looking longingly at them now, we were on a ship, on passage, to faraway places! Or so we thought!

The port after lifeboat being cleared away in order to examine the propeller.

I turned in and lay in my bunk trying to relax.

It proved extraordinarily difficult however, as the vibrations in the ship were uncommonly strong. The mates must have got the ballast arrangements all to pot, I thought. There'd have to be some adjustment there. Vibration or not, weariness began to win and, 'dousing the glim', I settled down to sleep. I was called at a quarter to eight when the steward brought me coffee, and looking through the port glasses, the sea seemed to be slipping by only very slowly. There must be trouble down below, I thought, as I swung my legs over the edge of my bunk. Putting on my uniform I went out on deck looking for someone to ask what was happening. The ship was indeed only crawling along like a wounded animal and, judging by the lie of the land off the starboard side we'd not gone very far since I'd turned in. I went to the saloon for breakfast. The Second Mate was already there and he unfolded a curious tale from the night's events.

The bump, as we'd left Grangemouth, had been our stern hitting a quay wall at the entrance to the locks. As the weather had been so foul when we sailed it had been deemed prudent to take the ship out by the stern instead of turning her in the basin first. In the dark, and battered by the wind and rain, things had not gone too well, and we'd caught the quay rather fiercely. Although we'd not done any evident damage to the hull it was just possible that the propeller had been involved. This was very feasible as the ship, being in light condition and therefore high in the water, and pushed off the target of the lock mouth by the wind, her counter could have cleared the quay sufficiently enough to allow the propeller to get dangerously close to the wall. If damage had been done there, it was a serious matter indeed, and clearly some questions would be asked in high places! John, who as Second Mate had been in charge of operations at the stern, naturally looked rather glum. Plainly the weather was going to be the devil in the piece, but doubtless the company would want something more substantial than the wind on which to vent their displeasure if any was to be vented, and ship's officers come rather high on the list for that. I felt for John, and assured him that I was sure he'd got nothing for which to blame himself. With a possible inquisition of sorts looking as if it was looming up I was very pleased that we'd had no problems in the engine room, and that I'd so carefully noted the precise time of the bump in the movement book. In the cold glare of official scrutiny things would look better if they'd all been done properly, and down below that had certainly been the case.

Jon came in having finished his watch, and he now added more tit-bits to the tale. The vibrations had really been exceedingly severe in the engine room, and the Chief had been down fretting about the tail shaft and the great bearings which carried it. Speed

The propeller exposed in the dry dock.

147

had had to be adjusted to keep the vibrations to a minimum, and as nothing was amiss with the main engine itself suspicions had focused ever more sharply on the propeller. Jon and I talked excitedly about this, seeing engineering heroics in the great traditions of the sea coming our way. We'd have to change the propeller for our spare, located on the after main deck, we decided, and we debated how we'd get it over-side and round to the stern, canted high by flooded for'ard tanks. Then we had a moment of realism, wondering who would chip all the paint off the spare one! I had an uneasy feeling that instead of swinging valiantly on bos'ns chairs under the stern, covered alternately by glory one minute and surging seas the next, we'd end up scraping paint and little else! In the event of course, there was to be none of any of it. News came round that we were stopping the ship at nine o'clock in order to cant her a little by the head sufficiently to expose the propeller blades, and then a lifeboat was to be dropped, in order to examine them while the prop was turned by the turning gear in the engine room.

Duly at nine, the engines were stopped, and the port after lifeboat was cleared away ready for launching, while the mates saw to the distribution of ballast to bring the head down. The examination confirmed our fears; two of the blade tips out of the four on the propeller, were indeed badly bent. The company was informed by radio telephone, and their reply was swift and to the point, reflecting perhaps the intense displeasure with which they'd received the news! We were, they said, to proceed south at the safest speed we could manage, and in the meantime arrangements would be made during the day for an emergency dry-docking on either the Tyne or in Sunderland. At midday as we limped slowly south, docking confirmation arrived. It was to be in Sunderland, and by the time dinner was being served, the ship, with her tail between her legs, was slowly closing the port. All was ready for us, and with mild surprise, so unexpected had been the whole turn of events, we found ourselves by half past seven, safely tucked in Greenwell's dry dock at Sunderland.

WIVES ARE RE-CALLED; THE PROPELLER GOES FOR REPAIR...

The dockside phone soon came in for some frantic use and became as clammy as a campaigning politician's handshake through all the feverish use. The wives who'd probably only just got home to unpack from Grangemouth, could promptly re-pack and join the ship again! Wally was to leave us in Sunderland, and in his place a new Third engineer, Malcolm Dixon joined with whom I was pleased to share the rest of the voyage as his watch-mate.

With the dry dock pumped out, the propeller could be seen exposed in all its glory. Staging was erected, and the dockyard workers soon had it prepared for drawing off the tapered end of the tail shaft, but watching the work as it progressed one realised that the expansive thoughts Jon and I had entertained about doing such work at sea, were merely that – thoughts! Removal was a big job indeed! Blocks, tackles and slings were all rigged and, with the supportive help of a dockside crane, the damaged propeller was eased off the shaft, and eventually put to rest on wood blocks on the quay wall. The damage was impressive, and many came to look, and marvel. As we expected, there was something of an inquiry into the incident, and in our engine room log book, pencilled marks around significant entries bore testimony to the thoroughness of the investigation. Curiously, very little official information seemed to become general knowledge, but we guessed that the villain of the piece had indeed been the weather, and that no blame was being attached to any individuals. I was very relieved for John, the Second Mate.

Now removed, the propeller was taken by road across to Liverpool, to a specialist firm able to effect its repair. In the meantime, we enjoyed the leisurely rest of our unexpected 'holiday,' until the propeller would be returned. The days slipped by. Then one day, a great low-loader growled purposefully into the dockyard precincts, bearing a very beautiful and shiny, repaired propeller. It was back! The dockyard workers quickly got cracking on the work of its installation to put it back where it belonged, and their activity was the cue for

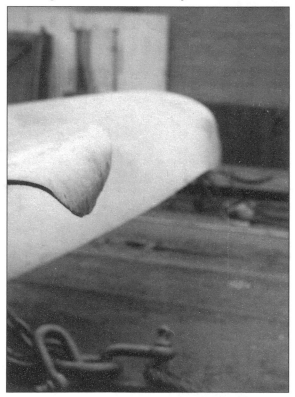

activity of another sort as, once again, the wives who'd rejoined us, packed to go home. Things all went smoothly, even rapidly, and there was clearly an anxiety on the company's part to get us off in order that we could start earning money for them instead of it being soaked up in dry-dock fees any longer!

With the propeller on, the dock was flooded again and orders were given for everything to be prepared for sea. A night sailing was expected and accordingly, Ken and Maurice on their eight to twelve watch, got the 'job' ready so that when Malcolm and I came on at midnight all was set for our departure. 'Stand By' was rung at 01:08 hours, with 'Full Away' at 03:06, and so in the early hours of the 24th of April 1964, the Border Keep was at last off on her voyage.

The damage sustained by two of the blades.

The log book destination was initially for Port Said and the fact that once we'd entered the Mediterranean and had to do a bit of port-hopping there first, taking in places such as Tripoli, Venice, Ravenna, and Termini Imerse in Sicily, it in no way altered the fact we were on our way to the Middle East and, far beyond!

SOME EVENTS AT SEA

BAD WEATHER; AN UNUSUAL 'STOP'; AN OUT-OF-SORTS PASSENGER...

At one point in the voyage we loaded a cargo at Aden for delivery to Kwinana in Western Australia. As we sailed and set course out, past the famous Horn of Africa and on into the Indian Ocean, the weather which had been still and hot in Aden began to change and eventually we found

Bad weather building up. The ship rolls to starboard...

ourselves running with a real monsoon storm. Huge seas formed and, deep laden as we were we soared and plunged in dramatic style. Even the mates, ones normally scornfully dismissive of any suggestion that the weather was rough, admitted that indeed it was, entering the stark acknowledgement in the log book as: 'rough sea and heavy swell.' From the engine room point of view we hoped that we wouldn't have a breakdown in such weather and fortunately in the usual sense of the word, we didn't. There was one difficult moment however when one morning at half past seven during the four to eight watch, the on-load generator engine suddenly began to falter, and the ship had to be stopped. It was realised that the seas breaking over the main deck were so severe that water had penetrated the goose-neck vents to the oil settling tanks causing the fuel supply to become erratic. I felt sorry for Jon and the Second whose watch it was but they managed to drain the water from the contaminated settling tank, prime the system and restart the generator. The ship was under way again by eight am, and I was filled with admiration at the able way they'd coped with a very tricky situation.

One person aboard who we lost sight of the moment the weather turned a trifle wild was Kath. She was the First Mate's wife and, as they'd just got married before the trip the company had graciously allowed her to

... and then to port!

accompany him on the entire voyage as a honeymoon treat. Thus Kath had stayed aboard when other wives who'd been with us while the ship was coasting had had to leave once the orders to go 'deep sea' had arrived. Kath enjoyed life on the ship in calm weather but it was miserable for her when it was bad and she simply went to ground in their cabin until things settled down again. However, when the sea was at its wildest in our monsoon storm, and I had occasion to deliver a message to the bridge, I caught sight of Kath as I passed the after door of the mate's accommodation on the boat deck. She was flitting like a ghost across the alleyway inside and I hailed her to see how she was. Turning, and holding the alleyway's grab-rails, she stumbled towards me as I waited, braced in the open doorway. She was very pale, and clearly not very happy, so I tried to cheer her up. "Hi Kath, how are things?" I asked, brightly. She grimaced by way of reply. "My," I said, "this is dramatic isn't it?" gesturing at the great running seas and, as I did so I saw her expression as she watched the colourful funnel of the ship sinking like a falling lift as the stern dropped in a trough and a great wall of water reared up behind to tower over our tiny ship. Poor Kath! Clasping a hand to her mouth, she hurriedly turned and vanished unsteadily but urgently, back along their alleyway to give her undivided attention to her long-suffering tummy! We were not to see her again until the wind dropped, the seas eased and the ship stopped her cavortings.

A VERY RAPID TURN-ROUND AND AN OTHER UNUSUAL 'STOP'...

The ship had been in Far Eastern waters and had then received orders to return from Japan to the Persian Gulf to load another cargo for Kwinana again. Thus, after a long haul from Matsuyama in the Inland Sea of Japan we arrived at Banda Mashur, an oil terminal situated at the northern end of the Gulf. 'Finished With Engines' was logged at 20:52 hours. Loading had already commenced by the time I went below, shortly after, at midnight. Down below, I was surprised to find there was no maintenance work to be done because, I was told, the port's fire regulations required the main engines to be kept in a high state of readiness in case an emergency dictated a need to move the ship rapidly off the berth. And, besides, I was informed, we were going to be off again soon anyway! Indeed we were! After breakfast, I went to stretch my legs on the jetty to which we were moored, the jetty effectively constituting the port itself for apart from a hut or two on the shore there didn't seem to be anything else but desert! I sat on the jetty swinging my legs over the edge and idly watched the rivets of the hull plating slip below the surface as the ship sank steadily with the cargo flooding into her tanks. Then I realised the movement had stopped. Checking the Plimsoll mark on the hull I knew she was down 'to her marks' and therefore fully loaded. As it was barely nine am it meant that we'd loaded 16,000 tons of oil in a mere ten hours or so! Shortly after, the pilot came aboard and 'Stand By' was rung at 10:28 hours; we were off again on another long haul, south, to Australia.

This little story illustrates vividly the difficulties faced by many seafarers, especially tanker crews, in that after a long haul with seven day a week watch-keeping work, a terminal port where a respite break might justifiably be expected in fact offers nothing but the prospect of a quick turn-round in order to get the ship out to sea again! The pilot was dropped soon after 15:00 hours and 'Full Away' rung at 15:12, and there we were, in well under twenty fours hours, Kwinana bound!

On this occasion the weather in the Indian Ocean was kind to us, the log book entries referring to a 'slight sea' or simply, 'rippled seas.' The sun shone, its light positively dancing on the glittering waters of the ocean, and Kath was to be seen enjoying things to the full. For us down below the calm weather

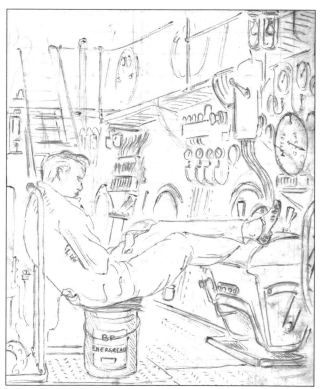

was to be an advantage for one afternoon, having just taken over the watch at noon we were startled by what seemed to be a single rifle shot being fired in the engine room. Alert as Redskins at the snapping of a twig Malcolm and I flew to the control station, our eyes raking over the gauge board and ears listening for any change in the familiar sounds of the machinery working. Strangely, almost eerily, everything seemed perfectly normal but the alarming sound must have had a cause so it was decided to stop in order that we could investigate it. The direction of the noise had suggested the problem was at the top of the engine and a thorough check on the top pistons eventually revealed the cause. A grease nipple block on one of the

A sketch made at 02:30 hours, of the Third engineer taking a nap. Broken sleep patterns, and little shore leave are very exhausting, hence a hasty nap when it's possible. The engine is fully working as revealed by the pointer on the revolution indicator; and although Malcolm looks to be asleep, the slightest change in any of the multitude of sounds around, will see him instantly alert!

transverse beams had come adrift and waving loose on it's copper pipe as the piston flew up and down, it had suddenly found itself trapped between the beam and a stout steel tie bar uniting the two sides of the guide unit. This had caused the whole corner of one of the cast iron guides to snap, the snapping being the explosive crack we'd heard. We set about effecting a butt-strap repair and refixing the grease nipple block securely, and then resumed our passage to Kwinana to see if any shore help could improve on our effort.

On arrival we discovered that there were no engineering facilities available to help there but links were established with a major dockyard at Melbourne which was to be our next port of call. Staff there said over the telephone that they were sure they could assist us but preparations for our arrival would be greatly helped if we could send all available information on ahead to them. By then, some awareness was around that I had a bit of an artistic flair so, while others set to compiling measurements I found myself 'commissioned' to do pictorial sketches of the damaged corner. The results were duly dispatched and I was pleased when dockyard experts meeting us said that from the sketches they really felt they understood what they were being asked to deal with. Our repair, endorsed by the dockyard's masterly effort using the Metalock principle of fitting steel splicing pieces fitted in holes drilled on each side of the cracked parts, was to see our ship not just through the remaining months of our voyage but, as far as I'm aware, to her final end at the breakers in Taiwan many years later.

One of a number of sketches of a broken top piston guide which was sent to a Melbourne ship repairer to assist their planning prior to our arrival.

We were due to have some dockyard help in Melbourne as several of the main engine bearings were due to be opened up for Lloyd's Surveyors to examine them. This was welcome help and the time involvement in this extra work meant we might well be in port a little longer than was often the case. This in turn meant our own 'in house' maintenance work could be spread more evenly, thus easing the pressure we so often felt we were working under.

It was thus in a faintly holiday mood I found myself ashore one afternoon, visiting the well stocked shop of the conveniently sited premises of the Flying Angel Club of the Missions to Seamen. My shopping done, before I left I looked around to admire the facilities there, remembering the time of my service as a 'Student Helper' with the Mission in Dublin and I compared the facilities we'd known there. As I looked around I was observed by a gentleman who seemed to sense my admiration and he came across to add his own, as well he might for he turned out to be the Chaplain. And here, authorship runs aground on a reef of ignorance. I have no surviving notes of the moment and the events which developed had such a surprise element about them as to eclipse much memory of the detail! Somehow or other, in the course of our conversation, the Chaplain found himself talking to a fellow priest who at that moment was just a seafarer visiting his club. He was completely bemused. What was going on? Was I working for the Mission in some new way he hadn't heard about?

Or worse, was he being subjected to a secret Mission inspection?! I remember doing my best to reassure him that I was not a spy! I tried to explain about my past, and how I was back at sea now to make 'amends' on the one hand, and to try to 'finish things off' on the other. As he listened I remember his gaze raking over me as he wrestled with the notion of a priest just abandoning his priesthood as I appeared to have done, but eventually he mellowed when I said that once I'd completed what I was doing the Church would lay claim to my attention once more. To describe him as surprised would, to put it mildly, be a serious understatement!

Celebrating the Holy Communion in the missions to Seamen chapel in Melbourne.

And then it was my turn to be floored by surprise. As our conversation developed and he seemed to be gaining a grasp of my unusual circumstances, he suddenly threw a bombshell suggestion into the ring. As it must have been a long time since I'd been able to celebrate the Holy Communion – something normally of great significance to any priest – would I like to have the facility of the Mission's chapel, he wondered. I could celebrate, and the Chaplain would be my altar server and congregation in one. I was stunned. When I'd come back to sea, for clarity of focus I'd felt it best to put the Church 'on ice' as it were, and concentrate on resolving the unfinished business. Now, suddenly, it was centre stage again, and I was thrown completely. I wanted to say 'No' for the simple reason I was totally unprepared on the one hand, and ignorant of the ways and practices of the Anglican Church in Australia on the other. Equally, I wanted to say 'Yes' for to a priest the offer of an altar is an immense privilege. Sensing my hesitancy on practical grounds the Chaplain urged me not to worry and, getting a Service book, we ran through the order which, he said, I would find remarkably familiar. It was true. Apart from a few isolated words and phrases I could have been holding a Service book in All Saints, Cheltenham! It was all agreed and, in a confused haze I went back to the ship.

The Service had been arranged for mid-morning on the following day in order to fit my watch keeping hours. The day came and, after breakfast I went to my cabin to get as ready as I could. Later, I slipped anonymously off the ship; I'd told no one of what was happening, and I didn't want any last minute confusions to give rise to silly ideas or suspicions. Arriving at the Chapel, and feeling as nervous as a kitten, the Chaplain took me through to a vestry where everything was ready. I'd got no Church 'uniform' of course, but he let me use anything that was available and which fitted, and thus in no time at all, we were ready to start. With some uniform on which serves to reduce the persona of the person and emphasise instead the role of the priest I had to admit to feeling a little more confident than when I'd arrived. From the vestry we went to the altar and the service was indeed the privilege it was, and always is, and which the Chaplain had envisaged for me. Such however was the 'surprise' of the whole thing, looking back, the details of the experience are completely lost in a haze of bewilderment with but one thing standing out vividly clearly, and that is the struggle I remember having over washing my hands! We washed frequently of course, but our hands in the engine room tended to become both hard and, oil-engrained. And then, even as I scrubbed, I thought of the Lord Himself and His grubby hands at work in the carpenter's shop, or on Calvary's blood-stained cross, and I remember thinking He wouldn't mind a bit of engine room grime from the Border Keep! A day or two later, when we were due to sail, I thanked the Chaplain for his pastoral care and hospitality and I left him, still feeling I thought a bit bemused, for after all it's not every day he'd get such a crew member surprise as I'd presented him with!

And so we sailed, but Melbourne still had one more surprise, this time for us all. Before we could say we were clear of the land we had a breakdown. The company of the shore workers had been a pleasant change in the engine room and they'd duly done their work in opening up some of the big bearings for the surveyors to inspect them. All having been well they'd been 'boxed up' again ready for sailing, and the dockyard men had packed their tools and with much friendly banter they'd left us to it. We'd duly sailed and it was during the evening eight to twelve watch, with Melbourne having just faded below the horizon astern, that the surprise came upon us. At twenty to eleven, just as Ken was walking past the fore end of the engine, he heard the most dreadful crash inside the No1 crankcase. Sprinting the remaining yards to the controls he stopped the engine immediately. On this occasion it was quickly apparent what the trouble was for there, for all to see, lying in the crank pit was an enormous bolt. It was one of the 'top end' bolts of the bearings sited on the forked end of the main connecting rod. That it had fallen out was bad enough, but what was more worrying was what may have happened to its fellow bolt. Examination of it revealed that with one bolt gone the bearing had sprung open and the companion bolt, for all its size, had actually been bent in situ. It was one of the bearings the dockyard workers had opened up and the usual questions flew about like wind-blown confetti. How had it happened? Who was to blame? Had anybody checked it? What other damage was there? From our examination of the dropped bolt it was quite clear that it had not been tightened, nor its nut split pin fitted, so it was the dockyard workers who were primarily at fault. There didn't appear to be any other damage so attention turned to the bent one. We carried new spare bolts but the problem was to get the damaged one removed. There was no way jacks could be brought to bear on it, and as hammering it was impossible it was agreed it would have to be cut through. Where the bearing had sprung it created a space which allowed a hacksaw blade to get at the bolt, but only the blade not the saw frame, and thus we set to work using hacksaw blades held with rags to allow something of a grip. It was painfully tedious work, the brunt of it being bravely borne by diminutive Jon who perched himself up among the great rods working like a furiously busy squirrel. Gradually, the high tensile steel of the bolt yielded to our efforts, but the work aside the most memorable feature of the night's work was that the Chief Engineer knocked up the Chief Steward and prevailed on him to give us the treat of a good 'fry up' meal! Once the damaged bolt had been removed, and the holes dressed smooth, a new one was fitted and, as the one which had dropped was itself quite serviceable it was put back. Nuts were properly tightened, and split pins fitted, and the others which had received dockyard attention were carefully checked. Once all was done steps were taken to start up again with the result that just after half past eight on the following morning we were under way again, 'Full Away' being rung at 08:48 hours.

Thus, after a stop lasting nearly ten hours, we were finally able to leave Melbourne and all its surprises astern. And nobody knew of those that had affected me; I said nothing about my chapel experience. It was something I felt I should keep between myself and the Lord; and anyway, in view of our breakdown I felt it even more prudent not to mention it. Others might interpret it as a sign of God's displeasure for some reason, and look around for a scapegoat. It had happened to Jonah of Old Testament fame, and he'd ended up in the belly of the whale. I certainly didn't want that!

THE 'TURNERS'...

After the success of our cargo pump rocker shaft repair, Jon and I thereafter seemed to be regarded as the ship's turners. Jon was astonishingly creative. He designed, and machined up, a little oscillating steam engine in no time at all! I had a progressive dabble with a model beam engine of the Stuart Turner design, castings for which I'd picked up second hand in a little tool shop Jon and I had found in Sunderland. There was much turning of ship's work, a notable feature of which being the regular making of new quills for the pipes carrying oil from the mechanical lubricators working off the back cam shaft of the engine to lubricate the cylinders. We had a lot of trouble with these lubricators and we were always dismayed when taking over the watch to find oil backing up in the sight glasses which revealed another blockage of carbon deposits in the cylinder outlets. But besides ship's work, we indulged ourselves in carrying out 'Government jobs' as they were known, this being an indulgent way of describing 'personal' jobs! I turned a little three-throw crankshaft out of solid brass bar, and the Captain made a polished wood base to mount it on. Another such job was fulfilling a request by one of our Indian crew to make him a joss stick burner. I drew up a design featuring a little tower of circular discs of reducing diameter, separated by turned distance pieces on a central column. The discs had small holes drilled around the tops of their circumferences for his joss sticks, and a neat onion shaped top

A joss-stick burner for one of our Indian crew members.

158

completed the piece which, I felt, would have looked quite at home in any temple let alone the crew man's cabin! I was busy machining one of the pieces for it one afternoon in a quiet moment when I was suddenly aware of the Chief standing on the top platform of the main engine and looking across at me on the lathe in the 'tween deck workshop. When he came over I began to expect that I was going to be quizzed over what I was doing but, to my surprise, Joe leaned on the tail stock and jokingly remarked, "That bloody lathe's done more revs than the main engine!" We laughed, and he moved off, and I realised later that he was actually distracted by a problem which was really vexing him. At that moment I knew nothing of it, but I would in the fullness of time.

That we'd worked our lathe hard did indeed become apparent towards the end of our long voyage. A lengthy shaft had to be turned and I had it in the lathe between centres with the automatic traverse engaged for the saddle. The ship was rolling heavily at that time, in a steep beam sea, and I noticed the curl of metal coming off the work seemed to vary in thickness! The truth suddenly dawned of course that the headstock bearings had become worn and, as the ship rolled, the work moved fractionally away from the tool and vice versa when she rolled back. We completed that job when the vessel was pitching instead, and we made sure a note was made for the lathe to be attended to when the ship would be in for her next docking and overhaul!

WATER SHORTAGE AND A BOILER ADVENTURE...

The reason for Joe's distraction when he'd spoken to me at the lathe, was over a shortage of fresh water. He'd come down to have a look around the engine room and he subsequently wrote a note about the problem to the Second. I read it when it was left on the engineers' desk during operations arising from it, and it began, 'Mr Graham, the position regarding fresh water in the ship is critical...' The problem arose from the fact that the regular double bottom tank dips revealed that we were actually losing water, and a blitz to stop even the tiniest of drips from valve glands, steam cocks, taps and flanges was undertaken. It was all to no avail and therefore the finger of suspicion was levelled at the boilers themselves. Leaks around some of the tubes was thought to be the likely cause and accordingly, with the furnaces shut down, the big hinged smoke box doors were opened and the fire tube ends in the boiler end plate examined. They were of course, all fine, so the real suspicion focused on the tubes' other ends, in the furnace combustion chambers themselves.

The burner carriers were therefore removed from the furnace fronts, planks brought down and inserted to lie on the corrugations of the furnaces themselves, and someone was then to be 'inserted' to crawl along inside. Once at the back that 'someone' had to stand up in the coffin-like box of the combustion chamber in order to examine the fire tube ends there for signs of salt encrustations which would bespeak a leak. If any were found, the person doing the inspecting, having taken in with him beside his lead lamp, a hefty piece of equipment comprising taper rollers with a lever drive, would insert them in the offending tube and by working the lever-drive, squeeze the rollers in an outward direction. They in turn would press against the fire tube expanding it to fit more tightly in the combustion chamber plating. As preparations were being made for this work I found myself wondering who would be 'going in.' Some, either by their sheer body size, or seniority, would not be involved, and looking around at those present only Jon and I fitted the bill! This was to be a new experience for me, and not a very attractive one at that! I'd heard of it being done of course, old sweats at the game referring to it as going 'up the back ends.' However, to insert oneself, even draped in damp sacking into the hot furnace of a boiler effectively 'live' with a pressure of 120lb per square inch on the gauge, and knowing you are surrounded by an enormous volume of scalding water and steam, was unnerving to say

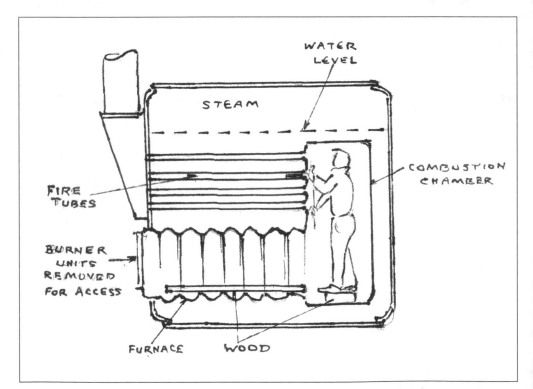

A diagrammatic sketch showing tube expanding being carried out in a combustion chamber. With three furnaces in each boiler there were six of these red hot 'coffins' to be visited!

the least. I discovered that however careful you were you couldn't avoid having some part of one's anatomy touch the hot metal, and to stand in the suffocatingly hot atmosphere of the coffin-like chamber hearing the pinging noises of stressed metal was quite distracting! There were of course, several tubes to be attended to with the cumbersome expanding gear and, as we couldn't stay overlong each time we went in, quite a number of such working visits had to be made. However, it was done, and it was all treated as just another aspect of the varied work of the marine engineer to be taken in our stride like everything else. Thankfully, our work paid off. The loss of water was considerably reduced, and the Chief was happy again.

COPING WITH THE HEAT GENERALLY...

The heat experience of our forays into the boilers was truly exceptional, but the working conditions generally 'down below' when the ship was in the tropics, were exceptional by any normal standards ashore. Daily readings of

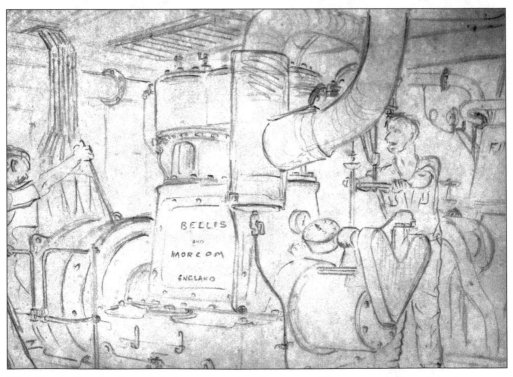

With the boilers back on full steam, we give the steam driven emergency generator a run. Jon Barsdell is at the main valve, while another engineer pulls the fly-wheel round.

the engine room temperature, taken in the control station area, were regularly between 110 and 120 degrees Fahrenheit, while on the rear, middles' platform of the main engine, under the exhaust trucking, much higher recordings could be made. This always seemed slightly ironic as it was one of the areas much work was required to be done on a regular basis, it being there that the cylinder lubricators were installed, and these, with their attendant pipe work and quills where the oil was admitted to the cylinder walls and which frequently became blocked with carbon deposits, required a lot of attention. It was also the position designed for the taking of indicator cards, these being graphical representations of the combustion pressures in the cylinders. Taking 'cards' was always seen as a hot and sticky job indeed!

In the tropics, going on watch was to indulge you in a sauna-like experience! It was as simple as that. One stepped into the oven-like heat of the engine room, instantly breaking out in a sweat that would not cease until you left. Once started, sweat would run endlessly, trickling down to drip off finger ends where it would sizzle briefly on the hot floor plates before disappearing, and it could even be poured from one's shoes! In such conditions, boiler suits were soaked in seconds, and those left to dry, draped over rails at the top of the engine room, were dry in as many seconds as it had taken

Hot work for the engineers. I am featured having a breath of air during a stop for piston maintenance in the Tropics. My boilersuit was once as white as that of the ship's Radio Officer who posed to make the contrast.

to soak them! Amusingly then, when they would come to be moved, they were found to be as stiff with dried salt as if they'd been through Widow Twankey's laundry having had an extra helping of starch thrown in!

And it always intrigued me that of the big cowled ventilators designed to bring air into the engine room, those provided with a fan induced boost to the supply, were actually positioned more to the advantage of the machinery, than the engineers!

However, with a good supply of salt tablets, and plenty to drink while on watch, everyone coped remarkably well; the heat was simply a fact of life!

ENVIRONMENTAL CONCERNS...

One night, in Singapore, when the ship lay at anchor, I came back by launch to take the night watch. At my cabin, pinned on the door, I found a note but I was surprised to see it bore but one order. We junior engineers frequently found notes on our doors, often with quite daunting lists of jobs to be done in the engine room. On this occasion however, I'd got one task, and a very simple one at that. The note read: '7ᵗʰ Engineer. Pump the tank tops off before 4 am', thus I knew it would be quite a peaceful watch and I would probably indulge myself with some 'government' (personal) lathe work, but, for all that, I felt troubled. Pumping off the tank tops, put another way, is to simply pump the bilges out. Any leaked water collects in the bilges which is the area under the engine room floor plates, the water collecting on those plates which form the top of the ship's double bottom, this area being divided up and used as tanks for the storage of important elements such as fuel, and fresh water. But besides any leaked water which will collect in the bilge there can also be the accumulation of any spillages of oil, and herein lay the problem. Pumping off the tank tops meant therefore, that if any oil were present, it would go out too with the water, thus polluting the sea. For years, such acts of pollution were accepted as a fact of life and the oceans could cope but, with the growth of shipping came an awareness that damage to the environment was an issue not to be ignored any longer. Many newer ships were thus being provided at the time of their building, with special tanks into which polluted bilge water could be pumped, and then such tanks would themselves be pumped out periodically into shore-based plants where the oils would be dealt with safely.

We had no such facility on our ship, and so it was 'easier' to pump the bilges 'over the wall' and leave Nature to cope as best it could. At sea, this was easily done of course, but, we were in Singapore Roads, one of a huge number of anchored vessels, and as policing of the harbour for acts of pollution was being taken ever more seriously, it was 'best' to do the act in darkness. Hence the significance of the cabin door's note of doing it before 4 am, as first light being a good hour later, any oil going overboard would be dispersed among the mass of shipping and its source therefore harder to pin down. I found it an uncomfortable task, but I really had no option but to comply. Fortunately, that night, there was no oil to speak of, so all was well, but for all that the deceit was troubling, and I could but only hope that better ways of dealing with the problem could, and would be found.

CHANGING THE CREW...

The timing of our voyage was bringing us at one point to the moment we would change our Indian crew. We were *en route* from Kobe in Japan, to the Persian Gulf, and a small detour was to be made in order to make a stop at Bombay. The excitement of the Indians on board knew no bounds. As we closed the coast, even though it was by then dark on our arrival day, many could be seen lining

the rails eagerly absorbing the sight of twinkling lights marking the land. Others were already stacking boxes, and bulging bags and cases, out on the after main deck ready for loading on the boat which would take them ashore on the following day. Eventually, we came to a stop in a wide bay and, just after ten in the evening, we dropped the anchor. From the Indians' point of view, we'd arrived; they were home! During the night, and in the early morning, more boxes and bags appeared, and we onlookers were astonished at the amount of luggage they'd accumulated during their year aboard. Clearly, they'd availed themselves well of the facilities travel had afforded them, and they'd obviously struck many a bargain in the local shops of our ports of call. There was an amazing assortment of goods, much of it clearly second-hand, but nevertheless obviously valuable and useful, especially the items of furniture

Changing the crew at Bombay; a cargo net of belongings is being off-loaded.

which appeared, along with assorted bikes. I was astonished, and I wondered where all the items had come from and, more interestingly, where it had been kept on board for I hadn't seen any of it! At first light, the stacking continued, and the main deck took on the appearance of a removal firm's yard! Those who had finished bringing out their belongings, lined the rail looking expectantly to the shore for signs of the boat which would be bearing our new crew, and which then would be taking them to the land, and their homes.

Meanwhile, a host of other boats had arrived, bringing a zealous crowd of traders and merchants – the 'bum boat' men, famed in every port in the world. In no time at all, they had transformed the crew's recreation room into a full blown bazaar, and we diverted ourselves buying intricately carved coffee tables, hand-crafted elephants, leather topped stools and a host of other 'treasures' to take home. Suddenly, a shout like a cheer, drew us away from the 'market' and once out on deck we realised that the crew boat had been spotted. Looking landwards, we saw it too, a vessel which appeared to be a cross between Noah's Ark and an elaborate Thames houseboat. It was wending its way slowly through the mass of anchored shipping and, as it drew nearer, our watching crew waved and clapped in delight.

As it finally came alongside, the contrast between the excited home-goers, and those who knew they were leaving home for a good year or more, was striking. Smiling faces contrasted most expressively with anxious-looking ones. I could see the new arrivals staring at our ship which would be their new home for so long; they were clearly wondering what it was going to be like, and I for one was determined to make friends with them as soon as I could, especially those who would be working with us in the engine room. It did trouble me at times that some of my fellow countrymen treated the Indian crew rather shabbily, and I felt it unfair as on the whole, they were always hard working and anxious to please. Certainly I knew, they might make mistakes and bring you a plank when you wanted a box, or a length of wire when you wanted a rope, but I found that with a bit of patience and a dash of humour, they would truly work their socks off for you.

Getting the new crew aboard was not a drawn out business, as compared with those who were leaving, they had little with them by way of luggage. Then, with the 'Ark cum houseboat' clear, it was the moment for those leaving to get their gear, and themselves aboard. Cargo nets of boxes and bags were craned out, using one of the ship's derricks, until finally, with a tooting of whistles, ropes were cast off and the cumbersome vessel veered slowly away with its excited passengers, heading for the land. The new crew had quickly established themselves in their accommodation at the stern of the ship, and those facing their first calls of duty got to work, for indeed there was to be no delay. The ship was due to sail immediately, and even as the shore-bound boat disappeared amongst the shipping, we were getting ready to raise the hook and get under way. 'Stand By' was rung at 12:04 and, shortly after, with the anchor snugged home in its hawse pipe, we were under way leaving Bombay astern, and heading for Abadan in the Persian Gulf.

We were well into our long voyage and the initial puzzlement at the discovery of my being ordained had long ceased to be of any consequence. I had now long been accepted as simply one of the ship's engineers, and I in turn never made any reference to religion or the Church unless it came up naturally in conversation. However, I kept my own personal discipline of spiritual responsibility alive with the use of a little daily guide to some regular reading of scripture, and the maintaining of an equally regular moment for some quiet thought and prayer. This, I was to discover, had been observed and noted!

After our evening dinner, those not on watch invariably gathered in someone's cabin for a chat over a beer or two but, at one bell for the First Watch (the eight to twelve), I'd make a move to get my head down for the few short hours until I'd be called at one bell for the Middle Watch of twelve to four. Before I'd actually get in my bunk however, I invariably went out on deck, often going up to the boat deck above, to lean on the rail and in a moment of peacefulness say my prayers for the day. One night as I was doing exactly that, I was startled to realise someone had joined me in the dark. "You come here to say your prayers, don't you?" a voice asked quietly, above the noise of the sea surging past. When I confirmed it I was astonished when my visitor went on to say, "That's what we all thought!" Observed one is indeed, I thought! Then he went on to say he was actually very troubled over an issue in his life and he wondered if I could tell him as a priest if I thought God could help him. It turned out to be a long evening and my few short hours of sleep were much reduced, but it was a richly rewarding moment for me for it showed that my priestly role was now being accepted as comfortably as my engineering one had eventually been!

THE VOYAGE'S END AND A NEAR DISCOVERY...

1964 passed into 1965, and in February we came north through the Suez Canal into a bitingly cold Mediterranean. A flurry of calls at various North African and Western Mediterranean ports followed, with some surprisingly rough weather to cope with, not to mention the icy cold winds sweeping down across Europe from the north. However, there was something to cheer us up in the form of champagne! One port we called at was Barcelona where someone discovered there was an abundance of very reasonably priced champagne, with the result that dozens of bottles appeared on the ship to be taken home. When finally we left the Med and turned north for

'Land's End for Orders' we knew we were on the final stretch of the voyage and thoughts turned to what duty free things we could get from the ship's bond to take home to our families, as well as the treats like the champagne. Knowing my father liked a nip of Drambuie I got a nice fat bottle off the Chief Steward while others put in for other liquid goodies, as well as the inevitable cigarettes. Some of the quantities involved did exceed the customs allowance rules so the surplus would either have to be declared and the duty paid, or the time-honoured game indulged in of 'getting 'em through' secretly. This sounds a trifle dishonest but in fact it was little more than a game because everyone knew that what the customs men were really after were the sinister things such as consignments of drugs. The more innocent things like a bottle here or a carton of cigarettes there, if they'd been hidden and then found by the rummagers (customs searchers) were often regarded as their personal perks almost on the basis of 'finders keepers!' Somewhere during the voyage the Missions to Seamen had visited the ship, in Adelaide I think, and they had kindly left a consignment of books for personal reading, one of which was the story of Colditz and the remarkable achievements of the Allied prisoners of war held there. This proved a very popular book and was widely read, everyone being enormously impressed by the daring things the prisoners did under the very noses of their German guards, even to the point of building a glider in the castle roof space and keeping the evidence of their activities securely hidden. On the ship, as we moved nearer home waters someone remembered the Colditz book and made the comment that if the lads could do what they did in the castle we could do the same on the ship, thinking now of course of the champagne rather than building a glider!

Thus the 'game' was on. Nearing Land's End our orders came that we were to take our cargo for discharge at Aalborg in Denmark and then it was to be the Tyne for dry docking. Down in the engine room we started thinking in earnest about where to put some champagne, while I decided to add my Drambuie to the game. Then someone hit on an idea. They pointed out that our No 2 generator had been running steadily since mid February and by the time we would arrive at Aalborg she would be due to be changed over letting the No 1 set take us on the final leg to the Tyne. Therefore they suggested, once No1 was running and safely on load, we could drain off the generator's little starting air reservoir, open the small oval inspection door and pop some champagne inside, box it up and Bob's your uncle! Weighing the idea up I had to agree that it sounded quite feasible and while reflecting on it my eye fell on the generator fuel filter body. With the filter removed I was sure it would offer a perfect home from home for the Drambuie!

Entering the Baltic area we began to encounter ice in the sea and the weather was indeed savagely wintry and bone-chillingly cold. There was however, one faintly romantic touch when during a twelve to four night watch the tannoy from the bridge burped and when we responded, the

Second Mate kindly informed us that we were 'just passing Hamlet's castle' of 'Alas, poor Yorick' fame. Down below as we were, and digesting John's information, we felt that at least our engine room was probably a good deal warmer than his castle however romantic!

When finally we docked at Aarlborg it was to find the harbour well iced over but happily not thick enough to impede shipping movements, and we were relieved as the end of trip fever was gripping us all and we just wanted to be out as soon as possible. Once the cargo was discharged we sailed, scrunching through the ice on what was to prove a long slow passage out to the North Sea. During the afternoon watch, at two o'clock, Malcolm changed the generators over, putting our No 1 set on load on the switch board and we were sure she'd see us comfortably over the next few days until we were home. Accordingly, with the generator running happily, our plan for the champagne and the Drambuie could be acted on. It was all done in a matter of moments. The little inspection plate on the air reservoir was replaced securely, and the fuel filter body took the Drambuie to its bosom as if it had been designed for it! Some fog in the North Sea slowed us up a little but at last, the memorable moment came when we made our approach to the Tyne and the Pilot boat came bobbing out to meet us. It was March 16th, a year

The end of the voyage on the Border Keep. The Tyne Pilot comes aboard.

and eight days since our departure. 'Stand By' was rung at 08:36 hours and it was accepted as also marking the 'End of Passage,' the counter reading for the revolutions of the main engine being logged as 8,036,610.

The long voyage was over; but not our problems!

We berthed initially at the tank-cleaning facility, and once we'd settled the engine room down everyone relaxed. A holiday spirit was in the air. At noon I went below to check around, noting that the engine temperatures were all being maintained at their normal readings, all was well in the boiler room and the generator was running sweetly. Leaving the Tailwallah to keep an eye on things I went back to my cabin to have another look at mail which had come aboard on our arrival. Deep in thoughts of home it came as a surprise then when an urgent knock announced a caller and the face of the Tailwallah appeared round the door bearing alarming news. "Fuel leak, Sahib," he said, "plenty fuel leak. No 1 generator!" ' Oh, no!' I thought. 'It can't be happening!' Dashing below I passed several customs rummagers in their blue boiler suits and armed with their powerful torches and long probes leaning on the rails at the top platform of the main engine peering down to where, far below, the on-load generator thundered away. They seemed to have guessed there was a problem. For my part, knowing we couldn't start our No 2 unit I was anxious to play down any sense of there being a crisis! Sliding down the ladders with as good an air of nonchalance as I could muster, I followed the Tailwallah round and saw what he meant. A pin hole had formed in the fuel supply line and a fine jet of oil was shooting out, to run darkly down the white paintwork of the hull plating nearby. Ideally of course, I'd start up the No 2 unit, parallel the two units on the switchboard, and then shut down the one with the fault. However, champagne was no substitute for starting air, nor Drambuie for fuel! Conscious of the piercing scrutiny of the rummagers above I made a snap decision; I'd try a repair with a bit of packing held in place with a jubilee clip, hoping against hope that the pipe would not simply collapse completely when I would tighten it up! If it did the game would be up, for the rummagers would know something must be fishy when the other set could not be started. Whistling a merry air, I got the necessary items, together with a screwdriver from the workshop and, whistling all the while, I set about making the repair. To my inexpressible relief it worked. The leak stopped! Leaving the Tailwallah to cope with wiping the plating down I climbed the ladders and breezed past the rummagers who I think still harboured their suspicions but could do nothing about them. I saw them later to find they'd cheered themselves up no end by the discovery of some cartons of Rothmans King Size cigarettes which someone had hung deep in a ventilation chute.

At 23:10 hours that night, 'Stand By' was rung and the ship, with the aid of a couple of Tyne tugs was moved off the tank-cleaning berth, and on to the Wallsend Shipyard. There, at 00:16 hours, 'Finished with Engines' was rung, and the entry was made in the log book, 'Vessel in Dry-dock.' Shore power was connected at 02:30 hours, and our work was effectively done.

It was time now to be thinking of going home.

I would very much have liked to stay with Common Brothers and their 'Border Boats.' I'd enjoyed the trip on the 'Keep' and I'd made some good and lasting friends, so I was sorely tempted to stay with the company. However, I knew that I not only wanted to work out the outstanding contract but also do what BP had suggested, and finish a qualification that my initial college experience had part begun. The Board of Trade rules for seagoing qualifications required candidates to sit examinations having two parts referred to as part A and part B. Part A was essentially academic featuring subjects such as mathematics, heat engines and engineering drawing and so on, while the emphasis in part B was entirely practical, dealing with engineering knowledge and naval architecture. With the apprenticeship scheme I'd joined the initial phase at technical college led to the sitting of an Ordinary National Diploma examination and this was regarded by the Board of Trade as of sufficient calibre to be awarded an exemption from the part A of their examinations. The part B however could not be attempted until at least two years of watch-keeping experience had been accrued. It was of course, with this in mind, that BP had advised that I stay with them to complete what I had begun. The voyage on the 'Keep' had given me one year of my required time and much as I'd like to have stayed with Commons I felt I ought to go on other ships for the sake of widening my experience, the 'Border Boats' being all very similar and powered, in the main, with Doxford type engines. Accordingly then, I left the Border Keep, bidding a fond farewell to friends I'd made, two of whom at least I'd keep in constant touch with, which was to be very gratifying.

In readiness to go home I went into Newcastle and hired a car. With the paper work done I was given the keys and escorted to an underground garage to the car. A steep ramp led up to the street and I suddenly had cold feet seeing the density of Newcastle's city traffic roaring past and realising I hadn't driven anything but a Doxford for over a year but it was a case of getting in and getting on with it! In the event it proved to be less difficult than I'd imagined, and I drove back to the ship to load up ready to drive off to Gloucester. As I pulled up at the gangway and got out I felt an instant touch of irony, for leaning on the rail watching me happened to be one our Indian ratings. It was Ibrahim, and I'd become very friendly with him for he'd shared our twelve to four watch working as a greaser and general helper. He'd told me that with the money he earned at sea (paltry as it was in comparison to our western rates) it gave him a status in his home village in India he would not otherwise have enjoyed. On one occasion chatting while we were on watch, he told me that such was his 'wealth' he actually owned his own bullock cart, and he could hire it out to others for extra income!

Power and status indeed! And there he was watching me zooming up in the latest Vauxhall car, handily hired just to drive home in! What astonishing cultural differences we do live with I thought, but wide as they so often are, the sense of friendship Ibrahim and I had achieved working together on the ship despite all the difference in the degree of our responsibilities, saw us simply sharing life as two human beings on an equal footing. That was, as it always is, well worth treasuring.

SOME OTHER SHIPS...

After a spell of leave at home, it was time to get afloat again and I applied to the 'Pool' office at nearby Newport docks to see what positions they could offer. As a result, I found myself flying out to Germany to join the MV Framptondyke of the Klondyke Shipping Company whose offices were in Hull on the East Coast. She was a much smaller vessel than I'd ever been on before, but she was listed as carrying out 'Foreign Trade' as distinct from only 'Home Trade' so watch-keeping experience on her would count towards the necessary sea time which I was anxious to build up. The ship was lying I was told in the Kiel Canal in northern Germany and I was to join her there. The flight from London landed at Hamburg and, once in Germany,

The MV Framptondyke of the Klondyke Shipping Company.   www.fotoflite.com

as I negotiated the problems of coping with airport facilities, public transport and taxi services, not to mention the buying of something to eat and drink, I marvelled at the courage and audacity of allied prisoners of war and their escape attempts. Not only were they coping with the sort of difficulties I experienced but also the hazards of recapture! I took my hat off to them.

Eventually, I arrived at the ship tired from the travelling but not too weary to pause and give her an appreciative once-over. She looked very small after the Border Keep, but very trim and neat indeed.

Once I'd been welcomed aboard I was surprised to find that those on board were hoping I'd go straight on watch as the ship was leaving immediately to transit the canal, heading then for Gdansk in Poland. However, my plea for a little rest first was accepted and, when I was 'put on the shake' it was to find us in Kiel itself at the eastern end of the canal.

Down below I found the engine room very modern in its appearance for the ship was only just over a year old. She boasted a beautiful nine cylinder Mirrlees main engine, and Rolls Royce engined generating sets. There was only one drawback and it was the noise levels! It really was quite deafening in the engine room but in those days little concern was shown for ear protection of any sort and you were expected to simply accept it as a fact of life on that sort of ship. I was given a tour round in order to get an idea of the overall layout of pumps and auxiliary systems, and I was given a demonstration of the main engine controls, then left to savour my first watch in a very different context to anything I'd known before.

Once clear of Kiel, the ship was sailing for Gdansk to load coal for shipment to New Ross in Ireland. I mentioned that I thought that a trifle odd as I'd been given to understand by the Pool officials that the company's primary interests were in the shipping of timber. However, those on the ship told me that the company did indeed have an interest in timber but would take any cargo charter going given the chance. And indeed they did. We took Polish coal to Ireland; loaded iron ingots in Cork for Bilbao; phosphates from Casablanca for Rouen; grain from Saint Malo for Leningrad; of timber there wasn't even a hint of sawdust, let alone a log!

I soon got the hang of the Mirrlees main engine, and the pump systems for ballasting, as well as those for the general services of the ship, but the noise levels were truly incredible. That they were something of a problem became very apparent when I got off the ship on arrival in Gdansk only to find I had a permanent ringing in my ears which took several hours to dissipate.

And, Gdansk proved to be an almost sinister place in the sense that Communist suspicion was endemic at that time...

A surly armed guard was stationed at our gangway and he scowled at us whenever we passed him, and there was an ever present feeling that we were in fact being 'watched' wherever we went. From our berth, to get to the city involved a trip across the dock on a little steam ferry and, on one occasion, waiting on the jetty for the return trip I became aware of a young man studying me overtly.

Eventually, he came over to me and, in surprisingly good English asked if I was from the UK. I told him I was on a British ship moored across the dock and we got into quite a conversation about ships, their destinations in the world and then, from that we got onto stamp collecting of all things! He wanted stamps of the world as he loved collecting but unfortunately such were the restrictive ways of his home country he could only obtain Polish or Soviet ones. I told him that as a matter of fact my father was a philatelist of some consequence and so when I would get home we'd send him some. He was excited at such a promise and then, while he wrote an address in my note book for me to send them to, it was my turn to study him noting the fact that he seemed to have a great many ugly bruises on his face. When he'd finished writing I asked him sympathetically if he'd been in some sort of accident. I was shocked when he said with a hollow laugh that he'd not been in an accident but in prison because, he explained, he'd been caught trying to escape from the country as a stowaway on a Swedish freighter! Good grief, I thought, what sort of country were we in? (When many months later I'd arrived back at home I did get my father to pack up a lovely consignment of stamps for him, and later still when we actually got a reply the letter said, 'You mention stamps but there were none in the envelope'! Clearly our package had been censored by 'Big Brother' which endorsed my bewilderment at why such a lovely people had to be subjected to so oppressive a regime. The irony of the oppression was greatly emphasised when I remembered that wherever you'd looked in Gdansk, there, among the drab, war-torn buildings, huge posters could be seen featuring happy smiling people their arms linked in the cheerful sharing of a fulfilling pride in their national achievements. My dock ferry companion's battered face had told a very different story!)

When the ferry arrived I left my friend on the quay looking quite forlorn as he gazed longingly after me and, past me, at the docked ships, all suggestive to him as possible passports to freedom! I felt very sorry for him and marvelled again, as I once had over Ibrahim on the Border Keep, at the staggering cultural differences that exist between people who, their race and nationality aside, are in fact all as one as human beings.

One amazing thing we all realised in Communist Gdansk was that whatever suspicions were officially harboured about western values there was no diffidence about getting our money! The Polish zloty appeared to be largely valueless and people would do anything to get their hands on sterling. Aboard the ship sterling was exchanged at the official rate and we were warned not to have dealings with money changers ashore who might be offering much more attractive sounding rates. They were, we were told, technically breaking the law and could be arrested. If the authorities chose to pounce on them and we were there too, we might find ourselves sucked into a situation which we would find difficult at best and frightening at worst – and no doubt vastly expensive as we'd probably have to pay hefty bribes to 'get out.' Thus suitably warned we were amazed to find ourselves targeted by money changers as soon as we walked out of the dock gates offering us anything up to six times the going rate! There they were, badgering us for sterling, almost under the noses of the surly, rifle-bearing guards, and after what we'd been told I fully expected trouble with a capital 'T' sensing that the soldiers were itching for a bit of action as they were as keen to get hold of sterling as anyone else through a bit of bribe-demanding! It was very uncomfortable, not to say unnerving! However, there was one place which we found where we could shop in peace. It was known as the Baltona and it was an extensive ship chandlery store to which local people had little or no access for the simple reason the store only took payment in sterling or dollars. The store's tool department was an Aladdin's cave of treasures and I was amazed at the give-away prices of quality brand-name goods. I bought a beautiful set of Britool metric spanners for an absolute song, and I vowed that if I ended up in Gdansk again I'd come armed with a good supply of sterling to go to town in the tool section in order to stock up, all with my home workshop of the future a clear vision in my mind.

SHIP TRANSFER...

I settled well into life on the Framptondyke. With only three designated engineers life was very different to that which I'd known on the bigger ships and it provided its own unique range of responsibilities and therefore experience. Settling into it then as I was, I was surprised when a message came from the company saying that they wanted me to transfer to the sister ship, the MV Revesbydyke, then loading in Liverpool for Brazil.

Bidding a sorry farewell to my shipmates, I flew to Liverpool from the continent via London, and took a taxi out to the port's famous Gladstone dock. There I found the Revesbydyke already deep laden with general cargo for Rio de Janeiro and Santos. And now I was surprised to hear at last the first reference to timber since joining a company with timber interests! Apparently the plan was that following discharge of the general cargo the ship would make for a third port of call at Itajai, and there load a cargo of special hard wood timber for return to Hull on the east coast.

Aboard the ship, a faint sense of excitement prevailed; clearly the voyage to Brazil was being seen as something of a novelty for this size of vessel. I was welcomed aboard and promptly urged to get cracking and turn to, as besides the loading of the cargo there was much work being done to enhance the ship's domestic facilities in anticipation of a transit of the tropics. Down in the holds a fascinating mix of cargo was being stowed by the stevedores; an orange painted fork-lift truck could be seen surrounded by some huge wooden crates one of which was marked 'sanitary ware' – presumably meaning lavatory pans! – while others carried engineering parts, hardware and household goods.

But it was the ship's 'household' side of things which claimed my attention once I'd got changed and into a boiler suit.

My first task was to install a big domestic refrigerator which would be invaluable when we got down in tropical waters!

From my new shipmates I discovered a good deal more about the company and their interests, and how they worked their ships. Although registered as operating for 'foreign trade' the ships were worked primarily in home waters trading with the Baltic (frequently for timber from there), the continent and occasionally, Mediterranean and North African ports. The trip to Brazil was a very new venture and being much longer demanded the addition of some more suitable facilities for the crew, hence the fridge I had to install. I was told that the ship I'd just left, and the one I'd now joined, had been built with the Brazil run very much in mind. The Revesbydyke was the slightly younger of the two sisters and was not then quite a year old, and the company's plan for them was that in the summer months they would go 'deep sea' taking general cargo out and timber home. It was anticipated that several such trips could be achieved during the summer and then, as the weather turned, the ships could revert once more to their Baltic and continental trading.

The run we were about to undertake was the very first in the company's scheme, and they would gauge all future action on its success or failure.

A few days after I'd joined, the last of the cargo was tucked in the holds and the hatches were battened down. Maximum bunkers had been loaded, together with a good deal of extra spare gear for the engine room; sailing in more distant waters meaning more self-reliance having to be placed in the ship's crew, particularly the engineers. Fresh water tanks had been filled to capacity and the cook/Chief Steward wrestled endlessly with the problem of the storage of his extra catering supplies. I gathered that once we'd sailed it would be a non stop run to the Cape Verde Islands off the West African coast and about 15 degrees north of the equator. There we'd make a bunkering and supply stop, and then it would be straight on down to Rio. With everything ready we prepared for sea and, on a quiet sunny morning, we slipped our moorings in a cosy corner of Gladstone dock and with our Mirrlees main engine turning over gently, we nosed towards the locks. Once clear of them, we headed out into the wide river Mersey and turned west for the open sea.

There certainly did seem a touch more drama to this sailing than those I recalled on the tankers of past experience. Perhaps it was because we knew it was a guinea-pig voyage fulfilling a new spirit of adventure on the part of the company, and perhaps it was also because once out in the Mersey's stream and clear of the docks and the embrace of the warehouses, our ship actually

The ill-fated MV Reavesbydyke. www.fotoflite.com

seemed very small indeed. Once the pilot had been dropped we were really on our own and our little ship turned to port down the Irish Sea heading for the wide Atlantic and beyond, and such was the 'Boy's Own' spirit of it all one could almost add, 'adventure!' However, if what was to befall me on the one hand, and the ship on the other, were to be adventures they didn't quite fit the usual understanding of the word!

We fairly romped down to the Cape Verdes. There was no bad weather to contend with, just long, Atlantic swells over which the ship swooped and dipped with the exuberance of a playful porpoise. I found myself thinking of the old shanty of windjammer days when crews sang of 'Rolling down to Rio.' With our Mirrlees instead of sails we were doing just the same! Our island stop was very brief. We'd no sooner arrived than the bunker barge pottered out to meet us, along with a couple of boats laden with necessities including some very welcome island fruits, and of course, a flotilla of bum boats which swarmed around us offering local craft gifts. It was all very entertaining but, we were making a passage to Rio and as soon as the bunker hose was disconnected the telegraph rang to 'Stand By' and we were off. Turning from the island it was a case of straight out to sea, and so 'Full Ahead' and 'Full Away' came ringing down almost immediately. Down below, I began settling the machinery down again in full running mode and, to my surprise, I began to feel sick! To my dismay, not to mention disgust, I actually was retching into the bilge near the shining propeller shaft whirling now so purposefully as our Mirrlees settled into her stride. I felt quite alarmed and puzzled. I was sure it couldn't be sea-sickness. Any tendency towards that had long been resolved in the Irish Sea! Was it something I'd eaten I wondered? However, checking with my shipmates when I came off watch revealed that no one else felt ill, and we'd all eaten the same food. I dismissed it but, after a couple of days it became clear I'd got a problem which couldn't be ignored. I felt feverish, and I could identify a sense of low, abdominal discomfort. Others, particularly the Captain, felt a need for some medical advice but here a real problem presented itself. The ship had only radio telephone equipment aboard which was essentially all she needed in the course of short sea trading in home and local waters. Now, out in a deep sea situation, she needed short wave radio facilities but the company had said that to economise on expense such equipment would only be fitted when the guinea-pig run had proved successful and the full shuttle service involving the two ships would be started in earnest. A call for assistance was put out on the radio telephone but it bore no fruit and none had been expected for no one would be listening on such a frequency out in the middle of the ocean! The only thing then, was to consult the 'Shipmaster's Medical Handbook' which the Captain produced, unused, from a drawer in the chart room. It was regarded with the wariness one might exhibit when handling a bomb. Everyone knew that in opening the pages we were walking into unfamiliar territory with the distinct possibility of creating some strange, even regrettable consequences! Following a comprehensive symptom guide it was felt my problem could be this or, even that or, very possibly the 'other!' However, in the end, a decision was made that I'd got appendicitis and the advice in the book advocated bed rest, accompanied by the administration of injections of penicillin and the seeking of medical opinion at the earliest possible moment. Accordingly I was confined to my bunk, and my fellow engineers went on a six on six off watch routine and, with the book's advice about getting medical attention as quickly as possible, they nudged our powerful Mirrlees to greater efforts. Rolling down to Rio we now certainly were with a vengeance! I responded well to the injections which were buttock-administered with rather more gusto than skill and, cosseted by a very solicitous engineers' steward who took to a nursing role like an out-of-time Florence Nightingale, I survived successfully until thankfully, we began to close the land and knew that help was now much nearer.

HOSPITAL IN RIO...

When it became possible to establish radio telephone contact with Rio, as well as docking details for the ship being discussed, arrangements were made for a doctor to be present to meet us as soon as we would be berthed; and, rather to my surprise, one was! As soon as 'Finished with Engines' was rung down (I could almost hear our main engine sigh with relief!) the gangway was slipped ashore and the doctor was aboard in a trice. He quickly confirmed our ship-board diagnosis and said a hospital admission would be arranged immediately. My shipmates, on receipt of the news, gathered to help me pack and, as it was realised I would not be rejoining the ship even as a convalescent, but would doubtless fly home direct, I was urged to take only the bulk of my personal effects such as clothing and washing gear, and I could leave other items like my tools and books in a box on the ship. I was assured they would be well looked after and, when in a few weeks time the ship would arrive back at home, I could come and collect them. I thought this was an eminently sensible idea as it would keep some of the weight of my travelling baggage down a good deal. And as I readied myself for taxi transit to hospital we heard news through the ship's agents that the company had arranged for a replacement engineer to fly out from the UK and he would join the ship in Rio if she hadn't finished her part discharge of cargo there by the time he arrived, or in Santos if she'd moved on there. Late in the afternoon of the day of our arrival in Rio, I was admitted to hospital and, by ten o'clock that night my appendix was out and in a bottle on a shelf above the wash basin in my room!

I had an uncomfortable night. Beside being in considerable abdominal pain I was much distracted by a good deal of shouting at intervals during the dark hours. However, it stopped eventually, the dawn came and, as the growing light streamed in at my window I was astonished when a galleon sailed in through the door! Shaking the drowsiness from my mind I realised it was a nun who had arrived, and the towering 'sails' were in fact an enormous white, tri-cornered wimple which adorned her head. She prattled cheerfully in Portuguese, and made signs indicating that she wanted me up and at the washbasin to clean my teeth. However, she stopped and assessed instead my sign language as I tried to explain that my abdominal pain was truly awful and I couldn't really stand up at all. There was a brief pause. I looked at her expectantly, and she in turn focused quizzically on my tum. Then, with a determined wave of her hand and a resumption of her prattling, she disappeared. Moments later, and still prattling, she was back with some things in a bowl. She gently turned me on my side and then, I was suddenly dismayed to feel what I later realised was a rubber tube being inserted in my 'stern tube', but as I gritted my teeth at the discomfort I was delightfully surprised when a great emission of wind brought instant abdominal relief! Turning back over I saw her smiling as she packed her kit back in the bowl. This was one nun who knew her onions, I thought, but her prattling was now clearly saying that with the 'wind', and therefore the pain gone, it was definitely time to be up to do the teeth. Getting up very gingerly, I went to the basin and there, as I dutifully brushed the pegs, I found myself gazing at a little jar right under my nose. What, I wondered, was a rather second rate looking worm doing in a jar on my wash basin shelf? Then, it suddenly dawned on me that it was my very own appendix! What a simply wizard souvenir to take home from my travels I thought, and I took it to the open window to examine it more closely in the morning sunlight. It was absolutely fascinating, while the sorry state it was clearly in said its removal had not been a moment too soon.

I was disturbed from my marvelling by a tap at my door. It was not the nun again but a blonde-haired young man. He spoke in a Scandinavian tongue but broke into English when he realised I was from the UK. He was a Norwegian seaman, and he explained that the whole floor we were on, in what was clearly a very big hospital, was given over to seafarers. He'd been in a few days already, and he proved a mine of information. One thing he revealed was that the shouting which I'd found so disconcerting during the night had come from a Russian seaman who had been badly injured when he'd fallen off over-side staging and been trapped between his ship, and the quay where it was berthed, in Rio's docks. The fact that the shouting had eventually stopped, and for which I'd been so pleased about was, he told, because the poor man had died in the small hours. I of course, promptly felt inwardly ashamed that I'd dared to have thought complainingly about it! After all, what was a mere appendicectomy compared to his unimaginable injuries? Other seamen on the floor included Argentineans, Indians, Chinese and several Greeks. They proved to be very jolly lot, drawn together by the common denominator of medical adversity, and this was soundly endorsed when one afternoon a

Greek face peered round my door with a compelling invitation to follow him to the lavatory! Suppressing any suspicion I followed him obediently and there, as I walked in, I was amazed. All the walking patients had assembled in the ablutions/toilet room, and one of them, the Second Mate off a Greek ship, held up a catering-size tin of peaches which had been brought to him as a parting gift from his shipmates as they were having to sail on without him. Once it was opened he indicated that he wanted it passed around so we could all share the delight of his gift! I looked round at the different faces and the nationalities we all represented, and I marvelled that a tin of peaches could have such a unifying effect as everyone smiled and chatted happily, even if largely incomprehensibly in our different languages, while equally happily slurping the lovely fruit! Besides being delicious in its own right there was a bonus in the Second Mate's gift as it brought a momentary variety to the hospital fare. The hospital's dietary regime was very strange in that it consisted of issues of steak at every meal time! I knew that being in South America we were in 'beef country' in a big way, but steak for every meal seemed surprising to say the least! The three steaks per day were always similar in size and invariably, I have to say, quite tender, but the only concession to variety was in the few vegetables that accompanied them; tomato in the morning, some beans and a slice of bread at lunchtime and potatoes with a green veg at dinner. We enjoyed the Second Mate's peaches no end, and thanked him most warmly for such a treat!

GOING HOME, AND DISTRESSING NEWS. A SHIP IS LOST...

A week to the day of my admission I was discharged. Bidding farewell to my fellow seafaring patients, another galleon-rigged nun, together with an amiable porter escorted me to a taxi which had been arranged by the ship's agents. Thanking them most warmly for all the help I'd received while in their care I climbed in and, soon after I was left at Rio's international airport to take an Air France flight to Paris en route for London, and home. The in-flight meal was, of course, steak! Afterwards, seeking to enjoy a post dinner cigarette, I found I had no matches. I eyed one of the buttons in the cluster above my head. One push would, I knew, bring instant cabin assistance but as it was an Air France flight I thought I'd ask in French. I rehearsed my request: 'Avez vous des alumettes, s'il vous plait?' I pressed the button, a ravishing stewardess appeared, I said my bit of French and she responded in perfect English, "You need some matches? Of course, sir, I'll get you some"! Had I made a mistake, I wondered; perhaps it was a British Airways plane I was on after all! At all events it was a good flight, and I transferred easily to London. There I was met by my father who drove me home to Gloucester and, as we walked in my Mother rushed to greet me with the exciting information that she was preparing a real surprise 'welcome home' meal of – STEAK!! My appreciation of this particular delicacy was beginning to assume the same regard I'd once had for corned beef after the weeks of that years before on the British Reliance!

I convalesced at home, and waited expectantly for news of the Revesbydyke's home-coming. My father and I mulled over the best ways (and the least expensive) of getting to Boston to meet her, but even as we debated travelling matters, the news of the ship when it finally came, was the last thing we'd expected to hear. We were appalled to hear that having arrived at her loading port of Itajai, and taken on her cargo for home, on sailing out she'd hit a reef and gone down! The ship was LOST!! It seemed almost unbelievable but, nevertheless, it was true; she'd gone as if she'd never existed! We gathered that the crew were safe, but I have to say that one of my first thoughts was, of course, about all the things I'd left aboard – my tools in particular! I was very sorry for many were in a sense irreplaceable, having a value beyond mere monetary terms, as they'd belonged to my father when he'd been in engineering before joining the Fire Service. And I never got back to Gdansk either, to have another go in the Baltona chandlery to replace the spanners and restock on other things. The shipping company never went back to Brazil!

I continued my convalescence and, just for good measure, I got married as well! And then it was time for another ship.

THE SHORTEST SIGNING-ON...?!

I contacted the Pool again. They had a number of positions to offer but they seemed very keen for me to take one in particular it being on the MV Pluto of the Bristol Steam Navigation Company. I knew this ship well of course, having affectionate memories of my visits to her and her crew in Dublin when I'd been with the Flying Angel there. I said to the Pool officials that much as I would like to sail on her for old time's sake if nothing else, I actually wanted 'Foreign Trade' seagoing experience and I was sure the Pluto was only 'Home Trade.' To my surprise they insisted that she was now listed as 'Foreign' thus sea time aboard her would count for the 'ticket' I was so set on trying for. On the strength then of their assurance I agreed to sign on. From earlier visits I already knew her engine room and I found myself quite looking forward to handling her neat little British Polar diesel main engine which I'd so often admired, now in a real working relationship. She was lying, I was told, at an outer pier in Newport docks, and my wife and I drove down from Gloucester the following day. The sight of her trim form brought back many memories of years before, and we laughed as I told Jean the story of her black-market condom dealings! Signing on was done very briskly, almost too briskly, for no sooner had I put the full stop to my signature than it became clear that I'd been right all along and the Pool wrong. She was indeed only 'Home Trade' registered, and that night, in the engineers' mess room it was agreed with many regrets and apologies, not to mention much laughter, that I'd have to sign off the following day! There can't be many seamen whose Discharge Book voyage record, has one as short as that! Jean arrived with our car to pick me up and I made contact immediately with the Pool office.

THE MV THACKERAY...

The staff at the Pool seemed remarkably unrepentant over their error but, as there was little point in pursuing it to make an issue of it I simply noted the other job appointments they were able to list. One was of a need for a Fourth engineer on the MV Thackeray of the Chine Shipping Company, and she'd just arrived at Portishead, near Bristol, with phosphates from West Africa. She was definitely listed as 'Foreign Trade' and I took the position straight away. Jean came down with me the following day when I went to join and, as we drove through the dock at Portishead to where we'd been told she was berthed, we almost wondered if she was on fire as there seemed to be

The MV Thackeray.   www.fotoflite.com

inordinate quantities of smoke rising from her direction. It was not smoke however, but dust from the phosphate cargo which was being unloaded by crane grabs. Little did I know then that I was to have a brush with death through that dust at a future date!

I was given a tour of the ship and I was very intrigued to note the builder's name plate of Henry Robb of Leith and the year of her launch which was 1957, and the fact that she'd then been delivered into the hands of the Chine Shipping Company in February 1958. Looking at the name Leith, and the year dates, my mind flew back to my days at theological college in Edinburgh when I'd found the nearby docks such a restorative haven at a troubled time. In those very waters the ship I was now aboard had been launched at her birth, and had I gone to college a little sooner than I actually did I might well have witnessed the event! With her bridge, accommodation and engine room in the by then, well established 'all aft' design, the unobstructed hull forward was divided into four large holds with steel concertina folding covers. I was told she had a cargo capacity of some 6,000 tons but looking at the scene from the sanctuary of the poop deck I thought a good deal of her present cargo was going straight over the side in intimidating clouds of gritty dust! It did occur to me that it was a good job the wind direction was as it was, and taking the dust away over the bows rather than over us, but that it could well be otherwise, with quite extraordinary consequences, we would discover at a future time!

Leaving the deck side of things, my shipmate tour-guides turned to the engine room and there I found the ship was powered by a sizeable, six cylinder Sulzer main engine, of the single acting two stroke crosshead type. Diesel generators provided power for the electric driven auxiliaries in the engine room, as well as for the deck winches and general lighting needs of the ship. There being no need for steam generation on the ship there was no boiler installation such as I'd known on the tankers of my earlier experience, but I was shown a chunky domestic oil fired boiler with the name 'Britannia' emblazoned on the front. It was situated in a port side 'tween deck compartment and it provided hot water for the galley, crew pantries and cabin use.

Having seen something of the ship I then gleaned a little information about the company. They had four ships, all named after great poets, the Thackeray and her sister ship Macaulay being slightly larger than the remaining two the MVs Longfellow and Tennyson. They were all handy-sized bulk carriers, and in my time on the Thackeray her charters concentrated on the shipping of cargoes of phosphates and mineral ores.

With the discharge complete we sailed from Portishead and headed south to the West African port of Dakar for another cargo of phosphates for discharge this time, at Belfast. The Sulzer engine ran very smoothly and I'd quickly mastered the controls for manoeuvring under instruction from the other engineers as we'd left Portishead. Once at sea we settled into the usual watch routine and, as Fourth engineer I kept the 8 to 12 watch which I found quite refreshing after so much experience of the sleep-depriving 12 to 4! The 8 to 12 gave a watch-keeper the nearest approximation to an ordinary night's sleep, and was therefore greatly valued!

The run to Dakar was uneventful and on arrival we engineers had only some maintenance work to carry out on the main engine's scavenge valves. It was regarded as merely a routine task to remove the covers, and the non-return disc plates for cleaning or renewal as necessary but, what on paper in the manual is described as a 'routine' task, in reality was an anatomical tangle of twisted fingers and contorted arms.

As we worked someone remarked that it was very plain that those who had designed the engine had never had to work on it! Scavenge valves aside however, the Sulzer engine was actually a beautifully crafted one and, like all two stroke designs, very compact in appearance. Such was the working of the two stroke principle there was nothing of the visual mechanical activity to watch such as the dancing springs of the valve gear as on four stroke engines, or the upper piston ballet as with the opposed piston types.

However, Sulzer engines did have one discreet visual treat in that through apertures in the engine structure between the cylinders and the crankcase, the shiny piston skirts could be watched flashing up and down as the engine worked. These apertures were known as 'lanterns' and had a twofold function. They allowed a constant visual check to be maintained on the condition of the skirts but, more importantly, they enabled a clean division to be maintained between the cylinders and the crankcase. Scraper rings fitted at the bottom of each cylinder collected dirty oil used in the lubrication of the pistons, this oil being collected in a tray at the bottom of the lantern aperture, while on the crankcase side scraper rings there prevented oil used for the lubrication of the bearings and running gear being drawn up thus avoiding contamination by combustion products.

The sight of the piston skirts' flashing movement was not, it has to be said, very exciting when compared to some of the other marine engines I'd got to know but, visual things aside, I quickly came to realise that the Sulzer was a powerful and reliable piece of machinery. And it had the bonus of being very easy to control, manoeuvring like a dream from the neatest of control stations.

This I found the more impressive when, having acquired the art of handling the controls in practice, I studied the operating manual giving the details of Sulzer's design for the starting and speed control of their engines. This revealed a seemingly incredible complexity of valves, relays, servomotors, pilot valves and safety interlocks, with the movement of one depending on another and, reading the text one marvelled that such a system could work at all, let alone do it as speedily and smoothly as it actually did!

With our cargo of 6,000 tons of phosphates safely aboard, we left the sun and the African exuberance of Dakar, heading north to the chillier realms of Biscay, and on into the Irish Sea, there finally to dock in Northern Ireland's fine city of Belfast.

Here I was surprised, not to say pleased, to find that we were in for a slow discharge which meant we had the unexpected pleasure of an extended stay in port to look forward to.

I rang my wife at home in Gloucester inviting her to join me on the ship, and she dropped everything there and made instant travel arrangements to come over. This seemed a most civilised arrangement – to be working away from home but to have one's wife able to share the life was very agreeable indeed.

The use of little Cole's mobile cranes working off the quay ensured that it was a slow discharge indeed, and I found the experience of a long stay in port quite novel after some of the quick turn-rounds I'd known on tankers. However, the cargo slowly disappeared ashore and orders came that, when ready for sea again, we were to sail around Ireland to Foynes on the Shannon near Limerick to load an ore cargo for New Orleans. Round Ireland seemed a nice coastal voyage, and reluctant to have to part from my wife in Belfast I went to see the Captain to ask if Jean could stay aboard and leave instead in Foynes. He agreed, and Jean knew an instant sense of excitement at the prospect of putting to sea with us.

The weather however, was to detract from any pleasure she would experience! While talking to the Captain on the bridge, he'd shown me weather forecast charts which had come in, and he'd said he was quite undecided whether to go north-about Ireland or, south-about, as storms and gales were promised for the sea areas of Malin and Rockall if we went north, and for Lundy, Fastnet and Shannon going south. The distance to Foynes was similar with either route and it was only a question therefore of choosing the least intimidating forecast.

With the ship riding light, with only some six hundred tons of sea water ballast in her double bottom tanks, bad weather promised a bumpy ride and he was keen to choose the least rough option from the charts before him. I'd peered over his shoulder at drawings showing isobars packed like sardines on every sheet. I'd thought it looked pretty grim whichever way we went. I didn't tell Jean about it!

We sailed from Belfast late one Tuesday evening and, the south-about route having been decided, once we'd cleared Belfast Lough, we turned to plough our lonely way down the Irish Sea. Throughout the night and the following day, the weather steadily deteriorated until, by 6 pm on Wednesday when we had the city of Cork abeam on the starboard hand, it was blowing storm force 10! The 'handy-sized' Thackeray, as light as a cork in her ballast condition, bounced and staggered all over the place. Down below, our splendid Sulzer coped superbly with the violent torque fluctuations in the propeller shaft as the prop itself came out of the water at one moment only to be deeply immersed the next as the ship cavorted about. The Sulzer's governor control system certainly worked smoothly and well, preventing the engine from racing dangerously when the stern lifted and the propeller had less water to bite on. It was a helecoidal gear-driven device, acting through a neat linkage system directly on the engine's fuel pumps, and I contrasted this harmonious method with Doxford's famous lever driven governor of the well known Aspinall type. This one not only acted on that engine's fuel pumps through long linkages to trip their suction valves from their seats but also, through long shafts and levers, on the mechanical fuel valves themselves, holding the valve needles firmly on their seats to prevent oil being admitted to the cylinders. It was a system that certainly worked, but it did it with such a heart-stopping clatter that one almost feared it was harming the engine rather than helping it!

I remembered how on my first ship to sea, the MV British Baron with a four cylinder Doxford, on one occasion in bad weather in the Indian Ocean, the Third engineer spent the four hours of his watch physically nursing the engine by hand, anticipating the working of the governor and pre-empting its mechanical shenanigans. 'It's kinder on the engine,' he explained, as he sweatingly handled the fuel controls and, through a human 'feel' for the machinery and the circumstances of its storm-bound working, eased its labouring like a midwife attending a straining mother-to-be. I didn't have to do that with our Sulzer, and I could give my attention to caring for all the auxiliary systems ensuring that the all important pressures and temperatures were kept as stable as possible in the wild conditions.

At the end of my watch I handed over thankfully to the Third and made my way wearily up to seek the sanctuary of my cabin and my bunk where, lying down, I hoped one might escape some of the constant buffeting of the storm. Opening my cabin door, I was appalled. In the violence of the storm cupboard doors had opened and drawers had slid out, their contents being strewn everywhere, with a packet of soap powder spilt whitely into the mix just for good measure. And everything was wet! A porthole glass had evidently been cracked by a boarding sea allowing water to percolate through. In our bunk, Jean lay flat and braced to each side and, as I stepped through the muddle of the gear on the deck, I heard a strangled whisper, "I'm dying!" "We all are," I said cheerfully, as I pushed her over and clambered in. And surprisingly, I slept the sleep of the just!

When I turned to at seven the next morning the storm was still raging but I sensed that the motion of the ship had changed. During the night we'd battered our way as far as the Bantry estuary on the south west corner of Ireland and we'd altered course in a northerly direction towards the Shannon. The course change had meant we were now running more with the storm than against it, and the ship was surfing the great seas rather than pounding into them. Once we'd passed Dingle Bay and then rounded the next headland with its prominent Brandon mountain we began to feel the benefit of getting under the lee of the land, and things progressively calmed as we worked into the Shannon River. Life aboard resumed its normality. Jean had rejoined the realm of the living and by the time we were on manoeuvres for docking at our loading berth at Foynes, she was cheerfully helping us in the engine room by taking on the chore of filling in the movement book recording the telegraph orders and their times. By the time 'Finished With Engines' was rung she'd been fully initiated into life 'down below' and the storm and its frightening overtones was forgotten. It was to be remembered the following day!

GETTING THE 'PASSENGER' OFF AND HOME; A RARE BUS RIDE...

As loading the cargo was not expected to take very long, the ore simply being decanted into the holds from cantilever conveyors, it was important for me to sort out travel arrangements to get Jean safely home to Gloucester. We were grateful therefore when the ship's agent offered to give us a lift into Limerick itself some twenty miles further inland. He dropped us in the town square and pointed out a Travel Agency. There, a helpful young man listened as I explained where we needed to get Jean to and, leaning back in his chair he said with calm Irish aplomb that it was all perfectly easy. Jean, he said, could take a train to Cork, catch the ferry to Fishguard and there join the boat train to Paddington changing at Cardiff for Gloucester, and she'd be home in a jiffy! It was the ferry bit that jiggered the plan! Memories of the storm and its fearsome discomforts had suddenly flooded back, and she asserted in the tone of voice that brooked of no argument that she was not going on another so and so ship, emphasising her well made point with a slam of her handbag on the young man's desk. He sat up with a jerk and looked at me quizzically. I shrugged helplessly. We'd not been long married but I sensed I was hearing the voice of a woman who, when her mind is set, one doesn't even *think* of disagreeing with her, let alone express it! I was quite flummoxed but, to his great credit, the young travel agent recovered his poise and threw up a new and, I thought, more adventurous plan. His suggestion was to fly. Jean, he said, could join an incoming flight from New York stopping at nearby Shannon airport en route to Heathrow for London. From there she could get into Paddington and catch a westbound train stopping at Gloucester. We agreed and, in a trice, he'd made some phone calls, issued some paper work and pointed out for us an airport shuttle bus waiting as if just for us, to depart for Shannon International even at that very moment. As for me he pointed out the stop at which I could catch a local service bus to get me back to Foynes and so, with hasty farewells said, I saw Jean on to the shuttle, and she was gone.

Her journey was faultlessly swift. Mine on the other hand, turned out to be a somewhat protracted affair. After a long wait the service bus duly arrived but seemed in no hurry to depart. When finally it did I was surprised when having gone but a short distance out of Limerick, it stopped in a village and a hefty pig came aboard as a passenger. It was stationed at the rear of the bus while some chickens, with much clucking and fluttering joined us as well, being stationed at the front. Eventually, our mobile Noah's ark moved off and happily, at the next village, the pig was led off into the care of farming people there, with whom our driver then rejoiced in sharing what was clearly a most convivial tea-break! And so it went on. It was only twenty miles to Foynes but it was perfectly clear that the journey time involved could, anywhere else in the world, have covered a two hundred mile haul! I feared I would miss the ship if the loading had gone as speedily as had been suggested that it might. I had no watch but a clock at the front of the bus had caught my eye and now with anxiety mounting at the passing of time, I kept looking at it only to begin to think its hands must be moving backwards rather than forwards. I toyed with the idea of having a word with the driver who by then was enjoying another natter over some villager's gate, but I couldn't bring myself to intrude. I realised that the bus I was on was a service bus in one sense, but rather more (and probably more importantly) a mobile expression of community life in another! Happily, at last, we got to Foynes, and equally happily for me, the ship was still there but even as I got aboard I found that the cargo was indeed in and preparations we about to begin for putting to sea again. I'd just made it!

I reflected on my remarkable journey, and now, without the worry over the time involved, I could see it as the delightful experience it was. It was one which spoke of life in an unpressured way; one lived purely on 'life for life's sake' terms rather than one where life is forcefully governed by the pressure to 'get on' and 'be successful' socially and professionally. The Irish could teach us all a lot, I thought – so long as there wasn't a ship to have to get back to before sailing time! (And I reflected even more on the timing of my unique bus journey of twenty miles when later, in a letter from home, I discovered that in the time it had taken me to get to Foynes from Limerick, Jean had actually caught her flight, arrived at Heathrow and got into London! Here were the two of life's principal perspectives neatly contrasted; dash and speed on the one hand, unhurried, laid-back ease on the other! Clearly there are times when a measure of speed is essential but sadly, for many, rushing and all its attendant stress has become a new and bitter norm of life, with ease ever harder to come by. Thus indeed, the Irish really could teach us all quite a bit!).

ACROSS THE ATLANTIC – A 'STIFF' SHIP...

We sailed that night, and once clear of the lee of the land we were soon butting into the apparently undying storm. Now, fully loaded, I expected the motion of the ship to be less violent than in our ballast run experience, and it was indeed different but still violent in a strange way. Instead of her light, cork-tossed sensation, the ship now seemed to have a curious kick-back effect in her rolling. I was reminded of course, that it was due to our cargo. The ore we'd loaded so briskly at Foynes was very dense, a tiny lump of it being surprisingly heavy, and we'd been warned that if we were out on deck during loading it was best not to loiter under the conveyor gantries; even only small pieces tumbling off, if they were to land on one's head could be seriously damaging! And indeed, on my return from Limerick when the loading had just finished, I'd registered that fact that although the ship was down to her marks, the holds had seemed surprisingly empty. I'd glanced in as I'd made my way along the main deck, and only tiny cones of ore occupied the bottom of each hold, but such was its density in relation to its volume, we'd nevertheless got 6,000 tons of it aboard. What it meant in movement terms was that it gave the ship a very low centre of gravity, with the result that when a sea rolled her over, the moment its influence eased, the low cargo weight would whip her back. In nautical terms this is known as a ship being 'stiff'. The opposite condition is referred to as 'tender' and this applies when certain cargoes, especially those being added as deck loading, give a high centre of gravity. In that sort of condition when a ship would roll she was apt to want to stay rolled! The Thackeray on the other hand, with her Irish ore deep in her innards, was very stiff indeed, rendering the discomfort inflicted by the bad weather even more so. Such motion, we all agreed, would make a pretty good fairground ride for those who liked a queasy challenge!

We plunged across the Atlantic on a great circle route taking us to the coast of Newfoundland, the course then for the Gulf of Mexico being straight down the eastern seaboard of America. Nearing Newfoundland we picked up the Labrador Current flowing south from chilly Greenland, and with a sea temperature only fractionally above freezing we suddenly found that we had a tricky job in the engine room adjusting cooler flows. We only needed the sea valves to be opened a fraction in order to cool the main engine oil and water systems, and I thought what a contrast it made with the reverse problem we'd experienced on tankers operating in summer temperatures in the Persian Gulf. There, the sea temperature could be so high that with the cooler sea valves fully open the engine systems could not be kept at their proper readings and the only way to achieve it was by reducing the revolutions! There was certainly no need for that on the Thackeray but, as we moved further south, we left the chill of the Labrador Current and began to feel the influence of the north eastern flowing Gulf Stream with its in-built central heating from its birth in Tropical waters. Thus adjusting the coolers was required again as the sea temperature crept up, and 'playing with the coolers' became a bit of a watch hobby!

IN NEW ORLEANS AND A TOOL BARGAIN...

Thus we arrived at New Orleans and, once docked, Yankee stevedores sporting hard hats and chewing great cigars trooped aboard. As the hatches were opened up ready for the work of discharging our cargo, I looked in again at the little cones of ore. They'd remained remarkably stable despite the wild movement of the ship during our crossing, and I marvelled at what I was told the ore was to be used for. Apparently it was to be crushed and then used in a water-base as some sort of coolant for drilling bits on oil platforms out in the Gulf of Mexico. However, fascinating as it all was, I had other interests in New Orleans. This was the world-famous home of Traditional Jazz and I really did want to see if I could sample some of it on its home ground so to speak. We engineers agreed our working times and apportioned the maintenance tasks that needed to be done before tackling the North Atlantic again, and I was very lucky to be given the opportunity of a shore break of an afternoon and evening.

A taxi whisked me into the city and the driver, talking round his cigar, pointed out features of interest on the way, one being a big store with the names of Sears and Roebuck emblazoned on its top. He enthused about it as if he'd got a share interest in the place telling me they'd got a great sale on right then, and I shouldn't miss it! I politely said that it sounded wonderful but, with Bourbon Street and jazz in mind the place held no real attraction for me; a store's a store, I thought and I would give it a miss. Moments later we were 'in town' and I was surprised to find that through bends in the road system, the drop off point had brought us to within a stone's throw of the driver's big store we'd seen from the freeway. I was about to ignore it but, a strange impulse suggested otherwise. I thought that perhaps, as I was so near, it did justify a quick look in for the sake of the experience, and I would then be able to tell folks at home how such a department store compared with our familiar Co-ops or Debenhams!

I went in. It was big, and no mistake, it was clearly having a boom time as the sales the driver had mentioned clearly gripped the place like a fever. It was not for me at all, and having walked through a couple of aisles devoted to household pots, pans and crockery, I went to find an exit. And at the one I approached I was arrested by a sign. It pointed to a tool section, and I thought I ought to check that out quickly before I fled the place and, my word, how glad I was that I did.

As I entered the display area, there before me was a stand laden with the contents of a large metal tool box, it being stood open at the bottom. It was a 'Sale Offer' and, doing some quick sums, I realised a '90 piece, Craftsman tool kit' of spanners, open ended and socket, plus a wide range of general hand tools, could all be mine for an absolute song in sterling terms. How I blessed the cab driver and his sales enthusiasm, for here I was able to pick up a tool bargain on a par with my Baltona chandlery experience in Gdansk! I bought a kit on the spot, and left the store walking on air despite the weight now in my hand! I wasn't going to lose this bargain when I'd get it back to the ship, I thought grimly; if this lot were to go down with a ship, I'd be going with it!

Despite my encumbrance I explored the city and found the place I sought – Bourbon Street. It positively brimmed with life, light, colour and blaring music, and I laughed at the exhibitions of the contra-rotating tassels on the nipples of strip girls tempting punters into this bar and that, there to behold the 'biggest tits in the business!' as their signs, and Bouncer's cries proclaimed! It was jazz I was after however, not tassels and juke boxes and, lo and behold, a block further down the street I heard it, thumping forth from New Orleans's world famous Preservation Hall! Tool box firmly in hand I went in, and there I spent a truly relaxing hour, utterly entranced by the music and the atmosphere.

Mindful of the time however, and the need to get back to my ship to relieve one of my fellow engineers, I reluctantly made to leave the Mecca of jazz buying as I left, a couple of LP records, one of which members of the band kindly autographed for me. Bearing them, as precious in their own way as my tool box acquisition, I hailed a cab and drove back to the docks, and work again down below.

There I had to tackle a ballast pump valve job, some lathe work and fuel valve overhauling, all of which was cheerfully done to the mental accompaniment of the beat of Preservation Hall's punchy and melodious jazz.

From New Orleans we sailed to Tampa in Florida for another phosphate cargo, destined if the orders remained unchanged, for Portishead. The weather was delightful. Balmy sunshine banished thoughts of wintry days at home, but a shore side café did on the other hand revive memories of home cooking. A clapboard eating place we discovered, served the most delicious apple and cherry pies – just like Mother used to cook! Mindful of our ship's cook's waxed cardboard pastry, we ate all the café's available supplies on the basis that when you're on to a good thing, make the most of it! Thoughts of home also prompted the idea of gifts for loved ones and, at a beach stall, I spotted a splendid sun hat made of plaited palm fronds; that would I felt sure, bring the 'feel' of sunshine as a gift to my wife on any winter's day! As loading proceeded, we engineers pumped the sea water ballast out, and as we popped up on deck to watch the outflowing discharge we enjoyed the tranquillity of our river dock berth and the wildlife that abounded. Prominent amongst the birds, we admired the beautiful pink flamingos as they strutted elegantly up

Memories were stirred of the Pacific isles visit made on a tanker, when we'd hoped to see silver sands and palm trees, and... but found ourselves a great nickel works!

and down in the shallows, or simply dozed in sun-soaked oblivion perched, precariously it seemed, on one match-stick like leg.

Cargo loading was speedily done at Tampa and once completed, with the hatches secured and 'Stand By' rung on the telegraph, we prepared to slip our Florida moorings and get under way once more ready to face the wild Atlantic. However, there was at least the diversionary interest that we were to make a bunker stop at Freeport in Grand Bahama as we passed through the Caribbean, before heading out north east and deep sea. 'The Bahamas'! What images such a name conjures up! – but I was cautious of anticipating scenic delights and affable Caribbean hospitality. I remembered how once on a tanker we'd had orders for the Pacific island of Noumea, and we'd foolishly allowed our imaginations to run riot with images of palm-shaded, silver-sanded beaches complete with flower bedecked girls dancing a welcome for us. Then, as 'Finished With Engines' rang down we'd all hastened up on deck to feast our eyes on our vision only to be dumbstruck at the sight of nothing but the stark gantries, rusting steel and dust-covered factory sheds of an enormous nickel works. But then of course, that's what we should really have expected for we'd come to deliver fuel oil for industrial use, not to enjoy holiday treats!

Grand Bahama was no better. Arriving off Freeport on a dull and overcast day, with the exotic island nothing but a dark smudge along the horizon, we

The view of Grand Bahama from the ship; not a hula hula girl in sight! – a great disappointment.

dropped the hook to await the arrival of a bunker barge. It duly came and, as I tinkered about with oil hoses and tank dipping as the fuel flowed aboard, I noticed a Royal Naval frigate nosing past us on her way into Freeport on a 'showing the flag' visit. They'd be in for a good ten days I thought enviously, with red carpets on the quay and bands playing, to welcome them in, as well as an endless round of shore functions laid on for them to enjoy during their stay. With the bunkers in, and the barge cast off, it was time for a working ship like ours to up anchor and be off; the citizens of Freeport would never even know we'd been near them! But, that's life in the Merchant Navy!

WINDJAMMER MEMORIES COME TO THE FORE...

Leaving the Bahamas and the Caribbean warmth astern, we forged into the Atlantic and, as we expected, the further north we sailed the weather steadily

The whaler Pequod/Rachel. Memories of her maze of rigging were curiously reassuring during events on the Thackeray.

deteriorated until, once again, we were riding rough seas. However, the motion of the ship was easier as her phosphate cargo gave her a more median centre of gravity than her ore one had done. Thus the days passed in turbulent but uneventful style until, that is, we had a phone call in the engine room from the bridge. The Third Mate had spotted through the wheelhouse windows that one of the big flood-lights high on the main mast and used when working cargo at night, had carried away and was swinging dangerously. 'Could the engineers turn-to and fix it?' was of course, the burden of his call. I volunteered to go, and the Chief came down to take over the watch for me, and I was joined by an off-watch colleague to help. In the workshop I gathered an array of tools, mindful of an old Second's advice about deck work: 'take everything you can think of as it's a long way back for more!'

and then together, we went to brave the elements out on deck. Fortunately, with the wind blowing from astern the ship was running with the seas, but they still rose menacingly over the bulwarks and some regularly crashed aboard to explode in a welter of white water against the high hatch coamings before streaming overside through the scupper ports. Wind-blown spray flew in the air and clearly it was going to be a damp experience even if we dodged the boarding seas, and I'd got dressed in the faithful oilskin coat and sou'wester which always travelled with me, but my companion had only a sweater and his uniform jacket on over his boiler suit.

However, it was less the weather and our clothing that mattered but rather the job we'd come to do. There, high on the main mast, as the Third Mate had reported, the great flood-lamp swung, hitting the mast with a nerve-jangling crash as the ship rolled. From the lee of the accommodation on the poop deck we weighed up the scene. The mast sprang from a mast house with the derrick winches mounted on, between numbers three and four holds, and we judged we'd have to time a run along the main deck to dodge the seas. I realised as well that we'd need some ropes to secure the swinging light, as well as for hauling our gear aloft, and a passing deckhand, intrigued by our task, hastened to fetch some for us from the aftdeck store. When he returned, we waited for a break in the boarding seas and, when one came we scampered down the ladder from the poop deck and legged it along the main deck with the haste of a groom and best man late for a wedding, arriving breathlessly at the mast house where we clambered up among the winches and safety from the seas.

The mast now towered above us and we stared upwards watching the mast truck at the top, and the derrick heads secured at the wide mast table below it, sweeping wide, disjointed arcs across the sky as the ship pitched and rolled. And of course, we watched the stricken flood-light, swinging and banging forlornly on its cables. From our new vantage point directly below, the light looked bigger and the mast taller, and my colleague, while happily at home in the engine room was now rather disconcerted by our open air challenge. "Bloody hell," he said, staring aloft while clinging to one of the winches for some sense of security, "I'm not going up there!" "Don't worry," I said. "I'll go up. You get ready to haul the tool box up when I reeve the line down." I looked up the mast again, and a memory of going aloft on another ship came flooding vividly back in a curiously reassuring way. I'd done it once, and it was on a windjammer at that! So I'd do it now on the Thackeray!

As I looked aloft I saw again, in my mind's eye, the mast and spars and maze of rigging on the Pequod/Rachel, the ship which featured as the whalers involved in the film of Herman Melville's epic story of the hunting of the great white whale, Moby Dick. At the time of that experience I'd been in my first year as an engineer apprentice at technical college in Swansea, and a course companion, Mike Evans, had told me one day that there was a windjammer in the harbour of his home town of Fishguard. Mike had explained that the ship was based there for the making of a film and, as we shared a common interest in sailing ships and the half-term break was at hand, we thought we'd better go and see what it was all about. We'd packed a sweater and a tooth brush and sallied forth from Swansea one Friday on the night train, along with the mails and the milk churns and, as the dawn was breaking we'd stepped forth onto Fishguard's dock and there she'd been – a real sailing ship with towering masts festooned with rigging and rolling gently against pontoons at the quay wall. We'd stood there, entranced, and I was so grateful to Mike for having told me about it. At college we'd quickly become good friends and although Mike was with Shell Tankers and I was with BP which meant we never actually sailed on tankers together, nevertheless our college friendship was to become one of those lifelong ones whose value deepens with the passing of the years; it was to have a very firm cementing in a surprise experience we were to find we'd have on the ship that had lain before us that morning. Later, we'd met the Harbour Master, a friend of Mike's and, as we'd talked, the Captain had appeared on the quay and we were pleased to be introduced. To my absolute amazement it had turned out to be no less a personage than Alan Villiers; he was a wind-jamming old sea dog if ever there was and his many books had been my delight for years, and there we were that day, face to face on Fishguard's quay! Villiers had a philosophy that it should have been a law as natural as adolescence for every lad (or lass) born, to ship out before the mast for a voyage on a Cape Horn square rigger before any step in life was taken; it would set them up for ever!

It might have been a bit sweeping but those who later lamented the passing of National Service felt a good deal of sympathy with Villiers' views. He was there because at that time there was something of a dearth of windjammers and desperate for anything in his line he'd taken the Captaincy of the big schooner 'Ryelands' which had been transformed into the lumbering whaler for the filming of Moby Dick. We'd said 'Good morning, Sir,' to him, as reverently as we might have done to God, and we'd promptly been astounded when the great man, in line with his policy of getting any lad to sea on anything with sails, had instantly elevated us from the status of mere quay-side gapers to being actual deckhands. He'd given us a no-nonsense command to 'Get aboard, report to the Mate and he'll give ye a job!' Aboard like shots, within an hour we'd found ourselves aloft on the mizzen helping with the lowering of yards and running gear which action, along with a change of name transformed the ship-rigged Pequod to the barque Rachel for a film sequence involving the meeting in mid-ocean of the two ships in the story. A little later, we were back again, then to actually put to sea and accordingly we'd been tarted up in costume and make-up in a nearby hotel which had been requisitioned as the film company's headquarters. Then, suitably adorned as whaling sailor men we'd walked down the hill to the harbour with the Captain, and he'd thrilled us to the core when he'd said wryly as he'd sized up the distant seascape that it would be rough out there that day. Mike and I had said 'Good Oh!' and our eyes had danced like the distant breakers with excited expectancy. It had all been too good to be true. There we were, actually about to go to sea on a real ship, as real sailors, and it would be real sailors' weather for good measure. We were to be in for a very rude awakening!

The ship had been moved to buoys in the harbour, and we had clambered aboard up her rigging chains from a launch, like a couple of old salts. We'd found the Mates and the Bos'n busy with the crew making last minute preparations for sea; hands were stood by the braces, and the fo'c'sle crowd were ready to slip from the buoys. An experienced hand was at the wheel, and the Captain who'd come out with us had taken his place of command on the poop deck aft. A big tug had nuzzled alongside and besides helping the ship to clear the harbour it was from her that filming would be done when we'd got under way. With the buoys let go we'd been taken gently in tow and for Mike and I our adventure had really begun and, near the harbour mouth, we'd been thrilled to hear a wind-blown cry from the poop to 'Set the heads'ls.' Men and ropes had gone a-flying and, besides ourselves with excitement at the thrill of it all we'd watched a thrashing mass of canvas become a sail, arched and straining to the wind like a well-banqueted tummy! It had been followed by another, and another, the tug had cast off, and the ship had been under way on her own but, as we'd cleared the long mole of the harbour, she'd met the sea. The ship's bowsprit had suddenly reared skywards, and then dropped as she'd fallen headlong into a great hole in the water! A stinging cloud of spray had swept over us and she'd then heaved dizzily up before plunging again with an awesome creaking of timbers and cordage. And something had gone wrong; what I thought I would enjoy, I was definitely not. Mike had turned out to be in the same boat too, which had been something of a comfort. We'd both turned a delicate shade of green and as things internally had got wildly out of hand for both of us we'd had in the end to make an unseemly dash for the side of the ship – only to be arrested by a shout from the poop which had boxed our ears with its very harshness: 'Other bloody side!' Together, we'd stumbled to the lee rail where we'd then spent a good deal of the rest of the day. I had certainly felt very ashamed and Mike had too. I had been stunned by the experience as I'd never ever thought of being seasick. If I'd thought of it at all I'd imagined my love of all things nautical would have provided a form of immunity from such a thing as befitted only paltry landlubbers; those people who never knew a ship's blunt end from its sharp one and who would insist on calling anything that floated a 'boat' be it a super tanker or a punt.

That first day had been a miserable one! The next day however, had proved very different. At our 'sick station' we'd suddenly been appalled when the Second Mate had come from the poop with orders from the Captain to get us aloft! What a bully my hero had become I'd thought but, once up the rigging and out on one of the yards in the madness of the gale, we'd found that fear for our very lives had overcome the malady; we'd been too busy hanging on to have any thoughts of being sick! And then we'd found ourselves responding, like lovers, to the magnificence of a sailing ship in a sea-way, running before an ocean wind. The 'God' on the poop had been restored to his rightful place in my affections; his philosophies had been proved correct, and Mike and I had found ourselves clinging to the jackstays of the great yards, and handling the attendant gaskets, all in the manner born. And danger then had brought not fear, but the immense satisfaction of a sense of achievement. Thus inspired by such memories, now looking up the Thackeray's reeling mast I hoped I would have the same sense of satisfaction and achievement if I could indeed manage to fix the broken flood-light.

The mast had a ladder welded to its after side which was far easier to climb than the Pequod's shrouds and ratlines! Putting the ropes our sailor had provided, over my shoulder, I began the climb, noting of course that the higher one went the wider the arc one swept through the spray-filled sky as the ship rolled! At the site of the broken light I hooked an arm through the ladder, thinking again how difficult the old sailor's adage of 'always keeping one hand for yourself and giving one to the ship' was, to actually apply in practise. All the jobs we ever did needed two hands and one often wished you'd been supplied at birth with three! However, working through the ladder as well as round it with my free arm I managed to get a line on the rogue light and belayed it securely. Then I passed an end of a long rope over a ladder rung, and fed it down to my colleague to tie the tool kit on, allowing him then to haul it up using the round rung as a pulley.

A view from aloft, taken from the main mast.

The problem with the flood-light was obvious, now that I was in a position to study it closely. The swivel pin holding it in its welded fitting had sheared, and once I'd got a chisel, a length of rod as a drift and a hammer to work, I was soon able, in between rolls of the ship, to knock the broken piece out. With a file, I dressed the edges of the holes, and that done, I shouted down to my colleague to 'nip' below for a long 7/8 inch Whitworth bolt from the engine room stores, and that would act as a temporary swivel until we could turn a new one on the workshop lathe.

While my companion dashed off on his errand I took stock of the scene. It was, in truth, a dramatic one. Height always adds an exciting perspective to any vista, and from up the reeling mast the surging grey seas streaked with white, looked awesomely impressive. And as I looked aft, seeing the after structure of the ship, with its colourful funnel lifting, dipping and swaying with the action of the sea, I noticed a line of white faces pressed to the wheelhouse windows as the mates and other spectators watched the entertainment of the repair work. From my wind-blown eyrie I gave them a wave, and someone raised a mug in reply. 'Lucky for some!' I thought. There they were, in the warm and dry, enjoying coffee and biscuits too no doubt, as they watched the antics on the mast. It was all a welcome visual diversion for them and, just for good measure, I did a jig for them while I waited for my colleague's return. In truth of course, the jig was less for the benefit of those in the dress circle of the wheelhouse and more for mine, as I flexed and arched my feet on the ladder rungs in an attempt to keep the circulation going! Then my attention came back to the task in hand for my colleague had returned waving a bolt like a trophy and, good fellow that he was, he'd had the presence of mind to remember to bring some grease. Using our makeshift pulley he slackened the line and lowered the tool box and then having added the goodies he'd brought, he hauled it up to me again. The most tricky part now had to be done. I had to get the flood-light's swivel boss back in the jaws of its mounting and get the bolt through. Casting the lamp free, and with one arm through the ladder, I wrestled with its swinging weight trying to manoeuvre it into place. I realised it was the sort of moment when I needed six hands let alone the three I'd wished for earlier but, timing things with the roll of the ship, it suddenly went home. I slammed the bolt which I'd already greased, together with a head washer, into place, and order was restored. I lathered it all with grease to make it easier when it would have to be dismantled and, having fitted a washer and two nuts lock-nutted to allow some play for swivelling without coming undone, the job was done. The tools were lowered to the deck, and as I began to descend I gave a wave to the spectator's gallery of the bridge getting a thumbs up in return, and I climbed down. Then, I found my legs had turned to jelly with the strain of perching on the narrow rungs for so long, but thoughts of the warm engine room and a hot drink soon got things moving properly again. Although a little unusual it had been for all that, just another job which had had to be done and, once back into the rhythm of work down below it was soon forgotten.

The voyage continued steadily until after romping past the Bishop Rock light off the Scillies, and rounding Land's End, we forged up the Bristol Channel to dock at last in Portishead. From a dockside phone I rang Jean at home and, on a grey and cold winter's day, she drove down from Gloucester to the ship. Once aboard she was very pleased to receive her Florida palm-frond sun bonnet! It looked utterly ridiculous at that most out-of-season moment, but it brightened things up no end by giving everyone something to laugh about.

While in Portishead many of us managed to get ashore for a meal. We seized such opportunities gratefully for in truth the ship was not one which could attract the seafarer's accolade of being a 'good feeder'. There was frequent grumbling about our meals, and Jean had not been overly impressed when served a fried egg swimming in the gravy of a roast dinner! But grumbles were merely that, grumbles, and we simply expressed them and thought no more about them. Thus it was a great surprise to discover that they'd actually been given some official recognition as the sudden appearance on board of the Company's Catering Superintendent revealed. I bumped into

The Thackeray, berthed

him in the cross-alley of the accommodation as I came out of the engine room and, seeing me in my white boiler suit and realising I was one of the crew, he button-holed me rather aggressively. Why were there so many complaints about the food he demanded to know, waving a bunch of past menus under my nose. He read from one at random as an example. It mentioned 'Tomato soup, Pork chops with *sautéed* potatoes and mixed vegetables, followed by Apple pie and custard.' It sounded fine, the Superintendent said. Taken rather by surprise by this alley-way encounter, I hesitated, wondering just how complaints had been passed to the Company to bring this fierce man down to meet us. I was tempted to mention what I thought was an amusing anecdote from my first two mornings on the ship. On the first of them, the engineers' steward had knocked on my cabin door and, popping his head in asked solicitously whether I'd prefer tea or coffee. I'd ordered coffee but, when it came it had tasted truly awful. Therefore, on the following morning I'd ordered tea. However, when that had arrived and been sipped it had seemed very little different to the previous day's coffee. I'd abandoned it to the washbasin! 'Warehouse sweepings' was what we enjoyed, others had told me darkly when I'd mentioned it, and I found that it was to a degree to be typical of the flavoursome standard of all the catering we experienced on a daily basis. Many people ashore to whom I'd mentioned the morning beverage experience had found the story rather amusing but, tempted as I was to relate it to the cross-patch Company official, I sensed he wouldn't see the funny side of it – or, in his present mood, the funny side of anything. He was rifling again through the menus in his fist and, before I could say anything by way of a proper answer to his original question, he launched forth again saying it was a scandal that anyone should complain when the menus revealed such varied and high quality fare. That was my chance at last to simply point out that there was often a very considerable difference in what appeared on a piece of paper, and what actually appeared on one's plate! I left him pondering such a truism as that most certainly was!

FIRE DOWN BELOW...

Leaving issues over the food aside, we did actually have a really serious problem. It was to do with the dust from the cargo. When I'd originally joined the ship in Portishead Jean and I had been amazed by the dust generated during the working of the cargo, but on that occasion we'd been relieved that the way the ship was moored and the wind direction prevailing at the time, the dust was being taken safely away over the bows and away from the accommodation. As we'd sailed up the Bristol Channel the wind had been in a similar direction but, to our dismay, it had changed, doing so even as we'd berthed, with the result that as soon as the crane grabs began their work, clouds of gritty dust were indeed blowing back, and getting in through any open ports and doors. We found ourselves scrunching along the alleyways and after decks, and orders went out that all ports were to be kept closed and doors shut securely after use until further notice. More seriously however, we realised we were 'scrunching' when we were walking on the plated platforms and negotiating the ladders in the engine room. Gritty dust and machinery make for an unhappy combination. It was getting in of course, through the part opened skylights as well as down the big cowled vents. These were quickly turned off-wind, and wooden blanking covers fitted over them. For the skylights, even though they could be closed right down over their frames, we realised however, that the wind would still be able to penetrate gaps in the cills and so it was agreed to cover their edges with sacking before cranking them securely shut. That solved the problem, and the greasers soon had the plates swept, and the engine tops all wiped down. Order was restored – until, that is, when we came to sailing day.

The grabs soon did their work and, with the holds swept out and the ballast flooded into our double bottom tanks, we began to get ready for sea once more.

The orders were for a ballast run back to Foynes, there to load another ore cargo for New Orleans, followed by more phosphate for the UK. It was a repeat voyage of the one we'd just done and all we could hope was that the weather would be kinder to us. Jean left for home, the sadness of our parting now being eased by the fact that when this trip would be complete I would at last have fulfilled the two years of 'that contract' time, the omission of which had so troubled me. With that done I could therefore think of paying off the Thackeray and getting home, probably for good. We said our quayside goodbyes, and she was gone. I dashed back to the engine room as we were sailing that morning and there was much to do. A tug had arrived alongside to help with the turning of the ship in the big dock basin, and the pilot came aboard having arrived in the docks by car. Down below I was given departure information from the bridge, and I was told that although I could expect 'Full Ahead' to be rung on the telegraph I was not to work the engine up to full revolutions. The reason for this I was told, was that we would be crossing the Bristol Channel and then slowing, or stopping, to drop the pilot off in a Pilot Boat which was due to rendezvous with us near Barry on the South Wales coast. That explained his vehicular arrival of course, in Portishead that morning. Soon after, 'Stand By' was rung down, and I made a quick check round at our main engine pumping systems, the compressors and the on-load generator, and then I stood by the controls at the fore end of the engine ready for manoeuvring orders to begin. They soon came. The strident ring of the telegraph and its moving pointer, suddenly demanded 'Dead Slow Ahead'. I responded promptly but, I'd no sooner kicked the engine on air than the telegraph rang 'Stop'. I hadn't even touched the fuel control!

Once again in that position, I found myself wondering just what those on the bridge thought actually happened in the engine room when they rang their telegraph handle. They sometimes requested engine movements that simply could not be fulfilled and one was almost left with the impression that they believed they manoeuvred the ship with the telegraph handle alone! I remembered how once on a tanker, southbound through the Suez Canal, when we'd arrived to take moorings at 'The Cut' to allow a northbound convoy to pass, we'd had a truly mad moment in the engine room. After a 'Stop' had rung down there was then a rash of orders for movements both ahead and astern with stops in between in such quick succession the perspiring Second at the controls of our big six cylinder Doxford, had stood back from the control station unable to do anything! He'd stared at the wildly swinging pointer on the telegraph saying, with a distinct air of resignation, 'Just keep ringing the bloody thing back – it'll at least keep 'em happy!' Then, keeping his hand ready near the air-start lever, he'd waited for an opportunity to use it properly. No doubt such telegraph hysterics that day were due to over excitement on the Canal pilot's part with the tenseness of the mooring work, but many engineers can tell of more normal situations when somewhat similar experiences have not been unknown.

On the Thackeray that morning, I got another 'Dead Slow Ahead', and this time I could actually start the engine for a measurable duration before 'Stop' rang down. Then there were some astern movements, and I knew we were being turned in the basin. Some gentle ahead orders followed until a protracted 'Stop' told me that we must be in the lock waiting for the levels to be adjusted to allow us to move out to the sea. Watching all the quivering gauge needles around me, I waited patiently for the off. Soon, 'Dead Slow Ahead' came, followed shortly after by 'Half Ahead', and I knew we were moving out of the lock. Then a 'Stop' told me that the tug was dropping off and, very quickly, I got what I next expected, 'Full Ahead'. Remembering the passage information given me prior to sailing, I opened the engine up gradually to about three quarters of her full speed and, having settled the controls I could relax a little until we neared Barry. Leaving the control station for a moment, I went to adjust the coolers, and as the air reservoirs were up to full pressure I shut the compressors down. Returning to the controls, a glance at the clock said coffee was due. I relaxed, leaning on the desk and watching the engine's revolution pointer, while in my mind's eye I saw the Welsh coast drawing nearer as we pushed ahead, Barry-bound. It was then that I noticed a smell!

I was suddenly as alert as a starved lion getting a whiff of prey, and remembering the Third on the old 'Reliance' and his nose leading him to our thrust block fire, I sprinted for the after end of our Sulzer to check ours – and the tail shaft bearings while I was about it. All was well however, so I made a quick checking tour taking in the on-load generator and all the motors of the running pumps, but all seemed well with them too; the generator's engine throbbed faithfully, and the motors whirred and whined as tunefully as ever.

But the smell was getting stronger; clearly something was amiss somewhere! Leaping up a ladder to the middles' platform, I raced along checking the flying piston skirts through the lantern apertures, and they seemed perfectly fine too. Running back along the platform I made for the ladder leading to the top of the engine intending to check the cylinder tops, and it was as I put my foot on the first step that the greaser appeared at the top about to come flying down. Seeing me coming up, he braked sharply and shouted the nerve-chilling word 'FIRE' I was up with him in the wink of an eye and I was absolutely stunned to find the whole upper space of the engine room solidly smoke-logged! The frightened greaser was clutching at my arm and pointing with a stabbing finger across at the port-side 'tween deck, while shouting as frantically as before, 'FIRE, Sir; boiler on FIRE!'

Breaking free of his grip I sprinted across and I could scarcely believe what I saw. Our domestic boiler with the proud name 'Brittania' cast so boldly on its brow, was now behaving like a fiery, fairy-tale dragon that needed no breaths between its bouts of nostril-flared flame-throwing! Our 'dragon' was issuing a constant and awesome jet of livid flame which roared out through the air-register spaces around the oil burner. The flame was then hitting the hull plating whose paint was blistering and burning merrily, and deflected upwards by the plate's curvature, it was licking hungrily round the unit's forty gallon daily service fuel tank, freshly filled only that very morning! It took but a split second to take all this in, registering at the same time that the flame emerging from the boiler was roaring around the fusible link that was its very own safety device! The soft metal of the link should have melted at the first lick of flame, and spring loaded connections would then have shut the oil supply to the burner safely off. Our fusible link, clearly a stubborn beast, was having none of that! The switch gear to close the system down manually, shutting off the fuel and stopping the forced draught fan was, of course, not just nicely to hand inside the compartment's door, but on the bulkhead beyond. The great gout of flame roared menacingly between, effectively cutting the switches off from any ready access. Weighing it up in the instant and not wanting to waste precious time looking for something to reach the switches with, I grabbed a nearby bucket and, upending it, I felt I could stand on it and just reach to do the necessary. Leaping on the pail and clutching the boiler's pressure gauge for support with one hand I did indeed reach the switches while being uncomfortably aware of the alarming sensation of having my thighs nicely singed by the intervening flame! Thankfully, it worked. The flame withered and died away with a sulky curl of smokey vapour and, apart from my bit of singeing, I was fine. A hand fire extinguisher dealt with the paint work of the hull and a solid spray round the fuel tank for good measure saw the fire effectively out – but my word, how hot it all was to be sure!

I dashed back down to the control station and slowed the engine before ringing the bridge and the Chief to apprise everyone of what had happened. With the alarm thus raised others quickly appeared, coughing and spluttering as they came down through the smoke! Everyone expressed absolute astonishment at what had happened. Clearly, an instant task was to vent the thick smoke and someone dashed back up into the 'smog' to find and operate the skylight crank handles. Once they were eased open, the smoke billowed out and, for a moment or two, we must have presented an alarming sight to any ship passing by or a ship-spotter watching from the shore! However, with the fire out and thus no more smoke being produced, what was there rapidly cleared. There was then an opportunity to take stock. The question on everyone's lips was 'how could it have happened?' – and it was the now open skylights which suddenly suggested the answer. In the rush of our departure thoughts on the sacking seals we'd put in place under them to avoid the cargo dust, together with the covers sealing the cowled ventilators, had not received any conscious recognition. It could only mean that once the main engine was running it was drawing air from the engine room space faster than any was finding its way in through any remaining chinks and gaps. This had meant the air pressure had been perceptibly lowered, insufficient to be sensed by the human presence but enough to draw the boiler flame back on itself creating the frightening and dangerous effect of the lunatic dragon!

Having then satisfactorily explained how the problem had arisen our attention turned to the other, and if anything, more serious issue of why the safety factor had failed. The fusible link which was plainly anything but fusible would have to be replaced as a matter of urgency; although, to be sure, we would never have a repeat of that morning's particular problem, lessons having been learnt all round! With order restored, and the greasers attending to the wiping down and clearing up, the boiler was flashed up again and the main engine brought back to our cross channel speed. Our rendezvous with the Pilot Boat was by then a little overdue but, once off Barry, we slowed back nicely and I could visualise the pilot, glad to get off our fiery dragon-hosting ship, climbing nimbly down to the sanctuary of his sturdy sea boat. As I imagined it veering smartly away in a flurry of foam, I stood poised to receive the 'Full Ahead – Full Away' signal. It duly came ringing down and, having nudged the engine up to full speed, my watch was ending and I could thankfully hand over to the Third.

It was as I wearily climbed the ladders and reached the top platform of the engine that I realised I'd been pretty lucky that morning. There were two doors to the engine room, one for'ard and one aft, but the ladders from the entry gratings of each door both led to the same top platform running the length of the port side of the main engine's cylinder covers. This platform therefore ran adjacent to the boiler compartment in the port side 'tween deck, and I realised that if the fuel tank there had 'blown' in the morning's fire, such would have been the resulting inferno I might never have got out of the engine room at all! Dismissing such morbid thoughts I went to get changed and then, sitting for a moment in my cabin, I found my knees knocking with an uncontrollable jitter-bug dance rhythm! I put it down to a shock reaction to the morning's dramatic events and to help it to pass I went for lunch. Descending the companionway to the saloon and thinking of food, I found myself suddenly wondering if we might be in for some culinary treats now that we'd had a visit from the catering superintendent but sadly, as the courses came and went we all realised things were just as before. Perhaps the superintendent who'd so enthused over the printed menus, felt we should draw on an imagined sustenance from their evocative and tempting phrases!

TO NEW ORLEANS AGAIN, AND STUDY TIME; A DISMEMBERED PUMP...

We arrived at Foynes in record time, the weather being at last calm. It was cold too, but we in the engine room didn't mind that! The loading of the ore was speedily done, and with no protracted bus journeys to make I enjoyed a more leisurely respite in port before we sailed to tackle the North Atlantic once again.

Once we'd left and were under way again, I squared up to the now imminent future which, if things went to plan, would see me at the end of the trip with enough sea-time in to not only have completed the missing two-year contract time but to allow me to present myself to the Board of Trade examiners to try for a Second Engineer's qualification. The sea-time factor looked after itself, simply accruing with the passing of time, but I knew I'd have to buckle to with some serious study for the three written papers, as well as the dreaded 'orals'. I'd been in touch with one of the Marine Engineering colleges in London and they'd kindly supplied me with an assortment of back papers for the Part B (practical) section of the Second's 'ticket'. Thus I got down to some serious off-watch wrestling with Electrotechnology, Naval Architecture and Engineering Knowledge. The electrotechnology was, as a subject, always the one I had most difficulty with. In my studies of it there were shades of my struggles with Greek when I'd been at Theological College, but this one I really had to pass and I did feel I could get enough of my mind around it to stand a chance of success. There'd certainly be no dispensations in the event of failure, that was for sure!

Besides the calculation type questions there loomed of course, the prime aspect of the 'ticket's' Part B, and that was the sheer engineering knowledge you could anticipate being examined on. Accordingly, I spent some time reviewing the experiences, particularly the unusual ones, gained from the various ships I'd served on. The Thackeray and the extraordinary engine room experience on our recent departure from Portishead, was a classic one, and it led to some practical considerations of another issue and one which might well have been very significant in that morning's, or indeed any fire situation. It was an issue directly related to the matter of fire-fighting. If the fire had developed more seriously I would have resorted to running our General Service pump in order to charge the ship's fire main system, but a dismaying thing applied in respect to the pump's back-up in the event of it failing, or being rendered unusable by dint of any failure of the electricity supply. At the after end of the engine room, near the engine's great tail shaft, was situated a small, diesel driven, emergency fire pump. We'd been nowhere near having a need to run it but the point was that if we had wished to, it would not have been possible. The unit was all in bits on the floor plates, and had been so for over a month!

What had happened was that nearing New Orleans on our first visit we'd been informed that Lloyd's surveyors would be coming aboard to inspect the pump and its engine. Accordingly therefore, it was carefully dismantled prior to our arrival, and the parts laid out neatly on clean rags spread on the adjacent floor plates, ready there for the surveyor's attention. In port, no-one came! When we sailed, questions arose as to what to do with all the bits, and as it was assumed we'd get a surveyor at some point, if not in Tampa then certainly back at home, we'd leave things as they were. Wooden shuttering was put on the floor plates around the assortment of parts to keep them all together, and we quickly absorbed their presence there as part of the engine room's general scene. No surveyor came in Tampa, and none in Portishead, so everything stayed unchanged – although on several occasions I'd noticed the shuttering had been disarranged by foot traffic on the plates, and I'd idly wondered if, when we would ever come to reassemble the unit, any of the parts would have become lost! It was on our second visit to New Orleans that the surveyor appeared, checked things over very quickly and gave it a 'pass.' Accordingly therefore, we could put it all back together, and it was then that we found that far from parts having got lost they'd in fact bred quietly amongst themselves for, initially at least, we found we'd got more than we could account for! Looking at it all from a potential examinee's point of view I felt that if I was to serve as a Second engineer with responsibility for an engine room I would have ordered the pump to be rebuilt when the surveyor had failed to turn up. Better an un-surveyed pump but one which might work, than one waiting to be looked at which most certainly wouldn't!

PAYING OFF IN ECCLES...

The voyage to New Orleans was routine and uneventful, and I didn't go ashore on this occasion, as with paying off now in mind I felt I would need all the money I could save. From New Orleans we went on to load at Tampa, and there the pie-shop we'd found before proved too great an attraction to miss and I paid it a most refreshing visit. Loaded, we sailed and, like our westbound crossing our return eastwards was also routine and uneventful. The ship sailed steadily, the watches were kept, and I kept my nose in my books of study as often as I could. Nearing home, a change of orders came in that our cargo was not for Portishead this time but for Eccles on the Manchester Ship Canal. At the mention of the name 'Eccles', images of my Mancunian mother sprang instantly to mind as she was a talented, homely cook, and regularly produced a topping line in Eccles cakes! And I was pleased too to have the chance to sail up that famous waterway with its masterpieces of Victorian engineering such as the Barton Aqueduct to marvel at.

The days passed and we were soon entering the Canal, travelling slowly and sedately to our berth at the quays of Eccles. There, arrangements for my paying off were put in hand. On my last evening on board, I was the duty engineer and, having checked the engine room I went to finish my packing in my cabin, keeping an ear alert for noises from down below. Not really expecting any I was then of course stunned when a terrifying bang shook the ship! Leaping into the alleyway heading for the engine room and wondering what on earth had happened below, I was brought up all standing by another nerve-shattering bang, followed in quick succession by another. In the alleyway I realised the noises were not from the engine room at all, but out on deck, and a sudden hail from a nameless voice urgently shouting to everyone to keep inside confirmed it. The noises had stopped, and the nameless voice proclaimed an 'All Clear' following it with a cry for all available sailors to turn to urgently.

Mystified, I ventured out on the poop deck to see what the fuss had all been about. There I realised what had happened. A big Brocklebank liner had just eased past us on her way up to the central docks in Manchester, and the displacement of water in the canal as she'd passed had caused us to surge on our moorings with such force that three of our wires had snapped like bits of cotton! The recoil of broken ends when such things happen can be quite lethal to anyone chancing to be in the line of fire, and very fortunately no-one on the ship, or the quay, had been caught. The urgent call for available sailors was of course to lay out new mooring lines; clearly, life on the Manchester Ship Canal could produce some interesting moments!

Leaving the sailors to it, I went back to my cabin, and at the end of my duty stint I was able to turn in and dream of events for the following day; I would be paying off, and going home! It was a moment with a strange air of unreality about it; the two years of that contract time whose omission had so dominated my thoughts for years, was now actually fulfilled!

The following morning, after my last meal in the saloon, I bade farewell to my shipmates. I would miss them. Their comradeship, and the shared skills of the tight team we'd been, were to become memories to be long and deeply treasured.

A taxi ride, and a train journey with a change at Birmingham, brought me back to Gloucester, and home. I had some official leave to enjoy, but of course it was thoughts of the examination attempt I was going to make which loomed ever larger in my mind.

I reported back to the Bishop of Gloucester, and he was pleased for me that I'd done what I'd set out to do. My leave passed, and eventually the bishop contacted me, offering me a position as a Curate in a Cheltenham Church. The vacancy I was being asked to fill was a rather unexpected one in that the priest who had been in the position had become seriously entangled with the

The Reverend Canon Keith R Corless.
Taken in 1990, working on my Stuart Turner single cylinder steam engine – representing how my diverse 'callings' came together...

wife of a parishioner who was actually away in training for the ministry at Theological College! When the story had become known he'd been promptly relieved of his post, and it gave the bishop an opportunity to get me back into Church and parish life. I'd told him about my examination attempt, and he'd been most supportive, sensing that for me it would truly crown the achievement of the fulfilling of the contract time.

Once established with my wife, at Saint Christopher's in Cheltenham, besides getting to grips again with parish life, I rounded off my marine engineering studies. Arrangements were made for me to attend the offices of the Board of Trade, or Ministry of Transport as it had become, at Pierhead in Cardiff. A week of examinations lay before me and I took lodgings in the Missions to Seamen boarding house near the Central Station in Cardiff. When I presented myself for the first paper, I was mildly surprised to find there was only one other candidate, and we commiserated with each other over our nervousness, becoming quite good friends as the week progressed. The week went by in a haze of papers, figures and calculations, ending finally, with the orals session. At the end, feeling drained and exhausted, I travelled back to my Church house in Cheltenham, and although desperately tired, inwardly I had a feeling it had all been successful.

After a fortnight, I had to ring the Examiner's secretary, a young lady I'd got to know quite well in my week in Cardiff, and she was delighted to tell me that I'd passed. The dent made by the phone receiver where it hit the ceiling bore its own lasting testimony to my elation!

I'd laid a ghost at last!

And I was, and still am, deeply grateful to all those whose patience, tolerance, encouragement and support had made it possible for me to do it, not least my wife Jean, the late Bishop Guy of Gloucester, my family and friends and parishioners, and the shipmates I shared so much with and learnt so much from.

My former shipmate, and good friend, Jon Barsdell has skilfully used modern technology to manipulate and superimpose three different photographs.
As if by magic, I can be seen operating my own model steam engine, seen in its actual size on the previous page! Sailing past in the background is the ship on which I sailed with Jon, the MV Border Keep.